C000186274

BEAUTIFUL IDIOTS AND BRILLIANT LUNATICS

A Sideways Look at Twentieth-Century London

ROB BAKER

AMBERLEY

For Olly

First published 2015

Amberley Publishing
The Hill, Stroud
Gloucestershire, GL5 4EP

www.amberley-books.com

Copyright © Rob Baker 2015

The right of Rob Baker to be identified as the Author
of this work has been asserted in accordance with the
Copyrights, Designs and Patents Act 1988.

All rights reserved. No part of this book may be reprinted
or reproduced or utilised in any form or by any electronic,
mechanical or other means, now known or hereafter invented,
including photocopying and recording, or in any information
storage or retrieval system, without the permission in writing
from the Publishers.

British Library Cataloguing in Publication Data.
A catalogue record for this book is available from the British Library.

ISBN 978 1 4456 5119 4 (print)
ISBN 978 1 4456 5120 0 (ebook)

Typeset in 10.5pt on 14pt Sabon.
Typesetting and Origination by Amberley Publishing.
Printed in the UK.

Contents

Author's Note

Thank you to the following for your inspiration, help and support: Beth Blunt (mum), Chris Bunton, Chris Cocks, Connor Stait, David Hepworth, Danny Baker, Ewa Scibor-Rylska, Helen Baker, Jane Awford, Jenny Stephens, Jill Shapiro, Justin Bairamian, Lindsay Smith, Louis Archard, Luca Leonard, Mary Baxandale, Mary O'Kane, Merlin Crossingham, Michael Burke, Miles Leonard, Paul Sorene, Bob Stanley, Peter Watts, Richard Gardner, Robert Ross and Wilfred Bairamian.

CHAPTER 1

The Empire Theatre on Leicester Square and the Arrest of Bobby Britt

Bobby Britt, Constance Carre and friends at the time of their arrest at Britt's flat on Fitzroy Square, 16 January 1927.

At one in the morning on 16 January 1927, Superintendent George Collins of the Metropolitan Police knocked on the door of the basement flat at 25 Fitzroy Square. A woman called Constance Carre answered, and was told that there was a warrant to arrest the occupants. Carre responded: 'But Mr Britt was going to give us a Salome dance!'

The superintendent and his fellow officers barged past her and quickly entered the flat. They came across a twenty-six-year-old man who was wearing, as a police report would later describe, 'a thin black transparent skirt, with gilt trimming round the edge and a red sash ... tied round his loins'. The same report added that 'he wore ladys [sic] shoes and was naked from the loins upwards'.

The oddly attired man gave his name as Robert Britt and said:

> I am employed in the chorus of 'Lady Be Good!'. These are a few friends of mine. I was going to give an exhibition dance when you came in. I have been here for about eight months and pay two pounds five shillings weekly for the flat. Carre is my housekeeper. I was a Valet to a gentleman for about nine years who died last November. I did not like that sort of life, so as I'm considered good at fancy dancing I decided to go on stage ... Some of the men I have known for a long time and they bring along any of their friends if they care to do so.

It eventually came to light that the police had been staking out Britt's flat for a month or so. Sergeant Spencer and Police Constable Gavin of D division had spent 16 and 17 December 1926 and 1 and 2 January 1927 essentially peering into the abode from the front and rear of the property. They noted the activities during various parties that Robert Britt held at his flat. Police Sergeant Arthur Spencer wrote: 'At 11.45 p.m. I saw two men, who I saw enter at 11.30 p.m., leave, they were undoubtedly men of the Nancy type. They walked cuddling one another to Tottenham Court Road, where they stood waiting for a bus. I stood close to them and saw their faces were powdered and painted and their appearance and manner strongly suggested them to be importuners of men.' Police Constable Gavin contributed to the report: 'I saw from the roof into a bedroom in the basement, where two men entered the bedroom; they both undressed and got into bed and the light was put out. I heard them laugh and scream in very effeminate voices.'

Londoner Bobby Britt, the youngest of four children, had been born in Camberwell at the turn of the century. As he mentioned to the police when they raided his flat, he was performing at the Empire Theatre in the dancing chorus of *Lady Be Good!*, the Gershwin brothers' first Broadway musical, which starred the brother-and-sister team of Fred and Adele

Astaire. The musical had been a huge success in New York and on 14 April 1926 had transferred to the Empire Theatre in Leicester Square, to perhaps even greater acclaim. In the end the comedy musical ran for 326 performances. Bobby Britt was dancing in easily the hottest show in town.

The Empire Theatre had opened in April 1884, on the north side of Leicester Square, as a variety theatre but also as a ballet venue, and had room for 2,000 seats. It had been built on the site of the historic Savile House which had been destroyed by fire in 1865. Savile House was notorious in its time for its *tableaux vivants*, or living pictures, which featured frozen-moment representations of well-known paintings where seemingly half-naked young men and women stood statue-like, and which included the 'fleshly embodiment' of *A Night with Titian* or *Venus Rising from the Sea*. The Empire had been designed in 1882 in the French Renaissance style by the highly reputed London architect Thomas Verity whose design included two large promenades which enabled people to stroll up and down while watching the stage below.

The first performance at the theatre was *Chilpéric* with music by Hervé and described as a grand musical spectacular with a fifty-strong corps de ballet. In 1887 the Empire was reopened as a popular music hall and renamed as the Empire Theatre of Varieties. In the early part of the twentieth century, the dancer Adeline Genée and the ballet company working under composer and director Leopold Wenzel were responsible for reviving the art of ballet in Britain, which had been steadily declining during the preceding century.

Exactly forty-four years after the Empire opened, almost to the day, *Lady Be Good!* opened at the Leicester Square venue. George Gershwin attended the opening night and huge crowds came to the theatre, just to stand outside. Later, with the Astaires, the composer partied at the fashionable Embassy Club on Old Bond Street, where he stayed until eight in the morning. The Embassy had opened in 1919 and had soon become the fashionable place to go after the Prince of Wales had become a regular (a couch was reserved specifically for his use). The music for the first-night party was provided by Ambrose and his Orchestra, who were back playing regularly at the nightclub after a lucrative period performing in New York. They had been persuaded back to London by a telegram from the Prince of Wales himself: 'The Embassy needs you. Come back – Edward.'

The reviews for *Lady Be Good!* were generally enthusiastic, especially as far as the Astaires were concerned. The *Manchester Guardian*, writing about the opening night, was initially worried that the audience may have been puzzled with the title as 'none of the numerous ladies involved in the plot were in the least in need of being told how to behave'. The reviewer enjoyed the performances of the Astaires, but thought that Mr Gershwin's music 'is rather disquieting. He has very little that is either new or captivating to say.'[1] *Lady Be Good!* established the Astaires as international celebrities and *The Times* enthusiastically wrote about them: 'Columbus may have danced with joy at discovering America, but how he would have cavorted had he also discovered Fred and Adele Astaire!'[2]

The Astaires had been a successful vaudeville act since 1905, and in 1926, when they both travelled to London to appear in *Lady Be Good!*, Adele was actually the bigger star of the two – Fred at this stage of his career played almost a supporting role. When the *Daily Mail* reviewed *Lady Be Good!*, which they thought of as 'a particularly fine brand of musical comedy', they singled out the sister: 'Miss Adele Astaire is the live wire of the piece. She dances so well, she sings in a way to give point to some ordinary lyrics, she shows a true sense of comedy, she laughs and romps her way into everyone's favour.'[3] Professionally, the siblings were completely different; Fred, a constant worrier, was never happy with his or his sister's performance and usually arrived at the theatre two hours early to limber up and practise, while Adele, a much more relaxed individual, would generally turn up a few minutes before she was due on stage.

Adele enjoyed her new-found celebrity status on both sides of the Atlantic, and particularly appreciated the attention she had started to get from rich tycoons' sons and wealthy young aristocrats. In 1932 she retired from the stage and her professional relationship with her brother when she married Lord Charles Arthur Francis Cavendish and moved to Ireland, where they lived at Lismore Castle. She had been dancing most of her life, but Adele made no attempt to hide the fact that the theatrical life wasn't really for her: 'It was an acquired taste,' she said, 'like olives.'

Thirty years before Fred and Adele danced on the stage of the Empire to such acclaim, Oscar Wilde had his character Algernon Moncrieff mention the theatre in the first act of *The Importance of Being Ernest*:

> Algernon. What shall we do after dinner? Go to a theatre?
> Jack. Oh no! I loathe listening.
> Algernon. Well, let us go to the Club?
> Jack. Oh, no! I hate talking
> Algernon. Well, we might trot round to the Empire at ten?
> Jack. Oh, no! I can't bear looking at things. It is so silly.

Oscar Wilde, who wrote his last and ultimately most successful play during August 1896, would have known the connotations most of the audience would glean from 'the Empire' reference. While Wilde had been writing the play, the Empire had been in the news for months, mostly because of the 'purity campaign' by the indomitable campaigner against vice Mrs Ormiston Chant. The *Daily Telegraph* gave it huge coverage, worried about 'the prudes on the prowl'. Laura Ormiston Chant had been persuaded to visit the Empire Theatre of Varieties after two of her American friends had had a particularly bad experience there. They had visited the famous theatre in Leicester Square in the hope of seeing coster songs sung by Albert Chevalier. They missed Chevalier but complained to Mrs Chant of 'the character and the want of clothing in the ballet' and, on the second-tier promenade, of being 'continually accosted at night and solicited by women'.

Prostitution and the theatre had, of course, always been pretty close bedfellows, so to speak. At Wilton's music hall, for instance, it was flagrant: the gallery could only be entered through the brothel inside which the hall had been built. In the 1890s the Empire in Leicester Square was justly famous as a variety and musical hall theatre, especially for its spectacular ballet productions and its *tableaux vivants* which were now almost traditional at that spot.

In reality, the dominant attraction, and what Wilde was almost certainly referring to, was the Empire's second-tier promenade. This was an area behind the dress circle where you could still see the stage if you wanted to, but which was essentially a place to pick up high-class prostitutes. The theatre charged half a crown for a rover ticket that gave you licence to enjoy the promenade. There was room to wander around, but there were also comfortable seats and what was called an American bar serving one-shilling cocktails such as the Bosom Caresser and the Corpse Reviver. The prestigious publisher Grant Richards described the second-tier promenade of the Empire as 'like the terrace of the Café de la Paix in Paris: if you sat there often enough you would see pass everyone you want to meet'.[4]

The promenade was known as 'The Cosmopolitan Club of the World', and the essayist and caricaturist Max Beerbohm described it as 'the reputed hub of all the wild gaiety in London – that Nirvana where gilded youth and painted beauty meet … in a glare of electric light'.[5] Enchanted Mrs Chant was not, and she was of the opinion that it was the risqué 'abbreviated costumes' on stage that encouraged and contributed to the indecent and indecorous air of the promenade. After a while, in order to investigate the promenade properly, Mrs Chant started to go in disguise. On the first three visits she had dressed 'quietly' but the uniformed attendant recognised her as out of place. For her next, more incognito visits, she wore her 'prettiest evening dress', although, she hastened to add, this did not extend to 'décolletage'. The women she observed who were 'very much painted' and 'gorgeously dressed' didn't sit down but walked about the promenade on the lookout for men. When the theatre was darkened for the 'living pictures' their behaviour was 'very objectionable indeed'.[6] Mrs Chant eventually told the London County Council, who were responsible for the licensing of the Empire: 'We have no right to sanction on the stage that which if it were done in the street would compel a policeman to lock the offender up ... The whole question would be solved if men, and not women, were at stake. Men would refuse to exhibit their bodies nightly in this way.'[7]

Mrs Chant's efforts were not in vain, and she managed to persuade the LCC in October 1894 to instruct the Empire to build a barrier between the theatre itself and its infamous 'haunt of vice' promenade. Although, when the Empire Theatre management put up canvas screens to hide the auditorium from the promenade, a rioting audience quickly tore them down. The crowd was egged on by the young Sandhurst cadet Winston Churchill, who shouted: 'Ladies of the Empire, I stand for Liberty!' Churchill later wrote about what he had said that night: '"You have seen us tear down these barricades tonight; see that you pull down those who are responsible for them at the coming election." These words were received with rapturous applause, and we all sallied out into the Square brandishing fragments of wood and canvas as trophies or symbols. It reminded me of the death of Julius Caesar.' Four days after the incident, Churchill wrote to his brother: 'Did you see the papers about the riot at the Empire last Saturday? It was I who led the rioters – and made a speech to the crowd.'[8]

Mrs Ormiston Chant would have been even more shocked and horrified had she known what was going on within the less prestigious and cheaper first-tier promenade. Oscar Wilde, however, almost certainly did know, and his 'Empire' reference almost certainly had other connotations to a more select part of his play's audience. At the cheaper price of only one shilling, the Empire Theatre's first-tier promenade was said to be *the* gay pick-up location in the whole of London. A letter to the council dated 15 October 1894, just six weeks after Mrs Chant's visit to the theatre, described the rough ejection of a man from the shilling promenade by Robert Ahern, the front-of-house manager. The letter writer described the man who was thrown out as a 'sodomite', as were perhaps half the occupants of that promenade, that it was the only venue for people of this kind, and that he 'could lay his hands on 200 sods every night in the week if he liked'.[9]

It's not known whether Oscar Wilde ever went to 'look at things' in the first-tier promenade at the Empire Theatre but at that time it was exactly the kind of place he would have frequented. Just a few months after Mrs Ormiston Chant's intervention at the Empire Theatre, and only two months after *The Importance of Being Ernest* premiered at the St James' Theatre in February 1895, Wilde was charged with gross indecency after a failed libel case with the belligerent little Marquess of Queensbury. Wilde was convicted under Section 11 of the Criminal Law Amendment Act 1885, and sentenced to two years' hard labour. The judge, Mr Justice Wills, described the sentence, the maximum allowed at the time, as 'totally inadequate for a case such as this'. Wilde's response was 'And I? May I say nothing, my Lord?' but it was drowned out in cries of 'Shame' in the courtroom. Five years later, utterly broken, he was dead.

Thirty years later *Lady Be Good!* finished its run at the Empire, on 22 January 1927. Bobby Britt was no longer in the chorus because exactly two weeks previously he had been formally charged with keeping a disorderly house. Or, to put it in slightly more detail, he was charged with permitting

divers immoral lewd, and evil disposed persons, tippling whoring, using obscene language, indecently exposing their private naked parts, and behaving in a lewd, obscene and disorderly and riotous manner to the manifest corruption of the morals of His Majesty's Liege Subjects, the evil example of others in the like case, offending and against the Peace of Our Lord the King, his Crown and Dignity.

After some legal arguments about exactly what a disorderly house actually meant, poor Bobby Britt was sentenced to fifteen months' hard labour for essentially being a 'nancy boy' and enjoying the occasional party. Four of his friends were sentenced to six months without hard labour. When Bobby was eventually released in 1928, let us assume that three years later he went out to see Oscar Wilde's *Salome*, perhaps to compare dances. The play, forty years after it was written – it was banned by the Lord Chamberlain on the basis that it was illegal to depict Biblical characters on stage – had its first public performance at the Savoy Theatre in 1931.

After his time in prison Bobby took the stage name Robert Linden and lived with his parents on Lansdowne Road in Stockwell. After the war he went to live with his sister in Amhurst Road in Hackney. Bobby went on to dance in many shows both in the West End and on Broadway in New York, working with Cecil Beaton, Frederick Ashton and Noël Coward. He danced at the initial BBC television trials at Alexander Palace, and he performed for the royal family at Windsor Castle. Britt eventually moved to West Sussex and became a proficient painter in his eighties and he died at the age of 100 in the year 2000.

After *Lady Be Good!*'s run came to an end, Metro-Goldwyn-Mayer Pictures, who had recently bought the Empire, promptly demolished most of the famous old theatre and built a large cinema in its place. A cinema on that location was particularly apt as the old Empire Theatre had been the venue, in March 1896, for the first ever commercial theatrical performances of a projected film to a British audience. The film programme, by Auguste and Louis Lumière, ran for eighteen months. The Empire Theatre cinema, in one form or another, still exists to this day.

To recreate the 'Naughty Nineties' atmosphere at the Empire Theatre, I have included the recipes for the cocktails Bosom Caresser and Corpse Reviver.

Bosom Caresser

Ingredients:
2 oz Brandy
1 oz Madeira
1 oz Triple Sec
1 tsp Grenadine
1 egg yolk

Directions:
Shake all ingredients vigorously with ice in a cocktail shaker.
Strain into a chilled red wine glass and enjoy.

Corpse Reviver

Ingredients:
1 oz Brandy
1/2 oz Apple Brandy (Calvados)
1/2 oz Sweet Vermouth
Garnish: Apple
Glass: Cocktail Glass

Directions:
Shake all ingredients with cracked ice in a cocktail shaker.
Strain into a cocktail glass and garnish with an apple slice.

Harry Craddock, who wrote the *Savoy Cocktail Book* in 1930, wrote that the Corpse Reviver No. 1 should be drunk 'before 11 a.m., or whenever steam and energy are needed'.

Cover of the programme for the Empire Theatre production of *Lady Be Good!* from April 1926.

"Pond's is so famous"
Every woman must know Pond's
declares
MISS ADELE ASTAIRE

"You know," said Miss Astaire, "your girls have lovely soft delicate skins, and that's a very good reason why Pond's should be so popular. If you have the gift of an attractive complexion you are naturally anxious to take good care of it by a safe, sure method. Pond's Vanishing Cream to protect in the daytime, and Pond's Cold Cream to protect at night. Merely washing the face and hands is not good enough, you need Pond's Cold Cream to keep the pores and little channels free and functioning properly."

Thousands of women are now following this complete method of Skin-care :—(1) *Pond's* *Cold Cream* or cleansing the pores ; (2) *Pond's Cleansing Tissues* for removing the cold cream ; (3) *Pond's Skin Freshener* to brace the skin and close the pores ; (4) *Pond's Vanishing Cream* to give a perfect finish and protect the surface of the skin from the weather.

FROM ALL CHEMISTS AND STORES

Pond's Vanishing Cream, Opal Jars, 2/6 & 1/3
                   Tubes - 1/- & 6d.
Pond's Cold Cream, Opal Jars, 5/-, 2/6 & 1/3
                   Tubes - 2/6, 1/- & 6d.
Pond's Cleansing Tissues, per box, 2/6 & 1/6
Pond's Skin Freshener, per Bot., 5/6, 3/- & 1/-.

Adele Astaire advertising Pond's Creams in 1926. While in England the Astaires endorsed Tibo toothbrushes, Phosferine Evan Williams Henna Shampoo, Amami Shampoo, Lakerol Bronchial Pastilles, Rayne's 'Dentelle' Shoes and Waterman's Ideal Fountain Pens.

Adele and Fred Astaire performing in *Lady Be Good!* in 1926.

Empire Theatre and Monseigneur News Theatre on Leicester Square, 1955. Six years later the interior of the Empire was extensively redeveloped with most of the original plasterwork removed. (Allan Hailstone)

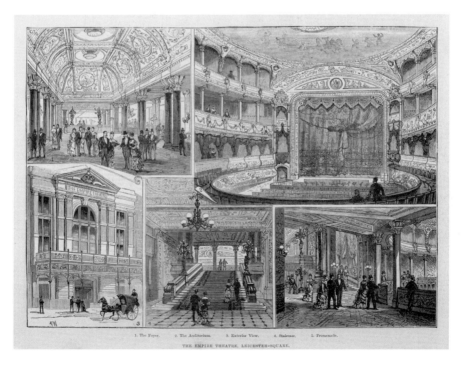

The interior of the Empire Theatre featured in the *London Illustrated News*, on the week it opened in April 1884.

CHAPTER 2

The Pop-Artist Pauline Boty and the Anti-Uglies

Pauline Boty in Ken Russell's 'Pop Goes The Easel'. (Courtesy of the Tower Library)

At 2 p.m. on Monday 8 July 1968, and nine days before the world premiere, three of the Beatles arrived at a press screening of *Yellow Submarine*. It was a very hot day and the film was being shown at the air-conditioned, 102-seat cinema situated inside Bowater House in Knightsbridge, a massive post-war office block that was distinctly 'carbuncular' in appearance. It had been built a decade before, in 1958, by the developer Harold Samuel for the Bowater-Scott Corporation, the world's largest newsprint company, and the building completely dominated the adjacent Scotch Corner junction.

John Lennon was the Beatle missing at the screening, and he was almost certainly at home under the influence of large amounts of marijuana, although Paul, George and Ringo jokingly posed for the photographers with a life-size cardboard cutout of John's cartoon character. Harrison told reporters that because of the bad reviews of the *Magical Mystery Tour* the previous year, the Beatles from now on would only appear in animated form. He then tried to avoid answering a question about the Maharishi Mahesh Yogi but McCartney interrupted and said that the episode had been just 'a phase' and that 'we don't go out with him anymore'.

Three hours later the three Beatles were driven to the EMI studios at Abbey Road, where they started on another version of 'Ob-La-Di, Ob-La-Da' (there had already been three days of aborted sessions). At the studio they were at last joined by Lennon. Richard Lush, an engineer on the session, described what happened: 'John Lennon came to the session really stoned, totally out of it on something or other, and he said, "Alright, we're gonna do Ob-La-Di, Ob-La-Da." He went straight to the piano and smashed keys with an almighty amount of volume, twice the speed of how they'd done it before, and said, "This is it! Come on!" He was really aggravated. That was the version they ended up using.'[1]

Bowater House, except maybe in size, was not an impressive building and now would be seen as typical of so much unimaginative post-war architecture that sprung up around London during the fifties and sixties. It isn't surprising, though, that thrift and speed often took precedence over quality and taste when so much of the capital still had to be rebuilt after the war. In 1959 Mies Van der Rohe was in London and in a taxi on his way to receive a gold medal from the Royal Institute of British Architects. His fellow passenger, the architect Ernö Goldfinger, waved dismissively at the newly built Bowater House and joked, 'This is all your fault.' To which Van der Rohe responded pointedly, 'I was not the architect of that building.'

Just after Bowater House had been completed in 1958, and not half a mile up the road in South Kensington, a twenty-year-old Pauline Boty began her first year at the Royal College of Art in South Kensington. Boty was at the School of Stained Glass. She had originally wanted to study painting but was dissuaded because, especially as a woman, it was far harder to be accepted at the RCA as a painter. It's worth noting that when in 1962 the new specially designed, and much-complimented, RCA building opened next door to the Royal Albert Hall, there were no women's toilets in the staff room.

Not long into Pauline's first term, the rector of the RCA, Robin Darwin (the great-grandson of Charles Darwin, incidentally), invited an ex-RAF pilot called Ian Nairn to give a talk about architecture. Nairn had made his name with a special issue of the *Architectural Review* called 'Outrage' a few years earlier in 1955 and the main point of his lecture was that bad buildings weren't just disappointing but should and must be seen as unacceptably offensive. To the young students his arguments were persuasive and they despaired that the general public seemed to be so indifferent to much of what was being built around them.

After the lecture Nairn and a handful of Stained Glass first-years, namely Pauline Boty, William Wilkins, Ken Baynes and Brian Newman, and also some other RCA students such as Barry Kirk, Ken Roberts, Ron Fuller and Janet Allen, thought it was about time something was done and the Anti-Ugly Action was born. On Wednesday 10 December, and choosing not to travel too far across the capital to make their point – not that they particularly needed to and they were art students after all – the Anti-Ugly Action, or the Anti-Uglies as they quickly came to be known, marched down towards Knightsbridge Green. They held aloft a long banner that said, 'Ugly Buildings are a Sin,' and were accompanied by trumpeters and a bass drum which beat out a funereal rhythm to everyone shouting 'Outrage! Outrage! Outrage!' On the way they stopped outside the recently completed Bowater House and clapped, waved and gave it three cheers in appreciation of the architecture. It's difficult to understand today their appreciation of this building as even Ian Nairn, who was actually on the demo that day, would later describe Bowater House as: 'A curate's egg. Walls with a good deal of trouble taken over the materials and proportion, yet a roofline which is laissez-faire at its worst. This perhaps should be the average. Alas, it is far above it.'

Their first target was Caltex House, designed by a subsidiary of the Alliance Assurance Company and completed the previous year in 1957. It contained, along with offices, a large branch of the Bank of Scotland and a retail parade of six shops. It was built on the old site of what used to be Tattersall's auction yard, which had been in and around the area since 1766 when Richard 'Old Tat' Tattersall opened his auctioneers near Hyde Park Corner, then on the very outskirts of London. As a nod to the horses that were once traded at Tattersall's, Caltex House was adorned by a metal-coated, reinforced concrete sculpture of horses called *Triga* by the Czech artist Franta Belsky. It was reported that a member of staff on the march (almost certainly Ian Nairn) said that Caltex House was 'chaotic' and that Belsky's horses were only suitable outside an Italian railway station. The students wrote slogans with white and blue chalk outside the building such as 'Pull it down', 'Alas for England!' and 'What a monstrosity'. The bank manager quietly protested to the students that while he approved of free expression, it cost quite enough to clean the marble walls of the building without having to wipe away chalk marks.

The second part of the Anti-Uglies' protest that day, called 'Operation Two', was outside Agriculture House at 25–27 Knightsbridge. This was a monumental neo-Georgian building which at the time housed the Farmers' Union headquarters, hence its name, and had been built not long before in 1954. With their heads hung low, the Anti-Uglies observed a minute's silence outside the building they described as Stalinist. People at the windows started shouting, 'Come up! Come up!' but no one accepted their invitation. Agriculture House had replaced two properties that had both been left empty after being badly damaged during the war. At number 25, between the years 1928 and 1939, there had been a prestigious London showroom of the fashionable furniture designers Betty and David Joel. The building, designed by the architect H. S. Goodhart-Rendel, featured a striking modernistic shopfront of plate glass and coursed slate with 'ship rails' to the first-floor windows. Next door, at number 27, had once stood the prestigious Alexandra Hotel where, it was once written in 1907, 'almost every European royal house was represented in its guest lists, together with innumerable statesmen, diplomats and celebrities'.[2] The journalist and former London editor of *The Manchester Guardian*, James Bone, recalled it in 1940 as 'that prim hotel of suites in Knightsbridge with its stiff, frail Ouidaesque air … probably the last hotel where country people still came up "for the season"'.[3] Both the Caltex building and Agriculture House were built in parts of Knightsbridge that had suffered badly during the Second World War from bomb damage. At around 12.30 a.m. on 11 May 1941, the Alexandra Hotel was hit by a single high-explosive bomb that smashed straight through five floors of the grandiose hotel and detonated in the heart of the building. The explosion resulted in twenty-four fatalities and sixteen people seriously injured. Three years later, in 1944, and up the road at Knightsbridge Green where the Caltex building still stands, a V1 missile exploded, razing the surrounding area and leaving twenty-nine casualties, including six dead.

Between 1955 and the time of the Anti-Uglies protest, new large office buildings had changed the appearance of the Knightsbridge Green area considerably. However, as far as re-building was concerned, the London County Council wanted to go further, much further. Plans were already submitted where the road junction at Scotch Corner was to be turned into a huge gyratory system comparable to those now at Marble Arch and Hyde Park Corner. The centre of Knightsbridge would have become a vast oblong roundabout stretching from the Green in the west to Harvey Nichols in the east. The roundabout would have contained a subterranean pedestrian concrete piazza, the same size as Parliament Square, with numerous shops and commercial units connected by subways to a vast 320-foot office tower on the southern side. The huge roundabout would have been overlooked by three massive tower blocks more than 400 feet high. The scheme would have meant the razing of the whole area contained within Brompton Road, Hans Crescent and Sloane Street. The relatively diminutive 308-foot-high Basil Spence-designed tower which is part of the present Knightsbridge Barracks in Hyde Park was originally designed to be just part of a 'visually appealing group' of LCC tower blocks. By the late sixties, in the light of changed economic conditions and fashion, but also the threat of even more traffic gridlock, the great majority of the plans which would have destroyed so much of Knightsbridge were thankfully dropped.

The day after the Anti-Uglies' protest *The Times* talked not of the terrible architecture but of the students' unusual clothes, describing them wearing 'the usual motley of lumpy coats, blue jeans, hats like tufts of gorse, and in one instance, green boots'. A more supportive John Betjeman, despite being already known as a conservationist, wrote of the protest in the *Daily Telegraph*: 'Art is coming into its own again after the worship of science and economics. What is more important, the art of architecture is at last coming in for the public notice it deserves.' It wasn't just the newspaper reporters who found the protest difficult to understand; members of the watching public were confused too. One of the shops at Caltex House was Bazaar, Mary Quant's second shop. During the demonstration a perfectly dressed shop-assistant-cum-model emerged from the recently opened boutique and asked what the chanting was all about. In a very well-spoken voice she responded to the Anti-Uglies' answer with, 'But you're all so ugly yourselves!'

This was patently untrue, at least as far as Pauline Boty was concerned, and she appeared in the *Daily Express* a few months later in the William

Hickey column next to a headline: 'Of all Things She is Secretary of the Anti-Uglies'. Boty told the *Express*: 'I think the Air Ministry building is a real stinker, with the Farmers' Union HQ, the Bank of England [a huge curved block along New Change by Victor Heal, which has now been demolished] and the Financial Times as runners-up.' And her own home? 'A 1930s semi in Carshalton, normally termed "desirable",' sighed Boty. 'I don't approve, of course, but I daren't say anything or daddy would be upset.'[4] The photograph accompanying the article was taken by Lewis Morley, then a frustrated painter but who would famously go on to take the iconic picture of a naked Christine Keeler astride a backwards-facing chair. He recalled, 'Someone decided Pauline should be photographed to publicise Anti-Ugly Action. I took several photographs of her that day, showing a blonde, vivacious girl, filled with joie de vivre. She was stunning, a major factor in why the article found a place in the *Express*.'[5]

Pauline was also interviewed at one of the protests by the BBC TV local Friday evening news roundup 'Town and Around' and was asked: 'What's a pretty girl like you doing at this sort of an event?' Instead of kicking him in the shins, Pauline smiled and said that the building was an expensive disgrace. The interviewer said that he had been told that it was very efficient inside. 'We are outside,' she countered.

At the time of the Anti-Ugly protests Pauline Boty, born in 1938 in suburban Carshalton in Surrey, was twenty years old. The youngest of four children, she won a scholarship to the Wimbledon School of Art when she was sixteen and went on to study there despite her father's very strong reservations about her choice of career. Due to her good looks, personality and blonde hair, her friends at the college called her the 'Wimbledon Bardot'. Brigitte Bardot was by now famous to the British public; she had appeared in *Doctor at Sea* in 1955 and had actually already made seventeen films when *And God Created Woman* made her an undoubted international star in 1957. It was directed by her husband Roger Vadim, who had been Bardot's lover since she was fifteen: 'She was my wife, my daughter and my mistress,' he once wrote. However, by the time the film was released, she was none of those things, and Bardot was living with her co-star Jean-Louis Trintignant, and was having an affair with the musician Gilbert Bécaud. Boty jokily enjoyed the comparison with the French actress and Charles Carey, Boty's tutor at the time, once recalled a younger student going up to her in the canteen at Wimbledon and asking her why she wore so much red lipstick: '"All the better to kisssss you with," she said, and chased him out of the room.'

In 1957 one of Boty's paintings was shown at the Young Contemporaries exhibition alongside Robyn Denny, Richard Smith and Bridget Riley, and the following year she was accepted at the Royal College of Art. Although studying Stained Glass, Boty continued to paint at her student flat and in 1959 she had three more paintings selected for the Young Contemporaries exhibition. The two years after her graduation, however, were perhaps Boty's most productive and by now she had begun to develop a personal 'pop art' style. Her first proper group show, 'Blake, Boty, Porter, Reeve', was held in November 1961 at the AIA gallery at 15 Lisle Street (where the restaurant Fung Shing is now). It has been described as the first proper British Pop Art exhibition, although the word 'pop' wasn't used in the contemporary reviews.

In 1962 Boty appeared in a film that was part of the BBC TV arts series *Monitor*. It was directed by Ken Russell and called 'Pop Goes the Easel', originally the title of a 1935 Three Stooges film. As well as Pauline, it featured the artists Peter Blake, Derek Boshier and Peter Phillips and is now a valuable contemporary look at the relatively short-lived British Pop Art movement. It was also one of the first British documentaries to use popular music as a soundtrack, and the James Darren song 'Goodbye Cruel World' was memorably used at the beginning of the film over shots of the four artists enjoying themselves at Bertram Mills Circus inside Olympia. It had been the title of one of Pauline's recent collages featured at the AIA gallery the previous November. Boty says in the film: 'It's a horrible thing when people just look at my paintings and walk away and that's it. I'd like my things to relate to everybody in the end. Things like beer cans may become a new kind of folk art; they're like paintings on pin-tables: something else that people haven't really looked at before.' The following year Pauline said of her paintings: 'My work is for looking at, not talking about. If they have some effect on you, I have probably succeeded.'

The fashion designer Ossie Clark, at the time an RCA student, wrote about Pauline in his diary during the summer of 1962:

The first time she noticed me, sunbathing in her bikini bottom sprawled out in the garden. Philip Saville was her current chap, beau lovers by the score. Freckles, innocent blue eyes, lips so full, a look direct eyeball to eyeball, melt away like Tom and Jerry heavy as mercury down a drain, or foolish as I did then – What subject should she paint? I'd suggested flags of the major powers, (Derek Boshier, Dick Smith, Peter Blake) China, Russia, America. 'Naa! S'bin done!' Green as the grass we lay in corn, in sunlight, as the storm clouds lift the golden rays from her smile. Those lips I was eventually to kiss, so soft like crying tears absorbed into a down pillow, maudlin, too pretty. Always swanking.

Philip Saville, mentioned in Clarke's diary, was a married television and theatre director who had a habit of turning his leading actresses into girlfriends. This time, however, it was the other way round and he encouraged Pauline to act, much to the dismay of many of her friends and art college contemporaries who thought that she should concentrate on her art. She appeared in television plays directed by Saville and appeared on stage at the Royal Court in a play called *Day of the Prince* by Frank Hilton. In January 1963 Saville directed a play broadcast on the BBC called *The Madhouse on Castle Street* which featured Bob Dylan's first British television appearance as an actor and singer, and indeed it was his first trip outside the USA. Phillip and Pauline picked Dylan up from London Airport and he stayed at Pauline's flat for four days. As was the BBC's wont, they of course wiped the recording, but Dylan, who played a character called Bobby the Hobo, was apparently too stoned to remember his lines and was only able to sing two of his songs.

It is said that the relationship between Julie Christie and Dirk Bogarde in John Schlesinger's film *Darling* was partly based on Boty's and Saville's love affair. Boty, ironically, would later herself audition for the role eventually played by Christie in the film that tried so hard to be hip and happening but now seems rather dated. In June 1963 Saville introduced Boty to a friend of his, the left-wing actor and writer Clive Goodwin. Ten days later Pauline sent Saville a telegram. It was opened by his wife, fearing an emergency, and she wasn't please to read: 'By the time you read this I will be married to Clive Goodwin. Please forgive me.' Boty described her new husband in an interview with the writer Nell Dunn (who personally thought Goodwin too dull for her) as 'The very first man I met who really liked women, for one thing – a terribly rare thing in a man … I mean here was someone who liked women and to whom they weren't kind of things or something you don't quite know about – and because you kind of desire them they're slightly sort of awful, because they bring out the worst in you, this funny sort of puritan idea, sort of Adam and Eve and everything.'[6]

The last picture that Pauline Boty painted was entitled *Bum* and completed very early in 1966. Kenneth Tynan had commissioned it during early preparation of his erotic revue *Oh! Calcutta!*. It was her last painting because in June 1965, two months before she filmed a bit part in the film *Alfie*, Boty found out that she was pregnant. During a prenatal examination, however, she was found to be suffering from terminal lymphatic cancer. She refused an abortion but also any chemotherapy that may have harmed her baby. Her daughter, who was called Boty Goodwin (so she would always have her mother's name), was born in February 1966. By this time Pauline was very ill and after just four days she handed her daughter over to her parents to look after.

Goodwin was devastated and never married again. In November 1978, he flew to Los Angeles for various business meetings, including one at the Beverly Wilshire hotel, where he met with Warren Beatty (who was living at the hotel at the time) to discuss the script for Beatty's upcoming film *Reds*. The next day, Goodwin, who had complained about a headache earlier, began vomiting in the hotel foyer before falling unconscious. The hotel clerk and a security guard assumed he was drunk and called the police, who handcuffed him, hauled him outside and took him to the Beverly Hills police station. Goodwin died later that night of a brain haemorrhage, alone in the cell, probably never having regained consciousness.

After her death Pauline Boty's paintings were stored away on her brother's farm and were almost thrown away more than once. For someone so well known in the art world during the early sixties Boty, along with her art, was almost completely forgotten. In the early 1990s the art historian David Mellor watched 'Pop Goes the Easel' and wondered what had happened to Boty's paintings. He tracked them down and some were exhibited in a 1993 Barbican exhibition called 'The Sixties Art Scene in London'. Boty Goodwin, who was now at art college in Los Angeles, came to the private view. Incredibly, the Barbican show was the first time Pauline Boty's work had been exhibited since her death. *Time Out* was not wrong when it included in their review of the exhibition the sentence: 'Boty's paintings shower with critical blows the macho stance of Pop.'

Boty Goodwin had been brought up initially by Pauline's parents but from the age of five by her father. She was eleven when Goodwin died and she moved back to Carshalton for the next few years. Boty eventually moved to Los Angeles in the late 1980s where, following her mother's career as an art student, she went to Cal Arts. Unfortunately the Boty/Goodwin family tragedies continued and in 1995 she died in her studio of a heroin overdose. She was only twenty-nine.

Over fifty years after the protests it's interesting to look at the buildings in Knightsbridge that upset the Anti-Uglies so. The Stalinist Agriculture House, never a particularly popular building, was eventually demolished in 1993 for two separate properties that architecturally don't seem to be much of an improvement, but which are of a size more respectful of the area. Along with its equine sculpture celebrating 'Old Tat' and his auction yard, Caltex House still stands and remains as stodgily unexceptional and dull as when it was built, despite a facelift in 2001. Bowater House, the building that the Uglies cheered as they walked past, was demolished in 2006 without many people mourning its loss. Its replacement, One Hyde Park, was called by its once idealistic architect Lord Rogers 'a twenty-first-century monument'. A monument to what, however, no one really knows but it seems to be some kind of celebration of the ostentatious ultra-rich and the ever-growing, widening gap between the rich and poor in London. In 2010, at the height of the credit crunch, a penthouse flat in the building sold for £140 million.

Somehow One Hyde Park has managed to make people remember Bowater House almost fondly. Firstly for the opening in its centre that enabled anyone to drive or walk though into Hyde Park, and secondly for the sculpture *The Return of Spring*, originally placed in the middle of the road for everyone to see and made up of three nude figures, a man, a woman and a child, running with their dog towards the park. It was the last work by the sculptor Jacob Epstein and he was still putting the finishing touches to it on the day he died in 1959. Ian Nairn was no fan and saw the sculpture as a 'sad end' to Epstein's career and said that it reminded him of 'an incestuous family fleeing into Hyde Park from the Vice Squad'.[7] The family now has less far to flee and Epstein's sculpture has been placed round the back of the buildings, near a small road that leads to Hyde Park. The road has been cleverly designed to look private so hardly anyone uses it.

If Pauline Boty was alive today and the Anti-Uglies were still protesting, One Hyde Park, a building architecturally more suited to Qatar and Abu Dhabi than Knightsbridge, would almost certainly have been first on their list.

'Outrage! Outrage! Outrage!'

Opposite above: Bowater House at 68–114, Knightsbridge in 1965. It was to be demolished just over forty years later.

Opposite below: High Row, 68–92 Knightsbridge in 1936. These buildings were demolished in the early fifties for Bowater House.

Above: Caltex House at 1, Knightsbridge Green and 44–58 Brompton Road built between 1955 and 1957.

Left: Caltex House in 2013. (Rob Baker)

Right: Pauline Boty self portrait, c. 1955. (Courtesy of Bridget Boty)

Below: Pauline Boty in her flat in 1962. (John Aston, courtesy of Matt Robinson)

Above: My Colouring Book, 1963, by Pauline Boty. (Courtesy of Bridget Boty)

Left: One Hyde Park, 2014. (Rob Baker)

Above: Security guard at One Hyde Park, 2014. (Rob Baker)

Right: Bum by Pauline Boty, her last painting, originally commissioned by Kenneth Tynan for *Oh! Calcutta!* (Courtesy of Bridget Boty)

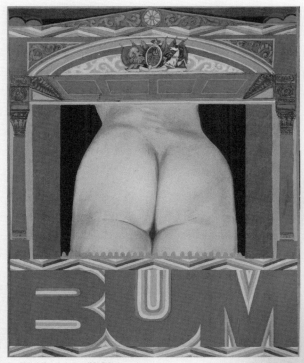

Plate 58 BUM, 1966, oil on canvas, 45.7 x 76.2 cm

CHAPTER 3

The Day the Traitors Burgess and Maclean Left Town

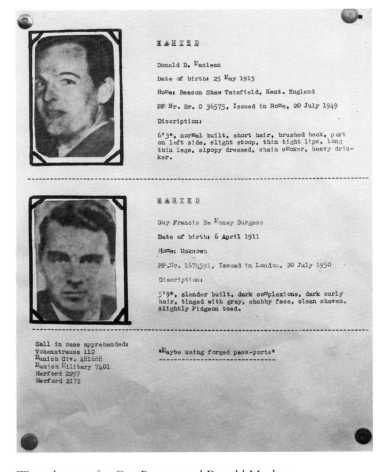

Wanted poster for Guy Burgess and Donald Maclean.

Guy Burgess woke up in his untidy, musty-smelling bedroom at around 9.30 on the morning of Friday 25 May 1951. Next to his bed was an overflowing ashtray and lying on the floor was a half-read Jane Austen novel. Since his return from Washington DC three weeks previously, where he had been second secretary at the British embassy, he'd been rising later and later. Burgess had left America in disgrace, and at the British ambassador's behest, after several embarrassing drunken incidents that included being caught speeding at 80 m.p.h. three times in just one hour, pouring a plate of prawns into his jacket pocket (and leaving them there for a week), continually chewing raw garlic like others would chew mints and being loudly vocal, not only with his anti-American views but also about his homosexuality. The FBI later described him, not inaccurately, as 'a louche, foul-mouthed gay with a penchant for seducing hitchhikers'.[1] Thoroughly disliked by most of the Americans with whom he came in contact, Burgess behaved as if he wanted to be sent back to England. Many people thought he did.

Burgess was born in Devon in 1911, the elder son of naval commander Malcolm Kingsford de Moncy Burgess and his wife, Evelyn Mary. Although he was just thirteen when his father died, his mother was affluent enough to send him to Eton, where his fellow classmates, apparently, thought him 'sophisticated, at ease, with a cool detached manner, an intellectually superior being'.[2] Burgess won an open scholarship to read modern history at Trinity College and he soon joined the Cambridge University Socialist Society. More importantly, he also became a member of The Apostles, a secret and elite debating society. It was there that Burgess was introduced to Kim Philby by Maurice Dobb, a communist don and fellow member. After graduating in 1933, Burgess held a two-year teaching position and in May 1934 he met Arnold Deutsch, a Comintern officer and recruiter for Soviet intelligence who would later that year travel to the Soviet Union. Around this time Kim Philby asked him to suggest other recruits, and Burgess suggested Anthony Blunt and Donald Maclean. This was the beginning of the Cambridge network of Soviet agents. As a cover for his Soviet Union support, Burgess openly renounced communism and also joined the rather Nazi-friendly Anglo-German Fellowship.

After leaving Cambridge, where he was more often than not described as 'brilliant' and 'charming', Burgess briefly went to work at *The Times* but in October of that year found himself a prestigious job at the BBC as a 'Talks' producer. He was helped by a reference from the renowned historian Sir George Trevelyan, who wrote: 'He is a first-rate man. He has passed through the communist measles that so many of our clever young men go through and is well out of it.'[3] While working for the broadcaster he got into trouble for abusing his expenses and when defending his exorbitant claims to his superiors, Burgess wrote: 'I normally travel first class and see no reason why I should alter my practice when on BBC business, particularly when I am in my best clothes.'[4] Either his cover as a Soviet spy was particularly sophisticated, or more likely, despite his communist sympathies, Burgess had always been a snob. When the police raided a drinking club one night during the war, he was purported to have said: 'I'm Guy Burgess and I live in Mayfair. I presume you, inspector, to come from some dreary little suburb.'[5]

Towards the end of the war in 1944 he moved to the news department of the Foreign Office and soon took on the position of secretary to the British deputy foreign minister, Hector McNeil. The job gave him access to hundreds of top-secret Foreign Office documents, which he happily photographed for the KGB on a regular basis. This continued until 1947 when he was sent to the British embassy in Washington DC as second secretary.

Four years later and now back in London, Burgess was living in a small three-roomed flat in Mayfair situated at Clifford Chambers, 10 New Bond Street, and opposite Asprey, the famous jewellers. The location was (and of course is) a particularly salubrious part of London and a long, long way from the Soviet Union and anything it represented. Burgess, the Soviet spy from such a privileged background, coped with this irony with surprising ease. At least until this particular Friday morning in 1951 when his world suddenly turned upside down.

Not long after he had woken in his untidy bedroom, Burgess had been brought a cup of tea by his flatmate Jack Hewit, known to his friends as Jackie. Son of a metalworker, Hewit had won a scholarship to ballet school, but his father forbade him to accept it, so he ran away from home and began dancing in revues. He met Guy Burgess while dancing in the chorus of a revival of the musical comedy *No, No, Nanette* and subsequently became Burgess's lover. Years later the two were still very close friends and had been sharing various flats in and around Mayfair for fourteen years. Hewit later wrote of that morning: 'Guy lay back, reading a book and smoking, and he seemed normal and unworried. When I left the flat to go to my office, Guy said, "See you later, Mop" – that was his pet name for me. We intended to have a drink together that evening.'[6]

As Burgess was waking up, Donald Duart Maclean was already sitting at his desk in Whitehall having caught his usual train from Sevenoaks some two hours previously. Maclean was the son of one of the most illustrious Liberal families in the country. His father, Sir Donald Maclean, had first entered Parliament as the Liberal member for Bath in 1906 and had been President of the Board of Education in the cabinet when he died in 1932. Nineteen years later Donald Maclean was head of the American department at the Foreign Office in King Charles Street. The job sounded important but care was already being made by the authorities that it should be of no operational significance. For several weeks now, along with three other men, Maclean had been under suspicion for leaking atomic secrets to the Soviet Union. In the last few days, however, the four suspects had become just one. Two years younger than Burgess, Maclean was exactly thirty-eight years old, for it was his birthday and he had already asked if he could take the next morning as leave (Saturday mornings were still worked by many civil servants in the 1950s) so that he could celebrate the whole weekend with family and friends at home in Surrey.

Between 10 and 10.30 that morning Herbert Morrison, who had recently become Foreign Secretary, was visited in his office by a senior MI5 officer and the head of Foreign Office security. After receiving and reading a few official papers, Morrison signed one of them. It gave MI5 permission to question Donald Maclean about links with the Soviet Union. The interrogation was to begin on Monday 28 May (not even a Soviet mole in the upper echelons of the Foreign Office justified ruining a perfectly good weekend). By now both Maclean and Burgess knew something was wrong and a few days previously had met for lunch to discuss the matter. Initially intending to eat at the Reform Club on Pall Mall, where Burgess was a member, they found the dining room full and walked to the nearby Royal Automobile Club instead. Ostensibly they were meeting about a memorandum that Burgess had been preparing about the threat of McCarthyism and American policy in the Far East, but on the way Maclean said: 'I'm in frightful trouble. I'm being followed by the dicks.'[7] He pointed out two men standing by the corner of the Carlton Club. Burgess later described the two men: 'There they were, jingling their coins in a policeman-like manner and looking embarrassed at having to follow a member of the upper classes.'[8]

Just three years previously Maclean had been posted to Cairo as one of Britain's promising young diplomats. He started drinking heavily and behaving in a way that couldn't be ignored by his superiors. At a party given by King Saud he urinated on the carpet and at another, smaller, gathering he was seen arguing furiously with his wife before seemingly trying to strangle her. Maclean was almost certainly either gay or bisexual and this, along with the weight of living two separate lives as a spy, was patently starting to take its toll. His wife Melinda once wrote to her sister saying, 'Donald is still pretty confused and vague about himself, and his desires, but I think when he gets settled he will find a new security and peace. I hope so ... He is still going to R. [the psychiatrist], however, and is definitely better. She is still baffled about the homosexual side which comes out when he's drunk, and I think slight hostility in general, to women.'[9] Maclean was advised to take medical leave in May 1950 but after six months the Foreign Office decided, extraordinarily, to make him head of its American department.

At around the same time as the Herbert Morrison security meeting in Whitehall, Burgess left his flat in New Bond Street. He had just received a telephone call from Western Union relaying a telegraph from Kim Philby in America about a car he had left behind in Washington. In reality it was almost certainly a coded message warning him that Maclean would be interrogated after the weekend. Burgess hurried to the Green Park Hotel on Half Moon Street just off Piccadilly and about ten minutes' walk from his flat. The hotel is still there, and with almost the same name (it has Hilton and London preceding it now), but when Burgess walked through the door in 1951 the street would have looked completely different. Although the hotel had survived the worst of the air raids during the war, much of the surrounding area was either a bomb or building site. Still to be rebuilt, in 1940 much of the terrace on the opposite side of the street had been destroyed by a German air raid, as had the entire east corner of the road at the junction with Piccadilly.

In the lobby of the hotel Burgess met a young American student called Bernard Miller whom he had befriended on his journey back from the US on the RMS *Queen Mary*. Burgess later described the American as 'an intelligent progressive sort of chap'. They had coffee in the hotel's comfortable lounge and then went for a walk in nearby Green Park. They had previously planned a short trip to France and Burgess had already booked two tickets for a boat that sailed that night. They hadn't been walking long before Burgess suddenly stopped, turned to his surprised American friend who had been animatedly chatting away about their trip, and said, 'Sorry Bernard, I haven't been listening, really. You see, a young friend at the Foreign Office is in serious trouble, and I have to help him out of it, somehow.' Burgess assured the shocked Miller that he would do everything he could to make their midnight Channel ferry but he couldn't be definite about it until a few hours later. By now it was just before midday and while the American went back to his hotel, Burgess went to the Reform Club for a large whisky. After half an hour he asked the porter to call Welbeck 3991 and ordered a hire car for ten days from Welbeck Motors. He also tried to call his friend Goronwy Rees but only got through to his mother. Characteristically, he 'forgot' to pay for the call and the amount owing, his name and the telephone number he called were written down on a note and pinned up on the members' noticeboard. It remained there for some time.[10]

While a worried and thoughtful Burgess was slumped in a large corner armchair at his club, Maclean left his office and walked up Whitehall and across Trafalgar Square to Old Compton Street in Soho. There he met a couple of friends for lunch at Wheeler's, which in 1951 had only been in existence for just over twenty years but was already a Soho institution. The owner, Bernard Walsh, a large and friendly Whitstable man, had started it in 1929 as a small retail oyster shop. He noticed how popular his oysters were in London's top restaurants so he bought a few tables and chairs and started serving them himself. He soon built a bar for the customers and before long Wheeler's was a full-blown restaurant. The war, despite much of Old Compton Street having been badly bombed, only made Wheeler's more successful. Oysters weren't rationed and it was easy for Walsh to sell them below the five-shilling limit on the cost of a meal imposed by governmental wartime restrictions.

By 1951, when Maclean and his friends visited for lunch, the restaurant featured a long counter on the left-hand side where a waiter or Walsh himself opened oysters at a frightening speed – up to six hundred an hour if the restaurant was busy. The back area had its own small bar and claret-coloured couches where the menu could be perused before sitting in the restaurant proper. The large green menu contained thirty-two sole and lobster dishes but no vegetables, save for a few boiled potatoes, and no desserts. During post-war austerity, when English food was at its dreariest and some of it still rationed, the meals served at Wheeler's seemed luxurious. Maclean and his friends stood at the busy bar and ordered a dozen oysters and some Chablis. Maclean seemed in good spirits and if the thirty-eight-year-old had something on his mind he wasn't showing it. Regular customers of Wheeler's at the time included Lucien Freud and his wife Elizabeth Blackwood, Francis Bacon, the writers Colin MacInnes and Cyril Connolly and countless other Soho artists, intellectuals and drinkers. Perhaps the *Daily Express* star journalist and broadcaster Nancy Spain was there that lunchtime. She often was during 1951 and from time to time was accompanied by the writer Elizabeth Jane Howard, who occasionally worked for her. Howard once recalled, after one such Wheeler's lunch, that Spain asked her to go to bed with her: '"Oh, come on darling. Just pop into bed with me and let's see how we feel." So I did. "Well?" The bright brown bird's eye was fixed on me. Eventually she said, "Well, it doesn't seem to be any good. Never mind." We got out of bed and put on our clothes. And that was that.'[11]

Wheeler's was too crowded to be comfortable and Maclean decided that they would eat the rest of their lunch elsewhere. He seemed unconcerned and almost nonchalant when he and his friends walked up Greek Street, through Soho Square and on to Charlotte Street. Here they had two further courses at a German restaurant and delicatessen called Schmidt's, situated at numbers 35–37. In 1951 this area of London was still known to most people as North Soho and the name Fitzrovia, named after the Fitzroy Tavern, would generally not be used for a decade or two. Incidentally, the word 'Fitzrovia' was recorded in print for the first time in an article by Tom Driberg, the Labour MP and also close friend of Guy Burgess. Donald Maclean wouldn't have called it Fitzrovia but he might have jokingly called Charlotte Street 'Charlottenstrasse' as the road occasionally was still called at the time. Schmidt's was the last vestige of the German community which had settled north of Oxford Street in the late nineteenth century. Frederic William Wile, the former Berlin correspondent for the *Daily Mail*, wrote about the restaurant in 1916: 'Frederick Schmidt's dining room is a crammed little apartment, not more than twelve or fifteen feet square, containing four marble-topped tables unadorned with tablecloths. It is for all the world like the *kneipen* or *destillationen* [low-class public houses] with which every street in the cheaper quarters of German towns and cities is infested.'[12]

Most of the staff at Schmidt's had been interned during both world wars and this is often given as an explanation why the waiters were described somewhere between 'curt' and 'the rudest in the world'. Schmidt's was also known for its cheap prices and this may or may not have been a reason why T. S. Eliot was a regular at the restaurant where, dressed in a navy blue suit, he would eat the Weiner schnitzel with chilled Moselle wine. The writer A. S. Byatt also often visited and described the establishment in her novel *Still Life*: 'In Schmidt's amazing delikatessen you could buy sauerkraut from wooden barrels, black pumpernickel, wurst cooked and uncooked, huge choux pastries and little cups of black coffee. In Schmidt's you paid for everything with little receipts at a central caisse presided over by an erect moustached lady with a black dress and lace.'[13] Ms Byatt was being kind: the woman behind the till dressed in black was usually described as 'bearded'. In 1951 the restaurant still served food using an old European restaurant custom where the waiters brought staple middle-

European main courses, such as eisbein with sauerkraut or frankfurters with spaetzle, from the kitchen and only then sold them to the customers. By 1976 the local German/Jewish community had long since relocated to Golders Green or Edgware and Schmidt's had to close down. It lay empty for years. By 2015 a Japanese restaurant called Roka was on the premises.

Maclean and his friends had a relatively long, relaxed lunch and, afterwards, while saying goodbye to them he gratefully accepted an offer to stay at their house while his wife was away in hospital having their baby. Melinda Maclean was only two weeks from having their third child and he said he'd call them the following week to arrange the details. As Maclean was saying goodbye to his friends, Burgess was probably calling on Welbeck Motors at 7–9 Crawford Street, half a mile or so north of Marble Arch, to pick up his hire car. It was an Austin A70 and was due to be returned on 4 June, ten days later. He paid £25 cash in advance – £15 for the hire of the car and £10 deposit. Burgess drove the Austin down to Mayfair where he parked outside Gieves at 27 Old Bond Street at about 3 p.m.

The 200-year-old tailors had only been at these premises for about ten years. The original flagship store, a few doors down at number 21, had been irreparably damaged by a bomb during the war. Incidentally Gieves & Hawkes, now possibly the most famous bespoke tailoring name in the world, only merged in 1974 when Gieves bought out Hawkes, also enabling it to acquire the valuable freehold of No. 1 Savile Row. The acquisition was particularly well timed because not long after the merger, the Gieves shop in Old Bond Street was again destroyed by high explosives. This time it was courtesy of the IRA but it meant that from 1975, number 1 Savile Row became Gieves & Hawkes. Which is exactly where the illustrious tailoring shop is today. Burgess bought a 'fibre' suitcase at Gieves and also a white mackintosh. Although very warm and almost 27°, thunder could be heard in the distance and it had started raining heavily. After paying for his purchases Burgess went to meet Bernard Miller again but after a couple of drinks he dropped the young American back at his hotel telling him, 'I'll call for you at half past seven.' Burgess didn't call for him and they never saw each other again.

Meanwhile Maclean had taken a taxi down to the Travellers Club, the club on Pall Mall that had long been associated with the Foreign Office and the Diplomatic Service. He had two drinks at the bar and cashed a cheque for £5. He did this most weekends so nothing appeared unusual. There wasn't anyone at the club he knew so he walked back to his office just after three. Burgess drove the hired Austin A70 back to his flat where he met Hewit who had by now returned home from work. While they were talking the phone rang. Burgess immediately answered it and made it clear to Hewit that he was talking to Maclean. After the telephone conversation a visibly upset Burgess left the flat almost immediately but not before he grabbed £300 in cash and some saving certificates. He also filled his new suitcase with some clothes and his treasured volume of Jane Austen's collected novels. He asked to borrow Hewit's overcoat and then left the flat without properly saying goodbye.

Burgess was next seen back at the Reform Club in Pall Mall where he had a quick drink and asked for a road map of the north of England (probably as a diversion). From there he drove the 22 miles to Maclean's home at Tatsfield in Surrey. While Burgess was on his way Maclean left the Foreign Office at exactly 4.45 p.m. and walked up Whitehall to Charing Cross station, where he joined the hurrying commuter crowd. The two MI5 'dicks' were still following him but only as far as the station, where they made sure he got on his usual 5.19 train to Sevenoaks and then they both went home.

The two friends arrived at Maclean's house within half an hour of each other and Burgess was introduced to Maclean's wife Melinda as Mr Roger Styles, a business colleague. Burgess must have been playing with the security services with this name and used two Agatha Christie novels, *The Murder of Roger Ackroyd* and *The Mysterious Affair at Styles*, to make up the alias. They all sat down for a birthday dinner at seven for which Melinda had cooked a special ham for the occasion. After the meal, Maclean put a few things into a briefcase, including a silk dressing gown, and casually told his wife that he and 'Styles' would have to go on a business trip and were unlikely to be away for more than a day.

At 9.00 p.m., with Burgess at the wheel of the cream-coloured Austin A70, they set off on the 100-mile journey to Southampton. The cross-Channel ferry *Falaise*, for which Burgess had already bought tickets, intending to use them for his trip with Bernard Miller, was due to leave for St Malo at midnight. After speedily driving though the deserted streets of Southampton they made it to No. 9 dock with just minutes to spare. In their haste they almost hit a lorry driven by Sid Hampton, an employee at the dockside garage. He described the scene to the press: 'They roared into the docks just before the ship sailed. The two men jumped out, banged the doors. One of them was carrying two cases, the other man one. I was about to tell them off for speeding in the docks when one of them threw a couple of bob on the ground. He shouted, "Buy yourself a drink." '[14] Hampton asked them what they wanted to do with the car they had just left on the quayside. As they ran up the gangway, almost as it was being raised, Burgess yelled back, 'I'm back on Monday.'

He wasn't of course, although it's said that he thought he would be, and Burgess and Maclean never set foot in Britain again. The writer and diarist Harold Nicolson, who had become very attached to Burgess after meeting him at the BBC during the war, wrote in his diary on 7 June: 'If I thought Guy was a brave man, I should imagine that he had gone to join the communists. As I know him though to be a coward, I suppose that he was suspected of passing things on to the Bolshies, and realising his guilt, did a bunk.' In an entry the next day Nicholson wrote: 'I fear poor Guy will be rendered very unhappy in the end. If he had done a bunk to Russia, they will only use him for a month or so, and shove him quietly into some salt-mine.'[15] He was never sent to a salt mine but Burgess, despite his political leanings, was much more suited to life on Old Bond Street in Mayfair and first-class travel on Pullman trains. He never learnt Russian and in reality he hoped a deal would be struck with the British government and he could return home.

Nothing was actually heard from Burgess and Maclean, as far as the British public was concerned anyway, for almost five years. On Saturday 11 February 1956 reporters from the Reuters agency and the *Sunday Times* were invited to a room at the National Hotel in Moscow. To the journalists' astonishment and surprise, Burgess and Maclean suddenly walked through the door and sat down behind a desk. They said nothing but the newsmen were handed a statement in which the two ex-Foreign Office men both admitted that they had been communists in Cambridge, but denied being Soviet agents. The only reason they had emigrated to Moscow, it said, was because of the perilous anti-communist stance of the present Anglo-American foreign policy. The two men then left without answering questions. Not long after the Moscow 'press conference' Tom Driberg, the Labour MP and an old friend of Burgess from his BBC days (he occasionally presented *The Week in Westminster* that Burgess used to produce), wrote to him requesting an interview. On 15 March 1956 Driberg received a telegram:

IN PRINCIPLE AGREE YOUR PLAN STOP MORE DETAILS BY LETTER POSTED TODAY STOP PLEASE ACKNOWLEDGE THIS WIRE AND ALSO LETTER WHEN RECEIVED IN CASE OF ACCIDENT STOP POSSIBLE OBSTRUCTION YOUR END ONLY STOP WARM GREETINGS GUY

On 10 August Driberg arrived in Moscow and stayed at the National Hotel. Two days later Burgess called him from the Moskva Hotel across the square and they arranged to meet outside the entrance. When Burgess saw Driberg he sighed and said, 'We've both got rather fatter since we last saw each other.'

Towards the end of his life, most of which was spent in a chain-smoking, drunken haze, a blonde electrician named Tolya moved into Burgess's Moscow flat and became the last of his many lovers. Burgess was just fifty-two when he died in August 1963 of liver and heart trouble. Maclean read the eulogy at the Moscow funeral while a band played 'The Internationale'. Maclean found it easier than his spying partner to assimilate into the communist system and became a respected Soviet citizen, although, tellingly, he was never allowed anywhere near the KGB and always worked from home. He lived twenty years longer than his spying partner but died of a heart attack in 1983. Melinda, his wife, had by now left him for Kim Philby, who had already become known as the Third Man, and who had absconded to the Soviet Union in 1963.

The names Burgess and Maclean will be forever linked but when Goronwy Rees sold his reminiscences of Burgess and Maclean to the *Sunday People*, Burgess was particularly upset that it was implied that they had been lovers. Burgess had once said, 'The *idea* of going to bed with Donald! That great white body, it would be like sleeping with Dame Nellie Melba!'[16]

Opposite: Guy Burgess and Donald Maclean.

Right: Guy Burgess at Eton.

Below: Clifford Chambers, 10 New Bond Street. The first-floor bay-windowed flat was the last address of Burgess before defecting to the Soviet Union. (Rob Baker)

Left: Jackie Hewit at his home he shared with Burgess in Clifford Chambers.

Below: Old Compton Street, *c.* 1951. When Donald Maclean walked to Wheeler's on this road, this must have been close to what it looked like. (*Daily Mail*/REX Shutterstock)

The delicatessen part of Schmidt's on Charlotte Street *c.* 1935. (Mary Evans Picture Library)

CHAPTER 4

Warren Street, Spivs, and the Gruesome Murder of Stanley Setty

Stan 'The Spiv' Setty, whose real name was Suleiman Seti.

On 8 March 2013 Camden Council permanently closed part of Warren Street to cars. The road had long been used, and for over a hundred years, as a rat-run for drivers hoping to avoid the congestion that would often build up at the junction between Tottenham Court Road and the Euston Road. Closing a road to traffic in central London is hardly unusual these days but in this case there was a certain irony. For much of the twentieth century Warren Street had been the centre of the used-car trade in London and was the oldest street car market anywhere in Britain.

It all started in 1902 when Charles Friswell, an ex-racing cyclist and successful engineer, astutely hopped on the running board of the new burgeoning car industry and opened Friswell's Automobile Palace at 1 Albany Street on the corner of the Euston Road. It was a five-storey building that could accommodate hundreds of vehicles in garage and showroom spaces, with repair and paint shops, accessory sales and auction facilities. It was known as 'The House of Friswell' and 'The Motor-World's Tattersalls'[1] and was a huge success.

Smaller car dealers started to open along the Euston Road, but as the traffic got busier it became harder and harder to park cars outside their main showrooms. Many of the premises, however, had entrances or exits that opened up on the parallel Warren Street (the road was actually built in the eighteenth century as an access road for the newly built properties on Euston Road).

By the start of the First World War most of the car sales were now taking place on the quieter Warren Street. The main dealerships were soon joined by 'small fry' or 'pavement dealers' – men who bought and sold cars of questionable origin on street corners, cafés, milk-bars and pubs. Frankie Fraser described Warren Street in his book *Mad Frank's London*:

> They'd have cars in showrooms and parked on the pavement. There could be up to fifty cars and then again some people would just stand on the pavement and pass on the info that there was a car to sell. Warren Street was mostly for mug punters. Chaps wouldn't buy one. People would come down from as far away as Scotland to buy a car. All polished and shiny with the clock turned back and the insides hanging out. And if you bought a car and it fell to bits who was you going to complain to?

In December 1949 the magazine *Picture Post* published an article about the used-car market in Warren Street. They described the road as the northernmost boundary of Soho and explained that the area thus 'attracted a fair amount of gutter garbage from the hinterland'. The reporters also feigned shock at the numerous cash deals that were going on: 'Bundles of dirty notes were going across without counting ... there is nothing illegal about a cash sale unless, of course, the Income Tax authorities can catch them – which they cannot – or thieves fall out and pick each other's pockets – or unless, of course, someone gets killed.'

And someone did get killed. His name was Stanley Setty, a shady Warren Street car-dealer with a lock-up round the corner in Cambridge Terrace Mews. He hadn't been seen since 4 October, when he had sold a Wolseley Twelve saloon to a man in Watford, for which he received 200 £5 notes. The next day Setty's brother-in-law called at Albany Street police station to report him missing, and it didn't take long before Setty's fellow traders and black marketeers noticed his absence from his usual patch outside the Fitzroy Café on the corner of Fitzroy Street and Warren Street.

Stanley Setty had been born in Baghdad of Jewish parents and arrived in England at the age of four in 1908. Twenty years later, he received an eighteen-month prison sentence after pleading guilty to twenty-three offences under the Debtors' and Bankruptcy Acts. In 1949 he was still an undischarged bankrupt and thus unable to open a bank account. Despite or, more likely, because of this, Setty dealt in large amounts of cash and he was what was called a 'kerbside banker'. It was widely known that, on his person, he never carried anything less than £1,000 and, if he was given a couple of hours' notice, he could produce up to five times that amount. His real name was Sulman Seti but to many he was known as 'Stan the Spiv'.

Spiv is a word that's almost non-existent today and a few years ago there were more than a few blank faces when Vince Cable showed his age when describing the City's much-maligned bankers as 'spivs and gamblers'.[2] After the Second World War, however, the word was almost ubiquitous. It was used to describe the smartly dressed black marketeers that in a time of controls and restrictions lived by their wits, buying and selling ration coupons and sought-after luxuries. When the war had come to an end in the summer of 1945 it was estimated that there were over 20,000 deserters in the country and 10,000 in London alone. These deserters, all without proper identity cards or ration books, had only one choice to make (if they didn't give themselves up and receive a certain prison sentence) and that was to be part of the huge and growing black market underground.

'Spiv' had been used by London's criminal fraternity at least since the nineteenth century and meant a small-time crook, con man or fence rather than a full-time and dangerous villain. The exact origin is lost in the London smog of thieves' cant, and is etymologically as obscure as the derivation of the goods the spivs were trying to sell. In the *Cassell Dictionary of Slang*, Jonathan Green suggests the word originally came from the Romany 'spiv', which meant a sparrow and was used by gypsies as a derogatory reference to those who existed by picking up the leavings of their betters, criminal or legitimate.

In 1909, the writer Thomas Burke had a short story published in the *Idler* magazine entitled 'Young Love in Bermondsey'. It features 'Spiv' Bagster, the 'Westminster Blood' who can 'do things when his dander's up'. Henry 'Spiv Bagster' Wilson actually existed and was a newspaper seller and petty thief. His many court appearances for selling counterfeit goods and illegal street trading were occasionally mentioned in the national press, and the *Daily Mail* wrote of him in 1904: 'Spiv Bagster the London news vendor was charged with stealing six shillings from a till in a dairyman's shop in Portslade. Spiv protested his innocence and the charge was dismissed. On the announcement of the magistrate's decision half a dozen of Bagster's companions in court shouted with satisfaction, and left wildly yelling hurrahs.'[3]

There is another theory about 'spiv' in that it could have come from the slang term 'spiff', meaning a well-dressed man. This turned into 'spiffy,' meaning spruced up, and if you were 'spiffed up' you were dressed smartly. Over time the two meanings of 'spiv' seemed to have mysteriously combined and in 1945 Bill Naughton, the playwright and author brought up in Bolton but best known for his London play and subsequent film *Alfie*, used the word in the title of an article he wrote in September 1945. Written for the *News Chronicle* just a few weeks after the end of the Second World War, 'Meet the Spiv' began: 'Londoners and other city dwellers will recognise him, so will many city magistrates – the slick, flashy, nimble-witted tough, talking sharp slang from the corner of the mouth. He is a sinister by-product of big-city civilisation.'

James Agate in the *Daily Express*, reviewing Naughton's article, described the spiv as: 'That odd member of society ... a London type. Which would be a Chicago gangster if he had the guts.' The word 'spiv' caught the imagination of the public of all classes. People who would have normally described themselves as law-abiding appreciated, albeit grudgingly, what the spivs had to offer. During the war and for another decade after, many people felt that without the black market it was almost impossible to have much quality of life at all. The spivs offered an escape from the overwhelming and suffocating strictures of austerity, rationing and self-denial. The sympathetic acceptance of the men with the flashy suits with the wide lapels and narrow waists only increased when the war came to an end. The wartime restrictions were now just restrictions, and the diarist Anthony Heap summed up the mood of much the country at the end of 1945: 'Housing, food, clothing, fuel, beer, tobacco – all the ordinary comforts of life that we'd taken for granted before the war and naturally expected to become more plentiful again when it ended, became instead more and more scarce and difficult to come by.'[4]

By 1946 the archetypal spiv character was better known. The columnist Warwick Charlton in the *Daily Express* wrote in November of that year:

The spivs' shoulders are better upholstered than they have ever been before. Their voices are more knowing, winks more cunning, rolls [of bank-notes] fatter, patent shoes more shiny. The spivs are the 'bright boys' who live on their wits. They have only one law: 'Thou shalt not do an honest day's work'. They have never been known to break this law.

When war came they dodged the call-up, bribed sick men to attend their medicals, bought false identity cards and, if they were eventually roped in, they deserted. War was their opportunity and they took it and waxed fat, sleek and rich. They organised the black market of war-time Britain. Peace had them worried but only for a moment. Shortages are still with us, and the spivs are the peace-time profiteers.[5]

Seventeen days after Stan 'the Spiv' Setty went missing, on 21 October 1949, a farm labourer named Sidney Tiffin was out shooting ducks on the Dengie mudflats around 15 miles from Southend. He came across a large package wrapped up in carpet felt and when he opened it up with his knife it revealed a body still dressed in a silk cream shirt and pale blue silk shorts. The hands were tied behind the dead man's back but the head and legs were gone after being hacked roughly away. It was later estimated by the police that the truncated body had been immersed in the sea for over two weeks and it was generally thought that without the head it would be impossible to identify. The celebrated (not least by himself) Superintendent Fred Cherrill of Scotland Yard's fingerprint department had other ideas. He managed to carefully remove the wrinkled skin from one of Setty's fingertips. He then stretched this over one of his own fingers to produce a print: a fingerprint that turned out to be a match for Setty's.

Within a few days the police found more evidence after they had instructed bookmakers around London to look out for the £5 notes they knew Setty had on his person the day he went missing. £5 was a lot of money in 1949 (in 2015 the equivalent is worth over £150) and at that time any £5 note withdrawn from a bank would have had its number noted by the clerk along with the name of the withdrawer. On 26 October, one of the Setty fivers was found at Romford greyhound stadium and on the next day five more were traced back to a dog track at Southend. The police were closing in and on 28 October a man was arrested and taken to Albany Street police station. It was not long after that the police started searching a flat at 620B Finchley Road, not far from Golders Green Tube station.

The man arrested was Brian Donald Hume, who had originally met the physically imposing Stanley Setty two years previously at the Hollywood Club near Marble Arch. Hume had been impressed with Setty's expensive-looking suit with the flamboyant tie and his general overall wealthy appearance: 'He had a voice like broken bottles and pockets stuffed with cash,'[6] Hume later recalled.

Setty realised that Hume could be useful for his illegal operations and they became 'business' partners, dealing with classic spiv goods such as black-market nylons and forged petrol coupons. They also traded in stolen cars which Hume stole for Setty to sell on after a quick respray. Hume was also useful as he had qualified for a civilian pilot's licence after the war and had been getting a name for himself within London's underworld as 'the Flying Smuggler'.

Hume was born illegitimately in 1919 to a schoolmistress who quickly gave her son to a local orphanage to bring up. He was retrieved after a few years and brought up by a woman he knew as 'Aunt Doodie' but who actually turned out to be his natural mother. According to Hume she never properly accepted him as she did her other children and he would later comment: 'I was born with a chip on my shoulder as big as an elephant.' In 1939 he joined the Royal Air Force Volunteer Reserve as a pilot but left in 1940 after contracting cerebrospinal meningitis. An RAF medical report at the time, however, described him as having 'a degree of organically determined psychopathy'. During the war he bought an RAF officer's uniform and used his knowledge to masquerade as Flying Officer Dan Hume, DFM. Hume passed off forged cheques at RAF stations around the country – 'it was a great thrill to have everyone saluting a bastard like me' – but he was soon caught and in 1942 he was bound over for two years.

On 1 October 1949, Setty's and Hume's thin veneer of friendship was stripped away during an argument at Hume's Finchley Road flat. Setty had recently upset Hume by kicking out at his beloved pet terrier when it had brushed up against a freshly resprayed car and the confrontation soon became physical. Hume, not a person who found it particularly easy to control his temper, was now in a violent rage and reached over and grabbed a Nazi SS dagger that was hanging on the wall as decoration. He later told a reporter: 'I was wielding the dagger just like our savage ancestors wielded their weapons 20,000 years ago … We rolled over and over and my sweating hand plunged the weapon frenziedly and repeatedly into his chest and legs … I plunged the blade into his ribs. I know: I heard them crack.'

Hume stabbed Setty five times, after which he lay back and watched his victim's last breaths. He wrote later: 'I watched the life run from him like water down a drain.' Hume dragged Setty's hefty lifeless body into the kitchen and hid it in the coal cupboard. The next day, while his wife was out, he started to dismember the corpse with a linoleum knife and hacksaw, eventually wrapping the body parts in carpet felt and adding some brick rubble for additional weight. The following morning Hume arranged to have his front room redecorated, and had the carpet professionally cleaned and dyed to get rid of any stray blood stains. What upset him most, however, was having to burn £900 worth of bloodstained £5 notes.

Later that day Hume took the carpet-felt parcels to Elstree airport and hired an Auster light aircraft to dump Setty's remains over the English Channel. It took him several attempts, and broke the plane's window in the process, before he successfully got the parcels to slide out of the small side-door. It was now getting dark and Hume decided to land at the closer Southend airport and hired a car home and paid for it, fatefully, with one of Setty's leftover fivers.

A week after his arrest, on 5 November, Hume appeared at Bow Street magistrates' court charged that he 'did, between 4th and 5th October, 1949, murder Stanley Setty, aged 46 years. Against the Peace'. By now there was so much evidence collected by the police, including fingerprints, identified torso, blood stains found in the flat of the accused and hire car paid for by the victim's proven money, that anyone involved in the case would have thought, realistically, that there could only be one verdict. The trial at the Old Bailey started on 18 January 1950 and Hume's defence was based around a story that he had originally contrived when interviewed by the police. He told the court that he had been paid £150 to dump some heavy parcels over the English Channel by three former associates of Setty's called Max, Greenie and The Boy. Hume's descriptions of the three men seemed so detailed that the story sounded credible to many in the courtroom.

The defence also called on Cyril Lee, a former army officer who lived within earshot of Setty's lock-up for three years. He was no friend of Setty's and admitted that he disliked the sort of men that had been habituating the garage at Cambridge Terrace Mews. He told the court that although they weren't 'the sort of people I would like to see round my doorstep', he had heard two people who were called 'Max' and 'The Boy' and also acknowledged that he had seen a man who looked like Hume's description of 'Greenie'.

The Judge, Mr Justice Sellers, spoke to the jury about the inferences and assumptions they had to make but also told them that if there was any doubt about what had happened then they were compelled to return a verdict of not guilty. On 20 January 1950, the jury retired at noon. In less than three hours they were ready to deliver their verdict and, to most people's surprise, it was that they had failed to agree on one. Hume was retried, but on 26 January 1950 and after the judge had instructed the new jury to return a not-guilty verdict for the charge of murder, he was found guilty of being an accessory after the fact. 'For no other reason than for money, the sum of £150,' said the judge, 'you were prepared to take parts of a body and keep the torso in your flat over night and then take it away and put it in the Thames estuary.' Hume was subsequently sentenced to twelve years in prison, but he didn't hide from the courtroom that he had expected less.

The Stanley Setty case received huge and sensational press coverage but whether George Orwell thought it had arrested any decline in the quality of English murders we will never know. On the morning of Donald Hume's sentencing Orwell's funeral took place at Christ Church on Albany Street, opposite the police station where Hume had been taken in for questioning less than three months before.

It was possibly the only time the two words were ever associated with him but Hume was released from Dartmoor two years early, on 1 February 1958, for 'good behaviour'. While Hume had been in prison he had been frequently visited by the *Sunday Pictorial* assistant editor Fred Redman, who wasn't alone in suspecting that Hume hadn't been telling the truth. At the time 'double jeopardy' existed in English law, which prevented a defendant from being tried again on the same charge following an acquittal or conviction.[7] Hume was secure in the knowledge that he could no longer be retried for the murder of Setty and was persuaded by Redman to sell his story to the (now-defunct) *Sunday Pictorial*. The newspaper's reporter Victor Sims interviewed Hume at a country hotel that overlooked the Thames estuary into which Hume had dropped Setty's torso ten years before. Hume lay on a bed and calmly told how he had killed and chopped up his former partner in crime. Sims later recalled: 'It was the most terrifying bloody day of my life.'[8]

The front page splash, which was said to have cost the newspaper £3,600 (more than £75,000 in 2015), began: 'I, Donald Hume, do hereby confess to the *Sunday Pictorial* that on the night of October 4, 1949, I murdered Stanley Setty in my flat in Finchley Road, London. I stabbed him to death while we were fighting.' Later in the article Hume admitted that he had murdered Setty alone and Max, Greenie and The Boy were just figments of his imagination. The astonishingly detailed description of the trio that had successfully fooled some of the jury was actually based on the three policemen who had originally interviewed him.

Four months after he had been released in May 1958 Hume, complete with a false passport and what was left of the money he had received from the *Sunday Pictorial,* fled to Zurich in Switzerland. To raise more money he committed at least two bank robberies back in England that were cleverly synchronised with flights from Heathrow, enabling him to flee the country before the police had even started their enquiries. Eventually Hume's luck ran out when he shot and killed a taxi driver after another attempted bank robbery, this time in Switzerland.

On 30 January 1959 Hume had entered the Gewerbe Bank of Zurich and pushed a hold-up note, written in German, across the counter. After one member of staff tried to ring the alarm he was shot in the stomach. Hume then hit another over the head with his gun. He tried in vain to open the safe before running off empty-handed. After fatally shooting a taxi driver, Hume was ignominiously brought down by a pastry chef who also managed to disarm him. When the police arrived it was not so much to arrest him but more to protect him from a crowd trying to lynch him.

It took a Swiss court to find Hume guilty of murder and at the age of thirty-nine he received a life sentence with hard labour. In 1976 he was judged to be mentally unstable by the Swiss authorities, which gave them the excuse to fly Hume back to England, where he was incarcerated at Broadmoor Hospital. Hume was eventually released in 1998 but it was just a few months later when his decomposing body was found in a wood in Gloucestershire. It didn't need the skills of Superintendent Fred Cherrill this time for Hume's body to be identified by its fingerprints and to confirm that Hume had died from natural causes.

Not unlike the Manson Family killings in 1969 that brought an end to the peace-loving hippy era and the summer of love, the shocking Stanley Setty murder changed the public perception of the typical spiv as a loveable rogue forever, although there was always something slightly comical about the spiv and indeed the exaggerated clothes and manners lent themselves to caricature. The spiv-like comedy characters continued to be part of British popular culture for the next couple of decades or so – notably Arthur English's *Prince of the Wide Boys*, George Cole's 'Flash Harry' in the *St Trinian* films, and Private Walker in the early *Dad's Army* episodes.

It was rationing that gave spivs their main reason to exist and during the general election of 1950 the Conservative Party actively campaigned on a manifesto of ending rationing as soon as practicably possible. The issuing of petrol coupons ended in May 1951, while sugar rationing finished two years later. Finally, in 1954 the public were allowed to buy meat wherever and whenever they wanted and this meant the end of all rationing completely. Two years later, when Brian Hume was released from Dartmoor prison in 1958, the proper era of the spiv had essentially come to an end.

Friswell Motors on Albany Street, 1911.

Poster advertising Friswell's, April 1907.

Donald Hume outside the Fitzroy Café on Warren Street. (Trinity Mirror/Mirrorpix/ Alamy)

CHAPTER 5

The Protests at the 1970 Miss World Competition and its Motley Crew of Judges

The judges turn round as the demonstration by members of the Women's Liberation Movement at the 1970 Miss World Competition begins. (*Daily Mail*/REX Shutterstock)

There were two separate protests at the Royal Albert Hall on 20 November 1970. One of them, the iconic flour-bomb demonstration directed at the Miss World contest by a group of young feminists, has become part of popular social history. The second, a potentially more serious event – something similar would certainly be taken as such today – has been almost completely forgotten. At around 2.30 a.m. on the morning of the Miss World contest a group of about four or five young people had gathered around one of the BBC's outside broadcast lorries that had been parked at the side of the Royal Albert Hall. They slid a homemade bomb under it and ran off quickly down Kensington Gore in the direction of Notting Hill. A small amount of TNT wrapped in a copy of *The Times* exploded a few minutes later, waking up some nearby residents, one of whom saw the youths running away. Almost in passing, the explosion was mentioned in the press the following day, but it didn't compare to the huge publicity the women's liberation demonstration garnered, not least because it was seen on television. The 1970 contest, in the UK alone, had over 23 million viewers – the second-highest-rated television programme that year.

The competition was almost half way through when about fifty women and a few men started throwing flour bombs, stink bombs and tomatoes at the stage while yelling, 'We are liberationists!' and 'Ban this disgraceful cattle market!' Leaflets were thrown all around, one of which showed a naked man tattooed with the slogan 'Morley is a Pimp'. Bob Hope, who was due to crown Miss World and was performing a routine when the protest started, quickly tried to flee the stage as the missiles flew by. He was hampered by Julia Morley, the wife of the organiser Eric Morley, who grabbed hold of his ankle in a desperate attempt to stop him leaving. Mr Morley got hold of Hope's microphone and yelled, 'Give the girls a chance!' It took only a few minutes for the police to restore order but in that short while the women's movement had in one fell swoop established itself in the country's consciousness, and in many ways the Miss World contest never really recovered. Historically the Royal Albert Hall was an apt place to hold a feminist protest: there had been over twenty suffragette rallies at the Royal Albert Hall between 1908 and 1918, making the venue an important part of the fight in the women's suffrage movement.

Meanwhile a clearly shocked Hope was persuaded by Eric Morley to get back on the stage where, for once not reading from idiot boards, he said, 'A nice conditioning course for the Vietnam!'[1] and then continued, 'These things can't go on much longer. They're going to have to get paid off sooner or later. Someone upstairs will see to that. Anybody who wants to interrupt something as beautiful as this must be on some kind of dope.'

The national press got very excited with both the contest and, of course, the protestors. *The Sun*, which the day before the event had written, 'We're in for a long, hard winter' because the 'lovely Miss World girls have abandoned the mini-skirt for the midi,' two days later criticised the Women's Lib hecklers: 'If you can't stand the cheesecake, stay out of the market.' The *Daily Mirror*, on the eve of the contest, had been very careful not to compare women with cattle but ruined it by using horses instead: 'You couldn't find a field of shapelier fillies than those coming under starter's orders tonight for the grand Miss World stakes.' The *Daily Mail*, sensibly you might think, thought it best not to compare women with animals of any sort and simply described the demonstrators as 'Yelling Harpies' and asked what was 'degrading about celebrating the beauty of the human body?' The staid *Guardian*, after trying to rise above it all by poetically describing the event as 'a bathetic banquet of bosoms and beams', then sniffily went on to say that contestants 'would barely stand out on a Chelsea shopping morning'. The *Daily Express* seemed to be shocked by the sex of the protestors: 'The trouble was caused by WOMEN – women with the slogan: "We're not beautiful or ugly, we're angry".' The *Express* continued, 'As [the contestants] celebrated or wept, as girls do, their tougher sisters outside were having an unladylike slanging match, as girls usually don't, with the departing audience.' The 'tougher sisters' outside had been handing out leaflets that said, 'Mecca are super-pimps, selling women's bodies to frustrated voyeurs until raging business men jump young girls in dark alleys. Our sexuality has been taken from us, turned into money for someone else, then removed, deadened by anxiety.' A confused Eric Morley could only counter with, 'The money is all donated to children's charities.'

The world's most famous beauty contest had started nineteen years previously in 1951 when Eric Morley was employed as a publicity sales manager for Mecca, then a small catering and leisure group. An ex-squadron leader called Phipps was at the time in charge of publicity for the upcoming Festival of Britain. He rang a former RAF friend, Group Captain Pickard, who was the managing director of Mecca catering, and said that he needed ideas to add glamour and 'razzamatazz' to the festival. 'My man Morley will come up with something,' Pickard replied. A few days later, over lunch at the Savoy, Eric Morley, who was already responsible for coming up with *Come Dancing* for the BBC in 1949 and who went on to popularise Bingo, suggested a Miss World Festival Bikini Girl contest. Squadron Leader Phipps thought this was a splendid idea and it all went ahead. A Swedish woman called Kiki Hakansson won the first prize of £1,000 and the competition was seen as a great success. When Miss Universe was launched in America the following year, Morley managed to persuade Mecca to make Miss World an annual event, with the proviso that bikinis were now to be banned. An odd decision for Morley, as only a year previously he had said, 'Even a girl with big hips can be made to look good in a bikini.' For the new Miss World contests he described the kind of young women he was looking for: 'Girls between 17 and 25, ideally five foot seven, eight or nine stone, waist 22–24″, hips 35–36″, no more no less, a lovely face, good teeth, plenty of hair, and perfectly shaped legs from front and back – carefully checked for such defects as slightly knocked knees.'[2]

The 1970 Miss World competition had started well. When the opening act of Lionel Blair and his group of male dancers, dressed in flared three-piece suits, brought their opening routine to an end the camera cut to Michael Aspel. The smooth presenter announced that while 'the girls are changing into their extremely expensive evening gowns', he would introduce the judges. Eric Morley, considering the vast television audience that was expected around the world, chose quite a motley crew.

The first judge on Aspel's cue card that night was, 'His Excellency, the High Commissioner of Malawi'. 'His Excellency' remained nameless but was warmly applauded by a Royal Albert Hall audience, most of whom almost certainly would not have had the slightest idea who he was nor the whereabouts of the country he represented. The south-eastern African country of Malawi, formerly known as Nyasaland, had been colonised by the British less than eighty years previously in 1891. The initial Victorian administrators were given just £10,000 per year – enough to employ ten European civilians, two military officers, seventy Punjabi Sikhs and eighty-five Zanzibar porters – to administer and police about 1.5 million people. Malawi gained independence in 1964 and became a republic two years later when Hastings Banda, the former prime minister, swept to power as the first President of Malawi in 1966. Banda called himself 'Ngwazi' but preferred the use of his full title: His Excellency The Life President (Paramount Chief) Dr Hastings Kamuzu Banda, the Ngwazi, Minister of External Affairs, Minister of Defence, Minister of Agriculture, Minister of Justice, Minister of Works and Supplies, Minister of Women's and Children's Affairs and Minister of Community Services. It didn't take long for Banda to make Malawi a one-party state and, just before the Miss World competition in 1970, had made himself president for life. In his particular case life didn't mean life and in 1994 he was ousted from power by a Malawian special assembly. Human rights groups estimated that at least 6,000 people were killed, tortured and jailed without trial during Banda's reign. Hastings Banda died around the age of ninety-nine (his actual age was uncertain) in 1997.

Next up on Michael Aspel's judges list, and shown chatting and smiling with the Malawian high commissioner, presumably unaware of any torturing or murdering his fellow judge may or may not have colluded with, was 'that well-known film producer and chairman and managing director of EMI – Nat Cohen!' The sixty-five-year-old Cohen lived alone in a multi-mirrored, suede-lined, split-level bachelor pad in St James's Place and in 1970 practically ran the entire British film industry. He was the son of a kosher butcher from the East End and had formed Anglo-Amalgamated Productions in 1945. Six months before the Miss World contest, Anglo-Amalgamated had been taken over by EMI, and as part of the deal Cohen was made chairman of the entire company. Cohen once commissioned two short films from the director Alan Parker, who would later write of him:

> Nat Cohen was an avuncular, vulgar man with a shifty, pencil-thin moustache who looked more like a Soho strip club spiv than a film mogul. His lowbrow taste in film production had secured him a sizeable wallet and hence his puffed-up position running EMI. He drove up and down Wardour Street in a cream Rolls-Royce with a number plate that said 'Nat 1' (just to rub it in the noses of all of us snobby and opinionated film industry oiks who were less than enamoured by him) to emphasise just who actually was the smart one.[3]

By 1973 Cohen was overseeing around 70 per cent of the entire British film industry and his most successful films, financially if not artistically, were *On the Buses* and *Murder on the Orient Express*. Cohen died at the age of eighty-two in 1988, two years after EMI Films was sold to the businessman Alan Bond in April 1986.

While Nat Cohen turned back round to converse again with the nameless Malawian high commissioner, Michael Aspel introduced the next judge on the panel: '… the premier of Grenada, the Honourable Eric Gairy.' The prefix 'Honourable', although diplomatically correct, in Gairy's case wasn't particularly apt. The Caribbean island of Grenada is located north-east of Venezuela and was a former French colony that was formally ceded to the British in 1763. A few nutmeg trees were left there by a merchant ship eighty years later, and to this day the island is responsible for almost 40 per cent of the world's annual crop. In 1950 Eric Gairy founded GULP

(Grenada United Labour Party) which, in 1951, led a national strike for better working conditions. The strike soon evolved into unrest throughout the island and it was announced that a general election would be held in October that year. Gairy's party won six of the eight seats contested and sixteen years later, in 1967, Grenada was granted full autonomy from Britain over its internal affairs, with Eric Gairy serving as the premier. Only a few months before the Miss World competition Gairy formed the infamous Mongoose Gang, sometimes called a private army but in reality just a nasty group of political thugs. Gairy used the gang for beating up and silencing critics, breaking up demonstrations and even murdering political opponents. By 1970 Eric Gairy was as suspiciously rich as his country was distressingly poor. In May 1973 Gairy visited London and persuaded Edward Heath that Grenada should become independent. Nine months later Gairy was granted his wish but not before his Mongoose gang killed Rupert Bishop, the father of his main political opponent, Maurice Bishop.

Two years later Gairy and GULP, among suspicions of tampered ballot papers, won all the seats in the 1976 elections. By now internal politics was boring for Gairy and he started to get obsessed with UFOs. In 1977 he addressed the General Assembly of the United Nations, where he urged the UN to establish an agency for psychic research into both UFOs and the Bermuda Triangle. The following year he tried to persuade the UN Assembly that 1978 should be called The Year of the UFO. Many in Grenada were acutely aware that their prime minister was becoming a worldwide laughing stock, and it was while Gairy was in the US at a UFO meeting that his long-standing opponent, Maurice Bishop, along with his New Jewel Movement, took his chance and mounted a coup. Many people were wary of Bishop's Cuban and Soviet connections and so the deputy prime minister Bernard Coard had Bishop illegally arrested. Within a few weeks Bishop and several members of his cabinet were summarily executed. Maurice Bishop's body has never been found. Bishop's death caused international outrage and ultimately resulted in the American-led invasion in October 1983. After living in the United States, Gairy returned to Grenada in 1984 and tried three times to regain power but all to no avail. After suffering a stroke, he died on 23 August 1997.

Michael Aspel continued to introduce the illustrious judging panel: 'Just one name for our next judge but we all know it so well, ladies and gentlemen – it's Nina!' Her full name at the time was Nina van Pallandt but even with the help of an added surname she's largely forgotten today. In 1970 she was still very famous for being part of the inexplicably popular Danish singing duo Nina and Frederik. Nina Magdelene Møller-

Hasselbalch and Baron Frederik van Pallandt, who was the son of a Dutch ambassador to Denmark, had been singing together since 1957 and had married three years later in 1960. After several execrable and almost racist calypso-tinged hits in the UK, the BBC curiously gave them a series called *Nina and Frederik at Home*. For the next few years they remained a popular cabaret act throughout the world but as a singing duo and as a married couple they separated in 1969. That same year, and as a solo artist, Nina recorded John Barry's song 'Do You Know How Christmas Trees Are Grown?' The track featured on the soundtrack of the James Bond movie *On Her Majesty's Secret Service* and Nina went on to perform it on the *Morecambe and Wise Christmas Show* that year. In the early 1970s Nina van Pallandt became known in the United States, not for her singing career, but as the mistress of Clifford Irving, the man gaoled for faking the autobiography of Howard Hughes. Nina helped expose Irving when she revealed that she was on holiday with him when he had said he'd been meeting Hughes about the book. In the film *Hoax*, which featured Richard Gere as Irving, Nina is played by Julie Delpy, although Nina herself appeared in another Richard Gere film, *American Gigolo*. She also appeared in Robert Altman's *The Long Goodbye*. Meanwhile her former partner Baron Frederik had got mixed up with a major Australian crime syndicate. In 1994 he was gunned down in the Philippines, along with his new wife, by a rival drug-running gang. It was Nina who flew to the Philippines to bring his body back to Europe.

Michael Aspel was much more comfortable introducing the next judge: 'Welcome home, the lady who's working on a film called *Quest* which seems the right title in this context – lovely star … Joan Collins!' Born in Paddington in 1933, Collins trained at RADA before joining J. Arthur Rank's 'Charm School' at the age of seventeen. She was soon appearing in British films such as *Tough Guy* and *Cosh Boy* and gained the nickname 'Coffee Bar Jezebel'. She moved to Hollywood in the mid-fifties but by the 1970 Miss World contest the decent roles were drying up. Her marriage to Anthony Newley had also recently come to an end. The movie that Michael Aspel had mentioned when introducing her was released the following year, almost without trace, as *Quest For Love*. The film, adapted from a John Wyndham short story, was a poorly directed science-fiction romance (not the most popular of genres and watching this film you can see why). Joan Collins' performance was by far the best thing about the film. She must have particularly liked the white dress she wore for a party scene in the movie as she was wearing it again for the Miss World contest.

The next judge on Aspel's list was 'His Royal Highness the Maharaja of

Baroda'. Just a few months after the maharaja stood up in the Royal Albert Hall, took a puff of his large cigar and bowed to the audience, the Indian parliament voted to abolish him, or at least his title, along with all official symbols of princely India, which included all privileges and remuneration. Fatehsinghrao Prataprao Gaekwad, to give the maharajah his full name, was often known in Britain as Jackie Baroda. He had managed the Indian cricket team during a tour of England in 1959 – it lost miserably – and was an occasional cricket commentator on the BBC – John Arlott, not known for his deference, called him 'The Prince'. In *The Guardian* the maharajah was once described (by a journalist who seemed not to have read the book) as a 'swarthy Gatsby and the last of the legendary cricketing princes'.[4] He had been born in 1930, unlike Gatsby, into a world where family wealth was extraordinary and almost incalculable. His father was once the second richest man in the world and whenever he appeared in public the British Raj would fire a twenty-one-gun salute. When Jackie Baroda got married to an Indian princess, the procession was led by a mile of elephants. Despite the lack of Indian government financial support, Jackie Baroda was hardly penniless when he died in 1988 at the relatively young age of fifty-eight.

After Jackie, Michael Aspel, happy that there was someone famous on his list again, quickly continued: 'Next, that recording star – by the time I get to Phoenix the contest will be over – Glen Campbell!' Campbell was in London for a celebrity adorned 'Royal charity gala, dinner and cabaret' at the Talk of the Town on Leicester Square. In 1970 he still had a very clean-cut and well-groomed image. In an interview with the *Daily Mirror*, published the day after the Miss World contest, he told the reporter that he was despondent about the current decadence in entertainment. 'I've vowed not to sing songs that have anything to do with drugs … I've got a wife and four kids. I don't want them to see me in anything I would be ashamed of. Artists have a special responsibility in what they're doing.' Within months Campbell left his wife, married another, divorced her and then had a tempestuous relationship with the country singer Tanya Tucker, twenty-two years his junior, all the while taking huge amounts of cocaine and alcohol. He was once arrested for drink-driving and leaving the scene of the accident. According to the police report, when he was asked for his name, he replied, 'Glen Campbell, the Rhinestone Cowboy!' He then insisted that 'he had never been drunk a day in his life, only over-served'. To underline his case he then kneed the officer in the groin. He was sentenced to ten days in jail. A republican for most of his life, in 1981 Campbell was once in a heated argument about his seat on a long-haul flight with a member of the Indonesian government. He told the politician that he was going to 'call my friend Ronald Reagan and ask him to bomb Jakarta'.[5]

There are no reports that Glen Campbell had any problems with the next judge who was sitting next to him. Aspel introduced him as, 'His Excellency, the ambassador of Indonesia!' As with the high commissioner, the ambassador either had a name that was unpronounceable or he wasn't deemed important enough to be given one. Indonesia, the country he represented, had been a Dutch colony from the beginning of the nineteenth century but Japanese occupation during the Second World War ended Dutch rule and encouraged the nascent Indonesian nationalist movement. Only two days after the surrender of Japan in August 1945, Indonesia declared independence. The Netherlands tried to re-establish rule, not without considerable violence, but it was to no avail and in the face of international pressure the Dutch formally recognised Indonesian independence in 1949. In 1965 there was an attempted coup by a communist group, but it was violently put down by the military and it is estimated that half a million people were killed. The head of the army, General Suharto, supported by the US government, became president in March 1968.

There was one small problem and it's a problem that still rumbles on today. After independence the Netherlands tried to retain West Papua, part of Indonesia, as her operational base in Asia. In 1961, however, Indonesia invaded the region. President Kennedy, very keen on strengthening relations with Indonesia as a bulwark against the rising threat of communism, persuaded the Netherlands to hand over West Papua. To placate the inhabitants of West Papua, it was all subject to a UN-supervised 'act of free choice' (AFC) vote that was scheduled for 1969. When the AFC vote was due, the Indonesian military declared that the Papuans were too 'primitive' to cope with democracy and handpicked 1,026 leaders to vote on behalf of the entire West Papua population of one million. They instructed them on how to vote and then threatened to kill them and their families if they voted the wrong way. Not entirely surprisingly, the thousand or so leaders unanimously voted by raising their hands in front of the UN observers. West Papua would remain part of Indonesia, and with the encouragement of the US government the vote was rubber-stamped by the UN. West Papua has remained under the control of the Indonesian state ever since.

Michael Aspel continued: 'Now the chairman of our panel of judges and also general manager of BBC Outside Broadcasts ... Mr Peter Dimmock!' Mr Dimmock, who looked like, and was, a former wartime RAF pilot, looked pretty calm considering what he had been through in the last twenty-four hours. The bomb that had exploded underneath one of the BBC's Outside Broadcast lorries was hardly mentioned the next day but must have caused logistical problems for Mr Dimmock and his team. In 1970, many people like Mr Dimmock had played some part in or lived through the Second World War and a small bomb exploding underneath an OB truck was almost brushed aside. As far as the perpetrators were concerned, the bomb was seen as a success, although completely overshadowed by the feminist 'cattle market' protests. The young men and women seen leaving the scene were members of a group of anarchists who would later call themselves the Angry Brigade. Admittedly the explosion caused no loss of life or any injuries, but from today's perspective the fact that it was hardly reported at all by any of the newspapers over the next few days is close to extraordinary. It was actually just the latest incident in an anti-establishment bombing and shooting campaign by a group of young men and women who had been in existence, in one form or other, since 1969, when in March they exploded bombs outside the Bank of Spain in Liverpool and the Bank of Bilbao in London. The following August they fire-bombed the home of the Tory MP Duncan Sandys and then twelve months later continued their campaign when they left a bomb outside the house of the Metropolitan Police Commissioner Sir John Waldron. The young anarchists were initially confused with the lack of publicity their bombing campaign was receiving but eventually assumed, almost certainly correctly, that there was a conspiracy of silence on behalf of the establishment, fearful that urban guerrilla activity would, in some way, become fashionable.

On 4 December 1970, just two weeks after the Miss World bomb, a car drove around Belgrave Square and machine-gunned the Spanish embassy. The young student militants again found there was nothing in the papers after the attack and, still suspecting an establishment conspiracy, they decided to issue a communiqué to the underground press, and for the first time the moniker 'Angry Brigade' was used. The name had been thought up after a drunken Christmas party and may have come from the 'We Are Angry' placards at the Miss World protest. Although Stuart Christie, an anarchist and connected with the Angry Brigade, later wrote that for some time they had toyed with the name 'The Red Rankers' in reference to the speech defect of the former Home Secretary 'Woy' Jenkins. So far the bombing campaign had utterly mystified the police and they had no clue as to who the perpetrators were, but they successfully managed to keep the bombs and the shootings relatively under-reported (the Miss World bomb was an exception). The situation immediately changed when on 12 January 1971 a bomb exploded at the home of the Right Honourable Robert Carr, secretary of state for employment and chief advocate of the hated (by many at the time) anti-union Industrial Relations Bill. The Angry Brigade released another of their communiqués stamped with the distinctive children's John Bull printing set, and, with this particular incident, too serious to be brushed under the establishment carpet, the Angry Brigade suddenly found that they had reached the nation's consciousness.

The Python-esque name, chosen by the disparate group of anarchists, was grabbed gleefully by the popular press. America had the Weather Men, Italy the Red Brigades, Japan the Red Army Faction, Germany the Baader-Meinhof gang, but in the UK they now had their own Angry Brigade. The newly named urban terrorists managed six more bombs, including an explosion on 1 May 1971 inside Biba in Kensington High Street. The fashionable swinging London boutique was seen by the 'Angries' as exploiting sweatshop labour. Soon after they released communiqué 8:

If you're not busy being born you're busy buying.

All the sales girls in the flash boutiques are made to dress the same and have the same make-up, representing the 1940s. In fashion as in everything else, capitalism can only go backwards – they've nowhere to go – they're dead.

The future is ours.

Life is so boring there is nothing to do except spend all our wages on the latest skirt or shirt.

Brothers and Sisters, what are your real desires?

Sit in the drugstore, look distant, empty, bored, drinking some tasteless coffee? Or perhaps BLOW IT UP OR BURN IT DOWN. The only thing you can do with modern slave-houses – called boutiques – IS WRECK THEM. You can't reform profit capitalism and inhumanity. Just kick it till it breaks.

Revolution.
Communiqué 8 The Angry Brigade

A few months after the Biba bombing, the police raided a house at one end of Amhurst Road in Stoke Newington, where they found various explosives, ammunition and guns. Most damning of all was a small John Bull printing kit with the words 'Angry Brigade' rather incriminatingly still set out.

The police soon arrested eight supposed members of the brigade and they quickly became known by the press, rather unimaginatively, as the 'Stoke Newington Eight'. The defendants were accused of carrying out twenty-five attacks on government buildings, embassies, corporations and the homes of ministers between 1967 and 1971. The Angry Brigade's campaign came to a definite end after, at the time, the longest criminal trial in English history (it lasted from 30 May to 6 December 1972). At the end of the trial John Barker, Jim Greenfield, Hilary Creek and Anna Mendleson were found guilty of conspiracy 'with persons unknown' and, despite the jury's request for clemency, they each received prison sentences of ten years. It was difficult for the jury to deliver anything but guilty verdicts after the judge, Mr Justice James, explained that active participation was irrelevant: mere knowledge, even 'by a wink or a nod', was sufficient proof of guilt. He went on to describe the Angry Brigade politics as 'a warped understanding of sociology'. At the same trial other defendants were found not guilty, including Stuart Christie, who had formerly been imprisoned in Spain for carrying explosives with the intent to assassinate the dictator Franco, and Angela Mason, who went on to become the director of Stonewall and the Government's Women and Equality Unit, and who was awarded an OBE in 1999.

In the end, despite having hips two inches larger than Eric Morley's ideal, the twenty-two-year-old Miss Grenada – '36-24-38 on the tape measure and five feet seven inches tall,' said Michael Aspel – Jennifer Hosten won the competition, in the process becoming the first ever black winner. In fact another black contestant – Miss Africa South, who was called Pearl Gladys Jensen – came second. Incidentally, Miss Africa South isn't a mistake: Eric Morley, that year, hoped to placate the growing disquiet about apartheid South Africa by admitting a black and a white contestant from the same country. Jillian Elizabeth Jessup, the white South African who was allowed the sash with the real name of her country, came fifth.

There were actually more than two protests at the Miss World competition at the Royal Albert Hall in 1970. The third protest wasn't anything about the treatment of women in beauty contests or the exploitation of Third World countries, but a collective disapproval of the result. After the contest had come to an end many of the audience gathered outside the Royal Albert Hall and started chanting 'Swe-den, Swe-den'. The BBC also received numerous phone calls complaining that the contest had been rigged. Four of the judges, it later came to light, had given first place to the Swedish entrant, a twenty-year-old model called Maj Christel Johansson, although, rather oddly, she only came fourth overall. Miss Grenada, the eventual victor, only got two first-place votes from the judges. Was it more than a coincidence that one of the judges, a Sir Eric Gairy, was the Premier of Grenada?

Miss Sweden, who was the favourite to win before the contest, probably didn't help her cause when two days earlier she had denounced the Miss World event, saying that she would have walked out if she wasn't under contract to the organisers: 'I don't even want to win. I was warned the contest was like a cattle market and I'm inclined to agree. I feel just like a puppet.'[6] Jennifer Hosten was far better at toeing the Miss World party line: 'I do not really know enough about what they were demonstrating against, all I know is that it has been a wonderful experience competing for the Miss World title.'

In 1969 Eric Morley had become the managing director of Mecca but he also became a director of Grand Metropolitan Hotels. Grand Metropolitan took over Mecca a few months before the 1970 Miss World competition. There were accusations, all denied, of course, by the parties involved, of a business deal between Eric Gairy and Eric Morley, based around a proposed Mecca casino and hotel complex on Grenada. Four days after the contest, the protests about the result were still dragging on and Julia Morley, although insisting that no vote-rigging had occurred, resigned from her post as organising director saying, 'Perhaps I was just not the right person to organise the contest. I have had enough.' Luckily for Julia Morley, her husband ran the Miss World organisation and after the fuss had died down she was reinstated a few days later. In one way or another, the Miss World competition never really recovered from the various protests at the 1970 contest and the BBC withdrew from televising the event ten years later.

In front of two unimpressed waiters, Jennifer Hosten, Miss Grenada, the day after being crowned the new Miss World at the Royal Albert Hall, 21 November 1970. (Trinity Mirror/Mirrorpix/Alamy)

The 1970 Miss World Judges: Eric Gairy, the Prime Minister of Grenada, is in the middle and from top left and then clockwise: Nat Cohen, Nina, the Maharaja of Baroda, Glen Campbell, Sir Peter Dimmock, the Ambassador of Indonesia, the High Commissioner of Malawi and Joan Collins.

CHAPTER 6

The Café de Paris and the Trial of Elvira Barney

Elvira Barney.

Visiting England, apparently on a whim and a year before she appeared in her first film *The Street of Forgotten Men* late in 1924, Louise Brooks became a dancer at the newly opened Café de Paris in Coventry Street. She was seventeen, and during a particularly cold and dismal winter, she reputedly became the first person to dance the Charleston in London. She was certainly the first to be noticed anyway. Brooks later wrote about her time in the capital: 'I was living beyond my means – who doesn't at seventeen? – in a flat at 49A Pall Mall.'[1] Although her dancing was a stunning success with the Piccadilly nightclub crowd – nobody had seen anything quite like it before – she was lonely. Despite trying and enjoying Christmas pudding for the first time then living off it for a week and making good friends with the housemaid, on 14 January 1925 she travelled on the White Star liner RMS *Homeric* back to New York. She left London almost as suddenly as she had arrived.

The Café de Paris had opened towards the end of 1924 after George Foster, an eminent theatrical agent who had once represented Harry Lauder, Charlie Chaplin and George Formby Senior, had been looking for a venue where he could introduce new cabaret artistes and dance bands. He came across a restaurant called the Elysée on Coventry Street, a few yards from Piccadilly Circus and, with Captain Robin Humphreys, bought the lease and had the good sense to take on Martin Poulsen, the Danish maître d' from the Embassy Club. The venue featured a glamorous staircase that led down to the basement-level dance floor and restaurant, which was said to be a replica of the Palm Court on board the ill-fated RMS *Lusitania*.

Business was initially quite slow until Poulsen contacted the Prince of Wales, who had once promised him that if he ever had his own restaurant he would attend. One Wednesday evening the prince made good his promise and dropped by. He was accompanied by his usual motley entourage that included Mrs Dudley Ward, his relatively long-term mistress whom he was occasionally wont to call 'Fredie-wedie', his equerry Major 'Fruity' Metcalfe and finally his aide, the one-armed Brigadier-General Gerald Trotter known usually to his friends as 'G'. The Prince of Wales was entranced by the oval, mirrored room and the relatively spacious dance floor and soon became a regular visitor. This invaluable early royal patronage made the Café de Paris the fashionable place to be and it soon became the habitual home of much of the 'Fast Set', the 'Smart Set' or the 'Bright Young Things'. Louise Brooks later wrote about this young group of aristocrats and socialites she had come across during her brief time in London, and described them as a 'dreadful, moribund lot'. Referring to

Evelyn Waugh and his novel *Vile Bodies*, she said only a genius could have possibly created a masterpiece out of such glum material.

In May 1932, and nearly eight years after Brooks danced in front of an adoring Café de Paris crowd, the celebrated thirty-six-year-old American singer Marion Harris was in the middle of one of her long engagements at the same West End nightclub. She had recently been appearing in the musical *Evergreen* and was known to British audiences of the time as the first white woman to sing the blues. Today's ears would perhaps agree with the more accurate description in a contemporary *Manchester Guardian* review when they described her as a '*Diseuse* with a very pleasant style and songs'.[2] Enjoying her success with the British public, she moved to London at the beginning of the thirties and performed regularly for the BBC. Her most famous song in this country, a hit in 1931 and recorded with Billy Mason and his Café de Paris Band, was 'My Canary's Got Circles Under Its Eyes':

> I thought he'd never do anything wrong
> Now he does snake-hips the whole day long
> My canary has circles under his eyes

The Prince of Wales was a fan of Marion Harris and would often come to the Café de Paris just to hear her sing. One night after she had performed, the manager came running into her dressing room to announce that the prince had been so impressed that he would like her to have a drink at his table. Miss Harris coolly declined, telling him, 'If your customers get to know you too well, they don't come back and pay money to see you. The illusion is destroyed.' Harris may well have been on the Café de Paris stage – the cabaret acts began their set at 11.30 – when just after midnight on 30 May 1932 an intoxicated couple arrived for a rather late supper. The lateness of the hour was not unusual. Margaret Whigham, the 'debutante of 1930' and later the Duchess of Argyll, remembered that in the early 1930s she would go with one young man for dinner, feign tiredness and be taken home at 10.30, only to go out again with another man to dance at the Embassy Club or the Café de Paris.[3] Elvira Barney and her lover Michael Stephen travelled by cab to Coventry Street after holding one of their numerous parties at the home they shared at 21 Williams Mews, just off Lowndes Square in Knightsbridge. After finishing their meal at the Café de Paris, they had further drinks at The Blue Angel in Dean Street before returning home in the early hours of that morning.

Not long after they had returned, neighbours heard screaming and shouting from the first floor of the couple's mews house. One neighbour said she heard, 'Get out, get out! I will shoot you! I will shoot you!' Not long after, the entire street heard a pistol shot echoing into the night and then the sound of a woman plaintively crying. In between the sobs, another neighbour heard, 'Chicken, chicken, come back to me. I will do anything you want me to.' Drunken dramatics were not unusual at number 21 and not one person bothered to get up and check what was going on. They had heard it all before. 'There was a terrible barney at no. 21,' a neighbour later told the police, with an unintended pun.

At about 4.50 a.m. a doctor was woken by a telephone call and he managed to hear through hysterical crying someone say, 'It is Mrs Barney. Oh, doctor, come at once. There has been a terrible accident. For God's sake, come at once.' When Doctor Thomas Durrant arrived at Williams Mews he came across Barney 'in a condition of extreme hysteria and continually repeating, "He wanted to see you to tell you it was only an accident. He wanted to see you to tell you it was only an accident."'[4] On the stairs, shot in the chest at close range, lay a distinctly dead Michael Stephen. Despite Elvira's protestations, the doctor insisted that they had to call the police. The writer Macdonald Hastings (Max's father) wrote about the fateful evening in his book about the firearms and ballistics expert Robert Churchill[5] and described how shocked the police were when they encountered the scene at the mews house for the first time: 'Over the cocktail bar in the corner of the sitting room there was a wall painting which would have been a sensation in a brothel in Pompeii. The library was furnished with publications which could never have passed through His Majesty's Customs. The place was equipped with the implements of fetishism and perversion.'

Shocked they may well have been, and despite Elvira at one point striking Inspector Campion in the face and saying, 'I will teach you to say you will put me in a cell, you vile swine,' the Metropolitan Police in 1932 knew their place and the murder suspect was only subjected to gentle questioning. She soon told them, however, that there had been an argument during which her boyfriend, Michael Stephens, had said he was leaving her, to which she had replied by threatening to kill herself with a revolver that she kept by the side of her bed. During their ensuing struggle when he tried to get the gun from her grasp the weapon suddenly fired into Stephen's body. She was unsure whose finger was actually on the trigger. It would be exactly the same story that she told all the way through her subsequent ordeal. After Elvira's parents, Sir John and Lady Mullens, arrived at the station, the police kindly allowed the main suspect of a likely murder case to go back home nearby at 6 Belgrave Square. The

1911 census, incidentally, shows that the Mullens shared their house with twenty-three live-in servants, and twenty-one years later several liveried footmen would have greeted the Mullens when they arrived home.

Three days after she had shot Michael Stephen, accidentally or otherwise, Elvira was arrested and charged with his murder. The police had no choice when, after questioning neighbours about the shooting, they found out there had been a witnesses to a previous altercation between Mrs Barney and Stephen. After one loud quarrel Stephen had stormed out of the house and started walking away, at which point a window on the first floor opened and a naked Mrs Barney was heard shouting, 'Laugh, baby. Laugh for the last time!' At which point she produced her revolver and shot at Stephen from the window.

Four years previously, a twenty-three-year-old Elvira, despite her parents' protestations, had married an American singer and entertainer called John Sterling Barney. They had met at a society function held by Lady Mullens where he had been performing in a 'top-hat, white-tie and tails' trio called The Three New-Yorkers. The three entertainers were relatively successful at the time and, indeed, often performed in cabaret at the Café de Paris. By many accounts, however, John Barney was a rather unpleasant man, and a friend of Elvira's called Effie Leigh once recalled, 'One day she held her arms in the air and the burns she displayed – there and elsewhere – were, she insisted, the work of her husband who had delighted in crushing his lighted cigarettes out from time to time on her bare skin.'[6] Violent rows had started within weeks of the marriage ceremony and after a few months the American went back to the United States, never really to be heard of again. Elvira, according to her biographer Peter Cotes, went off the rails and 'started sniffing the snow ... and became the demanding but generous mistress of a number of disorientated and sexually odd lovers'. The description goes someway to explain how, at the start of 1932, she ended up sharing her bed (and her not insubstantial bank account) with the drug-dealing ex-'dress-designer' Michael Scott Stephen, a man who was more than happy to accompany her as she 'drifted into flagrant immorality'.[7]

On Saturday 4 June, after spending the night in a cell at the Gerald Road police station in Victoria, a pale Elvira Barney, dressed in a long black coat with her fair hair covered by a black cloche hat trimmed with white, was driven to the Westminster police court on Rochester Road. She was charged with murder and accused of shooting Thomas William Scott Stephen, after which she was remanded for a week. After hearing the charge, Elvira staggered a few steps and collapsed into the arms of a wardress guarding her. Police officers carried her from the court and after doctors had attended her for an hour she was taken to Holloway Prison.

Sir John Mullens, with his society connections and wealth, managed to persuade the former attorney-general, Sir Patrick Hastings, to defend his daughter. In 1932 Hastings, in his early fifties, was at the height of his fame as king's council. In his book *Cases in Court*, published in 1949, Sir Patrick describes his first sighting of Elvira:

> She had been described in the Press as 'a beautiful member of the so-called "smart set"', but no doubt partly by reason of the ordeal which she had undergone, and partly in consequence of the life she had been leading, her appearance was not calculated to move the hearts of a jury; indeed she was a melancholy and somewhat depressing figure.

A month after she was charged at Westminster police court, Elvira's trial at the Old Bailey commenced on 4 July 1932. Despite Hastings' misgivings, she defended herself well, never once changing her story that it had all been a terrible accident. Her case was helped by the doctor who had first arrived at William Mews after the shooting when he said on the first day of the trial, 'In her mental condition after the tragedy she could not have invented the story she told me. She seemed passionately devoted to the dead man.' At the end of the trial Hastings made a final address to the jury, one that the judge – Mr Justice Humphreys – later called 'the best he had ever heard'.

While everyone was waiting for the jury to return their verdict, Elvira, waiting to be summoned, was standing halfway down the stairs that led up to the large dock. The *Daily Mirror* described the scene: 'She was ghastly pale and seemed as though she would break down completely. The two wardresses held her hands and she leaned heavily against the side of the stairs. The blood-vessels in her neck could be seen pulsating and throbbing as she ascended the steps.'[8] As soon as the jury arrived back in the courtroom, Hastings saw that they all glanced over at Mrs Barney. He knew that that was an almost infallible test that it would be a 'not guilty' verdict. When she heard that she had been acquitted, Elvira just stood in the dock looking intensely at Mr Justice Humpheys before she collapsed back into her chair. On his way out of the court the judge exclaimed, 'Most extraordinary! Apparently we should have given her a pat on the back!'

The jury may have acquitted her, but Fleet Street weren't in the mood to let her off so easily and they gleefully reported that Elvira Mullens (the name she had reverted to) had shouted on the dance floor of the Café de Paris soon after the court case, 'I am the one who shot her lover – so take a good look at me.' One strange aspect of this case was that Michael Stephen, the real victim, was always treated with an extraordinary lack of sympathy by both his family and the press. Sir Patrick Hastings was happy to describe him years later as 'worthless'. During the trial the former attorney-general depicted Elvira as 'a young woman with the rest of her life before her'. Unfortunately, the rest of her life lasted just four more years, and on Christmas morning in 1936 she was found dead in a Parisian hotel room after a typical long night of drinking and taking cocaine. It was reported that in the early hours she had decided to return to her hotel after complaining that she felt cold and unwell, and was last seen by a porter who had to help her up to her room. The next morning a chambermaid, after knocking several times, entered her room and found Elvira half on her bed, half off, and still dressed in a black and white checked dress and the fur coat she had been wearing in Montmartre the night before. She had been bleeding from the mouth. The years of drinking and drug-taking had finally taken their toll. Three days after her death the William Hickey column in the *Daily Express* described a recent meeting: 'I last saw Mrs Barney in a Soho negro nightclub. It seemed her proper milieu. It is surprising to read that she was only 31. She looked ten years more, fat, with tired eyes. Her defiant, almost truculent manner suggested that she was miserably unhappy.'[9]

At about the same time as Elvira's untimely death in a small Parisian hotel room, the American singer Elisabeth Welch made her cabaret debut at the Café de Paris. She described the Coventry Street venue at the time as 'the grand nightclub of London and all the big names of cabaret played there. It was very chic and very smart'. It was Welch, a year before Louise Brooks mesmerised audiences at the Café de Paris dancing to it, who had popularised 'The Charleston' in America when she sang the song in *Runnin' Wild* on Broadway in 1923. She arrived in London eight years later with Cole Porter's musical *Nymph Errant*. Soon she was singing in Ivor Novello's *Glamorous Night* and had her own radio series called *Soft Lights and Sweet Music*. She rented a smart art deco house in a mews off Sloane Street. Elizabeth Welch was one of several black musicians before the war who enjoyed London and made it their home. Another was a man who will forever be associated with the Café de Paris because he died there: Ken 'Snakehips' Johnson.

The Café de Paris, unlike the majority of theatres and nightclubs in the West End, remained open at the start of the Second World War. The rich and famous patrons presumably had influence over the wartime licensing regulations, but it was always said that the dance floor was so far underground that it was completely safe in an air raid, a 'fact' that certainly wasn't discouraged by Martin Poulsen, who called his Café de Paris 'the safest and gayest restaurant in town – even in air raids. Twenty feet below ground'. In August 1940 the Nazi propagandist William Joyce, Lord Haw-Haw, sneered at the well-to-do having fun in the West End, broadcasting one night, '... the plutocrats and the favoured lords of creation were making the raid an excuse for their drunken orgies and debaucheries in the saloons of Piccadilly and in the Café de Paris ... as the son of a profiteer baron put it, "They won't bomb this part of the town! They want the docks! Fill up boys!"'

At 9.30 p.m. on Saturday 8 March 1941, Johnson was still having drinks with some friends at the Embassy Club in Old Bond Street. His show at the Café de Paris started at 9.45 so he half walked and half jogged the usual eight-minute walk to the Coventry Street nightclub – not easy in a blackout (blackout time that night was between 7.27 p.m. and 6.53 a.m.). By now sirens were sounding and an air-raid had begun, but he managed to get to the stage on time and the West Indian Orchestra started playing 'Oh Johnny, Oh Johnny, How Can You Love' as usual. Johnson was a striking front man, his nickname coming from the long-limbed elasticity of his eccentric dancing.

Time magazine a few weeks later described the audience that night as 'handsome flying johnnies, naval jacks in full dress, guardsmen, territorials, and just plain civics sat making conversational love'. Five minutes into the song two bombs came crashing through the glass roof of the Rialto Cinema directly above the nightclub and exploded on the dance floor. Two days later *The Manchester Guardian*, after describing the bombing as 'fairly heavy' and careful not to name the Café de Paris because of wartime censorship, quoted a witness that night:

> The band was playing and the floor was crowded with couples dancing. Suddenly there was a flash like the fusing of a great electric cable. Then in the darkness masonry and lumps of plaster could be heard crashing to the ground. I was blown off my feet, but the sensation was that of being pressed down by a great big hand. Several people switched on torches and others struck petrol lighters when they had recovered from the first shock. I could see people lying on the floor all around ... The air was filled with smell of powder and dust.[10]

Among the chaos, next to the microphone through which he had just been singing and with a red carnation still in the buttonhole of his white dinner jacket, lay the leader of the band. There was not a mark on his body but his head had been blown clean off. Ken 'Snakehips' Johnson, only twenty-six years old, had tragically reached the end of his meteoric career.

A special constable with the splendid name of Ballard Berkeley, who would later become famous as the actor who played the Major in *Fawlty Towers*, was one of the first on the scene. He saw the decapitated Snakehips and elegantly dressed people still sitting at tables, seemingly almost in conversation but covered in dust and stone dead. He was shocked to see looters, mingling with the firemen and the police, cutting the fingers from the dead to get at their expensive rings. *The Manchester Guardian* reported that a nurse who was helping the wounded 'afterwards saw a man rifling her handbag. The articles stolen included a fountain pen and an RAF brooch given her by a pilot who is now a prisoner of war in Germany'[11]. Among the dead was Mr Café de Paris himself, Martin Poulsen, and of the musicians, Dave 'Baba' Williams, a Trinidadian saxophonist, had been cut in half by the blast. Survivors included the Grand National winning jockey and horse-racing trainer Fulke Walwyn, the author Noel Streatfeild (aka Susan Scarlett), and Howard Barnes, an advertising copywriter who lost his leg in the blast but who later became a songwriter (Nat King Cole recorded his 'A Blossom Fell').

Three years after the Café de Paris explosion, a house on Rutland Street, a few hundred yards away from William Mews, was razed to the ground by a V1 flying bomb. It was the home of Marion Harris, who had by then retired from show business after marrying a theatrical agent called Leonard Urry. Not that he had been a theatrical agent for long. When Harris first met Urry he was employed as a professional 'dance partner' at the Café de Paris. He was paid, essentially, for dancing with women who were on their own or had no one to dance with. Some might have called him a gigolo. Harris was completely traumatised by her home being destroyed and she soon returned to America. She never really recovered and she was soon admitted to a neurological sanatorium. Within a few weeks of her arrival in the US, on Sunday 23 April 1944, her room at the Hotel Le Marquis in Manhattan caught fire. She had fallen asleep with her cigarette still burning and the cause of death was asphyxiation and terrible burns.

After the explosion that killed Snakehips Johnson and about eighty others (the exact number isn't known), the Café de Paris remained closed throughout the Second World War. After a refurbishment in 1948, the famous West End nightclub reopened. It was again graced by royalty, notably Princess Margaret, the niece of the former Prince of Wales, and, although it came close, the club never really regained the sophisticated aura that it had garnered before the war. The only notable exception was on 29 September 1965, forty years after Louise Brooks danced at the Café de Paris with such acclaim, when Lionel Blair launched his new dance called 'The Kick' at the same venue. It wasn't a storming success.

Left: Michael Stephen.

Below: 21 William Mews in Knightsbridge at the time of the shooting in 1932.

21 William Mews, the house that Elvira Barney and Michael Stephen shared and where the shooting took place.

After being found not-guilty, Elvira Barney arrives at her parents' home at 6 Belgrave Square, London, 7 July 1932.

Marion Harris playing the ukulele. She began recording for Victor Records in 1916 and her biggest success there was 'I Ain't Got Nobody'. In 1920, around the time this picture was taken, she joined Columbia Records after Victor refused her wish to record W. C. Handy's 'St Louis Blues'.

The Aftermath. Café de Paris on the morning of 9 March 1941.

CHAPTER 7

The Deaths of Cass Elliot and Keith Moon in Harry Nilsson's Bed

Cass Elliot eating at her party at Crockford's Casino, celebrating the start of her engagement at the Palladium two days previously, 17 July 1974. (Joe Bangay/Evening Standard/Getty Images)

Marianne Faithfull pointed at a pale man sitting next to her and told a reporter, rather optimistically, that Oliver Musker, the twenty-seven-year-old Old Etonian she was seeing at the time and who had recently rescued her, albeit temporarily, from heroin addiction, was to become her second husband in the autumn. 'When all the leaves turn brown,' she said dreamily, 'it suits our mood.' She was quoting the Mamas and the Papas because they were both at a party at Crockfords, the Mayfair casino, as a guest of Cass Elliot, who was celebrating the start of a two-week engagement at the London Palladium[1] which had begun two nights before on 15 July 1974.

Elliot went on to receive good reviews for her shows in London that summer although nearly all of them mentioned her weight. The *Observer* wrote: 'Although she is a large lady, Miss Elliot does a thin girl's act, capering about like two Ginger Rogerses welded together.' The *Daily Express* told their readers that she had been dieting continuously and had given up alcohol for more than a year: 'Mama Cass Elliot is considerably lighter than when she was last in Britain. By 80 lb to be exact and is now weighing 14½ stone. She sang the Mamas and the Papas' favourites, 'Monday Monday', and 'California Dreaming' but got a little breathless during the song and dance routines.' After informing him that she would hit him in the mouth if he called her 'Mama' again, Cass Elliot told the *Daily Express* reporter David Wigg, after he had brought up her size yet again, 'I'd like to lose more because I'm getting older. These days when you approach middle thirties you think about heart disease.'[2]

Earlier that year the Palladium had proudly announced the rather unlikely boast that they were the only theatre in the world presenting twice-nightly variety bills. The main headliners on the bill of the summer season that year, other than Cass Elliot, included Frankie Vaughan, Vic Damone, Debbie Reynolds, Ken Dodd and Larry Grayson. Louis Benjamin, presenter of the *Royal Variety Performances* and managing director of the London Palladium, said: 'There are few stars who can fill a theatre for weeks on end. We cannot compete with Las Vegas or some of the Northern Clubs. A season at the London Palladium, though, is still a stamp of prestige.'[3]

It was all very middle-of-the-road fare. Cass Elliot was supported in her show by Black Lace who, in their programme notes, had written that they intended to become 'a top class concert and cabaret group' through the use of 'classy' material. After the band played their two hits, 'Billy Don't be a Hero' and 'The Night Chicago Died', the guitarist suddenly started singing 'Ave Maria' in full Italian-religioso style while the other members of the band gathered around the mike to give classy, harmonised support.

At the end of the last show of the two-week sell-out engagement, Cass Elliot received several standing ovations. When she went back to the Palladium dressing room for the last time she scrawled in lipstick over the mirror a message to Debbie Reynolds: 'Dear Debbie, if they are half as nice to you as they were to me, you will have a great time. Love Cass.'

Cass Elliott marked the end of her Palladium season with forty-eight hours of celebrations. She received a standing ovation and then went on to Mick Jagger's birthday party, held with Bianca Jagger at Tite Street in Chelsea. From that party – without sleep – she went to what the newspapers were still calling in 1974 'a breakfast-lunch' given for her by the singer Georgia Brown. She then went straight to a cocktail party given by the American journalist Jack Martin where Alan Bates, David Hemmings and Rachel Roberts were in attendance. She left this party at 8.00 p.m. saying she was tired and then she went back home.

During Elliot's time at the Palladium, 'home' was in Mayfair at her friend Harry Nilsson's apartment in Curzon Place. He had bought it two years previously in 1972 while he was particularly good friends with Ringo Starr; it was a two-bedroomed top-floor flat in a large eighteenth-century house at 9 Curzon Place, on the south-east edge of Mayfair. Nilsson and Ringo had become good friends during 1972: Ringo, although credited as 'Richie Snare', was the drummer on much of Nilsson's *Son of Schmilsson* released in July of that year. 'Ringo and I spent a thousand hours laughing,' Nilsson once said. They were part of a social set that included Marc Bolan, Keith Moon and Graham Chapman of *Monty Python's Flying Circus*. As rock stars can do, they met in the afternoon and when each arrival dropped by they would say, 'I hope I'm not interrupting anything?' Nilsson recalled: 'We would drink until 9 p.m. That's six hours of brandy. Then between 9 and 10, we would usually end up at Tramp, the most uproarious exclusive disco-restaurant in the world. Royals, movies stars, world champions, all frequented there. It was really a ride, meeting these luminaries and having total blow-outs almost every night.'[4]

Flat 12, 9 Curzon Place was where many of the 'total blow-outs' took place. It was different from the rest of the apartments in the building in that it was above the bay-window extension and had balconies on both sides of the building; from one it was possible to see the Palace of Westminster, while the other offered a particularly good view of the Bunny Girls coming and going to work at the nearby London Playboy Club. When Nilsson first found the place it looked old-fashioned and he was very keen for it to be completely re-designed. He decided to take on Ringo, who the previous year had set up a design partnership with the sculptor and furniture-maker

Robin Cruickshank, called ROR, which stood for Ringo or Robin. One of Ringo's earliest ideas was a Rolls-Royce Grille Table and a chrome-plated antique telephone that became the logo for Ringo's record company Ring O' Records. One of ROR's early clients was the Soho porn baron Paul Raymond, not known for his discerning or sophisticated taste, who asked them to design a patio for his apartment at Fitzhardinge House, a '60s building on the corner of Baker Street and Portman Square.

When ROR had completed their work the patio featured an illuminated fountain with underwater lights which pulsated in time to the music. Above this was a huge aluminium-and-glass-domed roof which slowly opened and closed at the press of a button. At one point Baker Street had to be closed to traffic while a crane lifted the domed roof into position. Raymond was so impressed with ROR's work that he got them to redesign the boat he had just bought. Fiona Richmond had persuaded him to call the yacht 'Get 'em orf' in Latin, and thus it was called *Veste Demite*.

Nilsson once remembered that, as far as his apartment was concerned, he had let the designer go wild: 'Robin made this great, amazing pad. It was … all glass and chrome and felt and velvet. And the price had doubled from the quote, and then Mr R. Starkey picked up the difference, or most of it. The first day I entered the flat it was completely finished. I had just come from America and I was shocked. I didn't know what to think. And then I thought for a second, and I loved it. As a little gift, Ringo and Robin and had made these special mirrors for the two-sinked bathroom. They were done in etched glass. One was a picture of an oak tree. But on the other, there was etched a hangman's noose.'[5]

As soon as Cass Elliot had got back to all the chrome, glass and velvet at Curzon Place after Jack Martin's party, she called her former Mamas and Papas band member Michelle Phillips, who later recounted: 'She had had a little champagne, and was crying. She felt she had finally made the transition from Mama Cass.' The next morning Cass's secretary Dot MacLeod and Joe Croyle, a twenty-five-year-old singer who had appeared with Cass in the Palladium show, had both come round to the apartment. Dot had been there all day but had deliberately tried not to disturb the singer because they knew she often slept very late. At about seven in the evening she opened the door to Elliot's bedroom and found the singer dead.

Cass Elliot died choking on a ham sandwich, everybody knows that. Except that she didn't. The myth began because the first doctor who examined her after her death, Dr Anthony Greenburg, in a late-night press conference, said, 'She was lying in bed eating and drinking a Coca-

Cola while watching television. She was half propped up by pillows and it seems that she choked on her sandwich and inhaled her own vomit.' Dr Greenburg added, 'She had been dead for some considerable time before her body was found.'

Dr Greenburg, Elliot's own physician, had overlooked the relatively important fact that the ham sandwich was by the side of her bed and untouched, but by then it was too late. The press reported his initial comments and the doctor unwittingly gave rise to the sandwich myth. A few days later at the inquest Gavin Thurston, the Westminster coroner, recorded a verdict of death from natural causes. 'There was left-sided heart failure,' wrote pathologist Professor Keith Simpson. 'She had a heart attack which developed rapidly.' Cass Elliott had been going on crash diets for years which in the end fatally weakened her heart. She was just thirty-two when she died.

Four years after the death of Cass Elliot at Harry Nilsson's flat, Keith Moon, after fitting in enough partying and convivial nights in his short life for a small town, died of an overdose of Heminevrin tablets in the very same bed.

Keith and his girlfriend, Annette Walter-Lax, had been to a party held by Paul McCartney at the trendy chrome and neon-lit cocktail-bar restaurant called Peppermint Park on St Martin's Lane, Covent Garden. By many accounts Keith was unusually quiet and sober and shared a booth with the McCartneys, David Frost, John Hurt and Kenny Jones – Moon's eventual replacement, ironically. At midnight, everyone went to the Odeon, Leicester Square, for the late-night premiere of the *Buddy Holly Story* that starred Gary Busey. Before the end of the film Keith and Annette caught a taxi back to Curzon Place. Keith started watching the film *The Abominable Dr Phibes* but fell asleep after taking several Heminevrin sedatives that had been prescribed to aid alcohol withdrawal. At about 7.30 a.m. he ordered Annette to cook him steak for breakfast. She complained but Keith retorted with, 'If you don't like it, you can fuck off.' Unfortunately they were his last words.

Annette, who had been sleeping on the living room couch because of Moon's incessant snoring, discovered him in the afternoon, face down on the bed, and he was found to be dead on arrival at Middlesex Hospital in Westminster. He was thirty-two and had died just three weeks after the release of The Who album *Who Are You*. On the album cover, he is seated on a chair back-to-front to hide his recent weight gain. The words NOT TO BE TAKEN AWAY are written on the back of the chair. Press assistant Paul Goodman was rather disingenuous the next day when he said, 'Keith drank whisky more than he took drugs – but he wasn't an alcoholic,' while his colleague Keith Altham added that the band had decided to carry on: 'They won't wind up. They feel they should go on ... because Keith was never a quitter.'[6]

It was Professor Keith Simpson, as it was with Cass Elliot, who performed the post mortem. Of the thirty-two Heminevrin tablets he found in Moon's stomach, twenty-six were undissolved. 'The quantity was enormous,' Professor Simpson wrote down, 'and constituted a vast overdose.' A half-empty bottle of 100 Heminevrin tablets was found at Moon's bedside at Curzon Place and the coroner recorded an open verdict. Moon the Loon was only thirty-two when he died, but dying young didn't come to anyone's great surprise – he was one of the greatest partiers ever. He once outlined his typical daily diet to a doctor: 'I always get up about six in the morning. I have my bangers and eggs. And I drink a bottle of Dom Perignon and half a bottle of brandy. Then I take a couple of downers. Then it's about 10 and I'll have a nice nap until five. I get up, have a couple of black beauties [also known as Black Birds or Black Bombers and are a combination of amphetamine, or speed, and dextroamphetamine], some brandy, a little champagne and go out on the town. Then we boogie. We'll wrap it up about four.'

It wasn't what a doctor would recommend for a long and healthy life but Keith had fitted in some fun during his relatively short life. He and Harry had become friends in the first place because of their mutual love of alcohol. They had originally met on the set of a film produced by Ringo Starr called *Son of Dracula* that was to star Nilsson. Nilsson had told Ringo that he expected no fee for appearing in the movie, but the ex-Beatles drummer paid for him to have cosmetic dentistry to straighten his crooked front teeth, historically one of the reasons that Nilsson had been very shy of appearing live. As well as Keith and Harry, other musicians were in the film including Marc Bolan and Peter Frampton. Keith remembered, 'We were supposed to be on the set at six, but it was nine before everyone was there. Then somebody brought out a bottle of brandy. Me, I think. Ah-ha-ha-HAHAHA! And Peter Frampton said no, no, too early, and some of the others said no. But 'Arry was standing there with an 'alf-pint mug. I knew at that moment it was destiny put us together. Ahhhh-HAHAHAHAHAHAHA!'[7]

After the death of a second friend in his bed, Nilsson quickly sold his flat to another Who member, Pete Townsend, and then moved back to Los Angeles permanently. Of course, like Cass, and especially Moon, Harry Nilsson liked having a good time and his consumption of drink and drugs were once described as Herculean. Marianne Faithfull once said of Nilsson: 'We used to do drugs together. And when I say drugs, I don't mean those airy-fairy drugs they do nowadays. I'm talking about narcotics.' Elton John, another person who knows what he's talking about in this respect, once described seeing Nilsson in a recording studio: 'He opened his mouth to sing, and blood poured out; he had done so much coke that his throat just haemorrhaged. And do you know what? He didn't even notice.'

Compared with his two friends, Elliot and Moon, however, Nilsson managed to live to the relatively grand old age of fifty-two. After surviving one heart attack in 1993, he died from another the following year. At his funeral the mourners felt after-shocks from the Northridge earthquake that was rumbling in the background. A joke went round that it was the result of Harry getting to heaven and discovering that there were no bars. Not long before his first heart attack Nilsson found out that his entire $5 million fortune had been embezzled, leaving him and his family almost destitute, and it was said that he never really recovered from the shock.

It's interesting to note that Mama Cass, a person who struggled with her weight nearly all her life, died from trying not to eat, with a heart fatally weakened by too many diets. Keith Moon, a man with a prodigious appetite for alcohol, died from an overdose of medicine prescribed in an attempt to stop him drinking.

In 2001, the building at Curzon Place containing Harry Nilsson's old flat was bought by a developer who completely changed the interior, and the three flats on Harry's floor were knocked into two luxury flats. The road has also changed its name to Curzon Square. The apartments would now, going into 2016, be worth several million pounds each.

Keith Moon attending the premiere of the new film *The Buddy Holly Story* in the West End with fianceé Annette Walter-Lax as guests of Paul and Linda McCartney. After dining with Paul and Linda at Peppermint Park in Covent Garden on 6 September 1978, he died a few hours later. (© Trinity Mirror/Mirrorpix/Alamy)

The building in Curzon Square (formerly Curzon Place) in which Harry Nilsson's apartment was situated. (Rob Baker)

Ringo Starr, Harry Nilsson and Keith Moon at the premiere of *That'll Be the Day*, October 1974. (Photo by Frank Edwards/Fotos International/Getty Images)

CHAPTER 8

Mary Richardson – Suffragette, Iconoclast and Fascist

Mary Richardson leaving court, March 1914.

In June 1934 at an anti-fascist gathering at Trafalgar Square, a fifty-two-year-old Sylvia Pankhurst angrily denounced Blackshirt violence. It had been only three weeks since Oswald Mosley and the British Union of Fascists had held their huge staged rally at Olympia for which the *Daily Mail* had offered free tickets to readers who sent in letters explaining 'Why I like the Blackshirts'.

The BUF rally had been designed to attract more recruits but also to impress the invited audience of politicians and journalists. Usually a stickler for punctuality, as most good fascists are, Mosley arrived on stage an hour late, but he quickly launched into a virulent anti-Semitic speech shouting about 'European ghettos pouring their dregs into this country'.

It wasn't long before a crowd of around 500 anti-fascists (including Vera Brittain and Aldous Huxley), all of whom had surreptitiously bought tickets for the meeting, started shouting abuse. Mosley stopped speaking and the hecklers were picked out by roving spotlights and then ferociously attacked by black-shirted stewards. Some hecklers were women and these were dealt with by female stewards who had been carefully trained to slap instead of punching. The *Daily Express*, not afraid to show where its sympathies lay, wrote about 'reds' gatecrashing the rally and gushed:

> Inside Olympia the most amazing meeting London has seen for two decades was taking place. As soon as Sir Oswald Mosley – a remarkable black-shirted figure, picked out by the glare of two dazzling search lights, started to speak he was howled down. In the audience that had rallied to his support were hundreds of women in evening dress. As fighting broke out in all parts of the hall many started to scream, left their seats, and made for the exits. Sir Oswald's voice amplified through twenty-four loudspeakers could be heard crying for calm. 'Keep your seats! Please keep your seats.' The women were reassured and sat down. Others, of bolder spirit, were standing on chairs watching the fighting through opera glasses and laughing with excitement.[1]

The committed pacifist and socialist author Margaret Storm Jameson described the same event, from a completely different point of view, in a letter to the *Daily Telegraph*:

> A young woman was carried past me by five Blackshirts, her clothes half torn off and her mouth and nose closed by the large hand of one; her head was forced back by the pressure and she must have been in considerable pain. I mention her especially since I have seen a reference to the delicacy with which women interrupters were left to women Blackshirts. This is

merely untrue ... Why train decent young men to indulge in such peculiarly nasty brutality?[2]

Lord Rothermere, the owner of the *Daily Mail* and the *Sunday Dispatch*, had for several months been promoting the BUF's cause in his newspapers. He wrote a now infamous article headlined 'Hurrah for the Blackshirts' in which he suggested that:

> Britain's survival as a great power will depend on the existence of a well-organised party of the Right ready to take over responsibility for national affairs with the same direct purpose and energy of method as Mussolini and Hitler have displayed. That is why I say Hurrah for the Blackshirts! ... Hundreds of thousands of young British men and women would like to see their own country develop that spirit of patriotic pride and service which has transformed Germany and Italy.[3]

The vicious 'Biff Boy' blackshirt violence at the BUF rally, however, shocked many, including Lord Rothermere, so it was unsurprising that during her passionate speech to the Trafalgar Square crowd Sylvia Pankhurst particularly criticised the brutality reported at Olympia. She also warned her audience about the treatment of women in Italy, saying that Mussolini had recently said, 'The chief business of women is to be pleasing to men.' At the end of her angry speech she demanded the arrest and detention of fascist sympathisers in Britain, one of whom, notably, was her erstwhile colleague and fellow member of the Women's Social and Political Union, Mary Richardson.

Twenty years previously Mary Richardson had campaigned, been arrested and imprisoned with Sylvia Pankhurst in the East End of London in 1913. She had joined the Women's Social and Political Union after witnessing 'Black Friday' on 18 November 1910, after Prime Minister Herbert Henry Asquith indicated that there would be no more time to read the Conciliation Bill (which would have extended the right of women to vote in Britain and Ireland to just over a million property-owning women). After a meeting at the nearby Caxton Hall, an angry WSPU sent 300 members who carried banners such as 'Taxed but Voteless' and 'Women's Will Beats Asquith's Won't' to lobby outside Parliament. The women who tried to force their way through a ring of policemen were physically attacked and even sexually manhandled by them. The public were shocked when the next day the *Daily Mirror* printed a large photo of Ada Wright lying on the ground with gloved hands over her face.[4] The violence shocked onlookers and later much of the public. A letter from a witness published by the *Daily Mirror* four days later described the scenes: 'The women were knocked about like footballs … I heard they [the police] had been given orders to ill-treat and wear out the women before arresting them. I consider the public have a right to know who gave that barbarous order. Hitherto the police have been friends of women but on that black Friday they completely lost their heads.'[5]

Richardson, as a suffragette, was arrested nine times and served several sentences in Holloway prison for assaulting police, breaking windows and arson. She was, however, particularly notorious for slashing the 'Rokeby Venus' in the National Gallery in March 1914. In a particularly militant period of suffragette activity in the months preceding the First World War, it is Richardson's vandalism of Velasquez's famous painting that is often still remembered today.

The *Toilet of Venus* or *La Venus del Espejo*, as it is more properly but rarely called, had been painted by the great Spanish artist Diego Velázquez sometime between 1647 and 1651. It is his only surviving female nude, an artistic direction not overly encouraged at what the art historian Kenneth Clark once called 'the prudish and corseted court of Phillip IV'.[6] The painting came to England in 1813 when it was bought for £500 by John Morritt, who hung it in his house at Rokeby Park in Yorkshire – hence the painting's popular name, which it has retained ever since. Morritt, a classical scholar and Member of Parliament, once wrote to his friend Sir Walter Scott about his new acquisition: 'I have been all morning pulling about my pictures and hanging them in new positions to make room for my fine picture of Venus's backside which I have at length exalted over my chimney-piece in the library. It is in an admirable light for the painting and shows it to perfection, whilst raising the said backside to a considerable height, the ladies may avert their downcast eyes without difficulty and connoisseurs steal a glance without drawing the said posterior into the company.'[7]

In 1906, the painting was acquired for the National Gallery by the newly created National Art Collections Fund. Henry James and Roger Fry both donated money, as did King Edward VII, who had greatly admired the painting and personally provided £8,000 towards its purchase. *The Times* described the Rokeby Venus as a 'work which the almost universal opinion of trained judges has pronounced to be among the great pictures of the world'.[8]

When Mary Richardson walked into the National Gallery on 10 March 1914 with a meat cleaver hidden on her person, the Rokeby Venus was undoubtedly the most famous painting in Britain. She had arrived at the gallery at about ten in the morning and for the next two hours she appeared to wander innocently around the building making occasional sketches of the paintings. No one noticed that she had also brought along a narrow butcher's meat cleaver which was hidden from view up her sleeve and held there by a chain of safety pins. She later wrote: 'All I had to do was release the last one and take out my chopper and go ... bang!'[9] As an ex-art student, she knew the gallery well and decided upon Velázquez's Rokeby Venus because, as she would later write: 'It was highly prized for its worth in cash ... the fact that I disliked the painting would make it easier for me to do what was in my mind.'[10] Richardson had actually submitted the idea of damaging a painting to Christabel Pankhurst some weeks before to which the WSPU leader, eventually, wrote back saying, 'Carry out your plan.'

The previous year three suffragettes had been arrested and two imprisoned for smashing the protective glass of fourteen paintings at the Manchester Art Gallery. Since then there had been added security in exhibition spaces and art galleries around the country. For this reason two detectives and a gallery attendant were in the room where the Velázquez masterpiece was displayed at the National Gallery. A nervous and agitated Richardson almost gave up on her premeditated plan but around midday one of the detectives went for lunch while the other sat down, crossed his legs and opened up a newspaper. Richardson noticed that this masked the painting from his view and she quietly released the cleaver from inside her sleeve and seized her chance.

Two years before she died, in an interview recorded in 1959 for the BBC, Richardson described what she did next: 'I went and hit the painting. The first hit only broke the glass it was so thick, and then extraordinarily instead of seizing me, which he could have quite easily, because I was only a couple of yards from him [...] he connected the falling glass with the fanlight above our heads and walked round in a circle looking up at the fanlights which gave me time to get five lovely shots in.' The attendant rushed forward but could only slip up on the highly polished floor and he fell face first into the broken glass. Two tourists also threw their guidebooks at Richardson but eventually the detective sprang on her as she was 'hammering away' and snatched the cleaver from her hand. Richardson offered no resistance and as she was being taken down to the basement she quietly told the visitors she passed, 'I am a suffragette. You can get another picture, but you cannot get a life, as they are killing Mrs Pankhurst.'

Mary Richardson had been jolted into action that morning because she had been particularly angered at the news of Mrs Emmeline Pankhurst's arrest the night before at St Andrew's Hall in Glasgow. Emmeline Pankhurst was at the time protected by a twenty-five-strong bodyguard of women trained in the martial art of jujitsu. They were taught by a woman, just four feet eleven inches tall, called Edith Garrud.

Garrud had started working with suffragettes a few years before in her own women-only training hall, based initially in Golden Square in Soho but later in the East End. She also taught her suffragette students how to use wooden Indian clubs which could be concealed in their dresses and used as a reply to the truncheons of the police. In 1910 Garrud wrote an article explaining how woman using the jujitsu had 'brought great burly cowards nearly twice their size to their feet and made them howl for mercy'.[11]

According to the *Glasgow Herald* there were 'unparalleled scenes of disorder' when the police tried to arrest Emmeline at St Andrew's Hall. She had initially avoided them by entering the building early but when she started to speak the police attempted to storm the stage. They were severely hampered not only by the barbed-wire hidden in the flower decorations but also Mrs Pankhurst's trained bodyguards. Emmeline Pankhurst in *My Own Story* described what happened:

> The bodyguard and members of the audience vigorously repelled the attack, wielding clubs, batons, poles, planks or anything they could seize, while the police laid about right and left with their batons, their violence being far the greater. Men and women were seen on all sides with blood streaming down their faces, and there were cries for a doctor. In the middle of the struggle, several revolver shots rang out, and the woman who was firing the revolver – which I should explain was loaded with blank cartridges only – was able to terrorise and keep at bay a whole body of police. I had been surrounded by members of the bodyguard, who hurried me towards the stairs from the platform. The police, however, overtook us, and in spite of the resistance of the bodyguard, they seized me and dragged me down the narrow stair at the back of the hall. There a cab was waiting. I was pushed violently into it, and thrown on the floor, the seats being occupied by as many constables as could crowd inside.

Mary Richardson would also have known that the day before Emmeline's arrest her daughter Sylvia Pankhurst had also been arrested. Sylvia had been travelling along the Strand on a 'motor omnibus' on her way to

Trafalgar Square, where she was to speak at a protest rally organised by the Men's Federation for Women's Suffrage. The bus had stopped outside Charing Cross post office but when Sylvia stepped on to the pavement plain-clothes policemen quickly surrounded her. Like her mother, she was arrested under the so-called Cat and Mouse Act (this was her sixth time). She cried for help but the police bundled her into the back of a taxicab and she was sent on her way back to Holloway prison.

The following day the *Daily Express* reported that the news of her arrest had caused 'intense indignation in the crowd' waiting at Trafalgar Square. They continued, 'Miss Patterson [sic] who acted as chairman, led a detachment towards Whitehall, waving a flag and shouting "It is deeds, not words!"'[12] The next day Margaret Paterson, who was the Poplar organiser of the East London Federation of the Suffragettes, and who had continually attempted to strike policemen with a short thick piece of rope loaded at the end with lead, was fined £2. Miss Paterson said to the magistrate, 'It had taken ten men and eight horses to arrest me. You ... drag people like Sylvia Pankhurst back again to prison. You have roused a fire in the East End and ten men and eight horses won't be enough next time!'[13]

It was to the Cat and Mouse Act that Mary Richardson owed her temporary freedom when she had been released the previous November after a long bout of forced-feeding. After her release she declared, 'The worst fight on record since the movement began is now raging in Holloway.' Richardson, one of the earliest suffragettes to be force-fed, had written about her experience in a 1913 suffragette leaflet, where she described a tube a yard long that ran through the nasal passage down the throat into the stomach: 'Forcible feeding is an immoral assault as well as a painful physical one, and to remain passive under it would give one the feeling of sin; the sin of concurrence. One's whole nature is revolted: resistance is therefore inevitable.'

The infamous 'Cat and Mouse' Act was the name given to the Prisoners (Temporary Discharge for Ill Health) Act passed by H. H. Asquith's Liberal government in 1913. Hurriedly enacted, it was meant to counter the growing public disquiet over the tactic of force-feeding suffragettes who were determined to continue their hunger strikes while in gaol. The law's intention was that suffragettes could hunger-strike to the point of emaciation and be let out of prison to recover, and then recalled, especially if found to be 'misbehaving', to serve the rest of their sentence. The act's nickname compared the government cruelty of repeated releases and re-imprisonments of suffragettes to a cat playing around with a half-dead mouse. The act did little to deter the more militant campaigns of the suffragettes and, if anything, made the public far more sympathetic to their cause.

Between July and October 1913 Mary Richardson was released four times under the Cat and Mouse Act. These were her convictions during this time:

July 8: Sentence of two months' imprisonment for a disturbance a t Bromley Public Hall
July 12: Released under Cat and Mouse Act after hunger striking
July 18: Sentence of two months for Home Office window smashing
July 2: Release under Cat and Mouse Act after hunger striking.
July 28: Twice arrested in the afternoon outside the London Pavilion when she was released on bail, and in the evening on a charge of window-smashing outside Holloway gaol
July 29: Sentence of two months' imprisonment
August 3: Sent for trial for smashing Colonial Office windows
August 12: Release under Cat and Mouse Act after hunger-striking
October 4: Arrest in connection with Hampton-on-Thames fire.
October 6: Remanded for a week.

The *Daily Mail* in October 1913 pointed out that Richardson 'has received three sentences totalling six months of which she has served only fourteen in prison four days of the first sentence and five days of each of the others'.[14]

Herbert Henry Asquith had been an opponent of women's suffrage since the 1880s, and his government's implementation of the Cat and Mouse Act caused the WSPU and their supporters to consider the prime minister with particular enmity. Even women in his social circle had been privately objecting to his attitude to the opposite sex. Winston Churchill's wife Clementine once complained of Asquith habitually peering down cleavages, while Lady Ottoline Morrell once told Lytton Strachey that Asquith 'would take a lady's hand as she sat beside him on the sofa, and make her feel his erected instrument under his trousers'.[15] Even the writer Cynthia Asquith, his daughter-in-law, found his sexual predilections so unmentionable that she violently inked over all references in her diary.

A few hours after Mary Richardson was apprehended in the National Gallery, she was brought up before Bow Street police magistrates' court, where she was charged with maliciously damaging the Rokeby Venus to the amount of £40,000. Richardson told the magistrate that she was amazed that anyone was willing to preside over the farce of trying her, as it was the tenth time she had been brought before a magistrate in one year. He could not make her serve her sentences, but could only again repeat the farce of releasing her or else killing her: either way, hers was the victory. The unimpressed magistrate said that he would not allow bail and committed her for trial.

Immediately after Richardson's 'outrage' the National Gallery was closed to the public and remained so for two weeks. The trustees of the gallery met that afternoon to consider what steps were needed to further protect their collection. One of the trustees was Lord Curzon, the former Viceroy of India, who on his return to England had led the campaign against women's suffrage in the House of Lords. In 1908 he had helped establish the Anti-Suffrage League, of which he eventually became president. The press widely publicised the attack on the painting and *The Times* wrote: 'One regretted that any person outside a lunatic asylum could conceive that such an act could advance any cause, political or otherwise.' Even the *New York Times* commented on the story the next day: 'The British Government is getting precisely the sort of treatment it deserves at the hands of the harridans who are called militants for its foolish tolerance of their criminal behaviour. Why should women who commit assaults and destroy property be treated differently from common malefactors?'

During the trial the next day Richardson told the court that 'My act was premeditated. What I did I had thought over very seriously before I undertook it. I have been a student of, and perhaps care as much for, Art as anyone who was in the Gallery on Tuesday morning, but I care more for justice than I do for Art, and I firmly believe that when the nation shuts its eyes to justice and prefers to have women who are not only denied justice but who are ill-treated and tortured, then I say that this action of mine should be understandable. I don't say it is excusable, but at least it ought to be understood.'

Mr Travers Humphreys, who was prosecuting, certainly didn't understand and described the slashing of the Rokeby Venus as 'senseless and wicked as one could well conceive. She had attempted to destroy, so far as lay in her power, a beautiful work of art presented to the nation by persons who, as subscribers, included women as well as men ... one regretted that any person who was not an inmate of a lunatic asylum could conceive that it advanced any sort of cause, political or otherwise, to do such an act of wanton and malicious damage'.[16] Richardson later said: 'The judge nearly wept when I was tried because he could only give me six months.': the maximum sentence allowed for damaging a work of art. How the judge felt when Richardson, after starting a hunger strike, only served a few weeks before she was released again, we can only guess.

At the outbreak of the First World War, Emmeline Pankhurst suspended the activities of the WSPU and instructed suffragettes to get behind the government and its war effort. Sylvia, opposed to the war, was horrified to see her mother and sister Christabel become such enthusiastic supporters of military conscription, and supported the International Women's Peace Congress, held in 1915 at The Hague. Mary Richardson published a novel called *Matilda and Marcus* during the war and also two volumes of poetry. In the twenties and thirties she stood several times as a parliamentary candidate for the Labour Party, most successfully in Acton in November 1922, when she received over 26 per cent of the vote although ultimately lost to the Conservatives.

In April 1934, Richardson politically changed direction when she joined the British Union of Fascists and declared that, in the light of her previous political experience, 'I feel certain that women will play a large part in establishing Fascism in this country.'[17] This was just four months after Lord Rothermere's 'Hurrah for the Blackshirts!' issue of the *Daily Mail*.

Her initial post was assistant to Lady Makgill, the officer in charge of the women's section whose headquarters was then based at 233 Regent Street (in 2015, the Lacoste shop next to the Apple Store) but which moved in January 1934 to 12 Lower Grosvenor Place, adjacent to the grounds of Buckingham Palace. The women's section of the Blackshirts had initially been set up by Mosley's first wife, Lady Cynthia, who was known as 'Cimmie' and, incidentally, was the daughter of the anti-woman's suffrage campaigner Lord Curzon.

Cynthia had married Oswald Mosley, then a Tory MP, in 1920, and nine months later gave birth, much to the consternation of Margot Asquith, wife of former Prime Minister H. H. Asquith, who told her, 'You look very pale. You must not have another child for a long time. Herbert always withdrew in time. Such a noble man.'[18] In 1929 Cynthia was elected Labour MP for Stoke-on-Trent, as was her husband but for the constituency of Smethwick. Two years later Oswald, unhappy with the direction of the Labour Party, formed the New Party in 1931 and subsequently the British Union of Fascists the year after that. Cynthia supported her husband in his political activities until she died in 1933 after an operation for peritonitis following acute appendicitis. The unconditional support she gave her husband was generous, for during their marriage Oswald had an affair with both Cynthia's younger sister and her stepmother.

The women's HQ was seen as crucial for nurturing both female interest and recruitment levels in the BUF. The female blackshirts were encouraged to train in jujitsu. The *Blackshirt* newspaper reported in 1934 that it was particularly popular in London, saying 'the ladies especially showing remarkable aptitude in this splendid form of defence so suitable to members of the "weaker sex"'.

The new main BUF headquarters, called 'Black House' and situated on the King's Road near Sloane Square, was practically out of bounds to women. The Fascist *HQ Bulletin* in 1933 stated, under the heading 'Lady Members', that 'Ladies are no longer allowed access to NHQ premises, except to attend mixed classes and concerts and at such times as may be from time to time authorised.' Despite this rule and others like it, the 'lady members' made up 20–25 per cent of the BUF membership, which was extremely high for a political party of the time.

It seems odd that an ex-suffragette, and such a militant one at that, would have put up with these rules, but in April 1934 Richardson became the chief organiser of the women's section. A young female BUF member remembered Richardson at the time: 'The moving spirit of this [women's HQ] was an ex-suffragette of great character. She was a fiery speaker particularly at street corner meetings and used to plaster her hair down with Grip-fix so that it would not blow about on these occasions.'[19]

Mosley, however, was aware of the value of his women members. He later wrote: 'My movement has been largely built up by the fanaticism of women; they hold ideals with tremendous passion. Without women I could not have got a quarter of the way.' In June 1936 the *Blackshirt* newspaper stated: 'Women have won the vote but not their rightful influence in politics. Politically, women have no freedom. Only when women represent Woman will woman kind attain its rightful influence.'

It was in fact a woman who, ten years previously in 1923, created the first fascist organisation in Britain. It may well have been the first time a woman had started and led any political party in this country. She was called Rotha Lintorn-Orman and she started the British Fascisti in response to what she thought was a growing threat from the Labour Party. The BF was actually the predominant fascist organisation in Britain until Oswald Mosley started the British Union of Fascists in 1932.

On 10 November 1924, the Fascisti held a rally consisting of almost 10,000 people in Trafalgar Square, most of whom, it was reported, were wearing black and silver British Fascisti badges. *The Manchester Guardian* reported that there was 'a large contingent of women' present, but it was a man, the monocled Brigadier-General Blakeney, who told a cheering crowd, waving black and white fascist banners and Union Jacks, that there 'is a great danger that aliens should be allowed to settle in this land, overcrowding the towns and taking employment from the workers'. The rally finally marched down Whitehall where several large black and white wreaths bearing the legend 'British Fascists for King and country' were left next to the four-year-old Cenotaph.

The British Fascisti ultimately lost members to the Imperial Fascist League and then to the BUF. Lintorn-Orman, stubbornly, would have nothing to do with the latter as she considered Oswald Mosley to be a near-communist. Lintorn-Orman's mother, who was actually the first-ever female Scout leader, had been pay-rolling the organisation from the beginning, eventually stopping the funding amid lurid gossip about her daughter that involved alcohol and drug-fuelled orgies. Rotha Lintorn-Orman died in March 1935 and her British Fascisti organisation wound up four months later. The Official Receiver reported: 'Throughout the company's history its accounts seemed to have been kept in a lax, casual manner, and though formed to organise Fascism in the country the company appeared to have been incapable of organising itself.'

In 1934 the BUF however, now with Richardson in charge of the women's section, seemed organised, efficient and most of all popular. The *Daily Mail* on 18 May reported, 'The recent development of the Women's Section has been particularly remarkable,' and a few days later the *Sunday Dispatch* wrote, 'The women's sections are adding – Beauty. The women and girls of Britain are flocking to the movement. Many of them are strikingly beautiful.'

After Sylvia Pankhurst's speech in Trafalgar Square in June 1934, Mary Richardson responded quickly to the criticism. In an issue of the *Blackshirt* newspaper published on 29 June she reminded her of their shared memories working together in Bow and being confined in Holloway at the same time. Richardson wrote:

How can she forget so easily and conveniently that the Suffragette movement, when she stood in the vanguard, was proud of its use of 'force and bludgeons', of dog whips, truncheons [carried and used by Mrs Pankhurst's bodyguard], stones in their multitude, and bricks and the hammers? Does she remember how for years her reply to her accusers was: 'We are attacked, we must hit back!' ... I was first attracted to the Blackshirts because I saw in them the outrage, the action, the loyalty, the gift of service, and the ability to serve which I had known in the Suffragette movement. When later I discovered that Blackshirts were attacked for no visible cause or reason. I admired them the more when they hit back, and hit hard.

Mary Richardson left the BUF sometime in 1935. For what particular reason it is not exactly known (her autobiography published in 1953 doesn't mention her political activity in the BUF at all). Lady Mosley, Oswald's mother, however, described Richardson as being full of 'dishonest inefficiency'. In 1935 Richardson spoke at a meeting of the Welwyn War Resisters, an anti-war group. The *Welwyn Times* on 19 December 1935 reported that she had told the meeting that she joined the BUF believing that it opposed class distinction and stood for 'equality of opportunity and pay for men and women'. She had found, however, that the organisation was riddled with hypocrisy and had been expelled in February for 'attempting to organise a protest'.

On 7 November 1961 Mary Richardson died at home of heart failure and bronchitis, aged seventy-eight. The *Daily Mail* reported her death using the headline 'Slasher Mary Dies Forgotten': 'Yesterday Mary Richardson died in obscurity in her guinea a week bed sitting room in St James's Road, Hastings, surrounded by dusty mementoes of the fight for women's suffrage, a faded flag, a "campaign" medal and a pile of manuscript that publishers did not want.'[20]

Throughout her life Richardson often went to see the painting that will forever be associated with her, usually when she needed to 'cheer herself up'. Nowadays you have to look particularly closely to see any marks caused by her meat cleaver. The National Gallery, presumably not to encourage any copycat protests, make no mention of her vandalism on the card next to the painting.

Christabel Pankhurst once said that: 'The Rokeby Venus has because of Miss Richardson's act, acquired a new and human and historic interest. For ever more, this picture will be a sign and a memorial of women's determination to be free.'[21]

Opposite above: The Toilet of Venus by Diego Velásquez (1647–51), the only surviving example of a female nude by the artist.

Opposite below: Velásquez's Venus was brought to England in 1813, where it was purchased by John Morritt for £500. Morritt hung it in his house at Rokeby Park, now in County Durham.

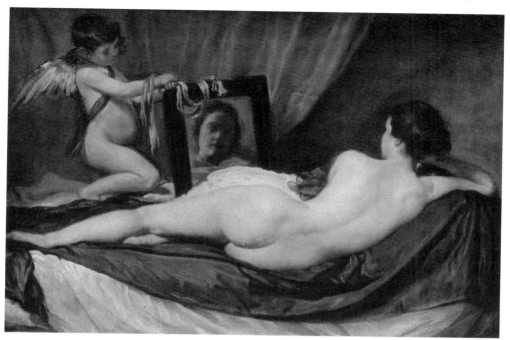

The slashed Rokeby Venus.

In September 1913 the Home Office ordered photographs to be taken of suffragettes without their knowledge. Film speeds were much slower at the time and it was easy for prisoners to ruin the results of any photograph they knew were being taken of them. After Mary Richardson's attack on the Rokeby Venus, the 'mug shots' were sent to all the art galleries so they could watch out for 'known militant suffragettes'. Mary Richardson is number 11 on the top left.

1937. 21 (83)

No. 5.

LORD CURZON'S
FIFTEEN GOOD REASONS AGAINST THE GRANT OF FEMALE SUFFRAGE.

LORD CURZON OF KEDLESTON has said that there are fifteen sound, valid, and incontrovertible arguments against the Grant of Female Suffrage. He summarises them as follows :—

(1) Political activity will tend to take away woman from her proper sphere and highest duty, which is maternity.

(2) It will tend by the divisions which it will introduce to break up the harmony of the home.

(3) The grant of votes to women cannot possibly stop short at a restricted franchise on the basis of a property or other qualification. Married women being the women, if any, best qualified to exercise the vote, the suffrage could not be denied to them. Its extension to them would pave the way to Adult Suffrage. There is no permanent or practicable halting-stage before.

(4) Women have not, as a sex, or a class, the calmness of temperament or the balance of mind, nor have they the training, necessary to qualify them to exercise a weighty judgment in political affairs.

(5) The vote is not desired, so far as can be ascertained, by the large majority of women.

(6) Neither is the proposed change approved, so far as can be ascertained, by the large majority of men.

(7) If the vote were granted, it is probable that a very large number of women would not use it at all. But in emergencies or on occasions of emotional excitement, a large, and in the last resort, owing to the numerical majority of women, a preponderant force might suddenly be mobilised, the political effect of which would be wholly uncertain.

This and next page: Lord Curzon (1859–1925) was a leading Conservative politician who had served as Viceroy of India from 1899 to 1905. He was appointed to the National Gallery board in April 1911 and became the President of the National League for Opposing Woman Suffrage in 1912. His 'Fifteen Good Reasons Against the Grant of Female Suffrage' were first mentioned in a speech in 1909. The leaflet is undated but was published between 1910 and 1914. His daughter Cynthia became the first wife of Sir Oswald Mosley. Her sister, mother and step-mother all had affairs with Mosley.

2

(8) The presence of a large female factor in the Constituencies returning a British Government to power would tend to weaken Great Britain in the estimation of foreign Powers.

(9) It would be gravely misunderstood and would become a source of weakness in India.

(10) The vote once given, it would be impossible to stop at this. Women would then demand the right of becoming M.P.'s, Cabinet Ministers, Judges, &c. Nor could the demand be logically refused.

(11) Woman, if placed by the vote on an absolute equality with man, would forfeit much of that respect which the chivalry of man has voluntarily conceded to her, and which has hitherto been her chief protection.

(12) The vote is not required for the removal of hardships or disabilities from which woman is now known to suffer. Where any such exist, they can equally well be removed or alleviated by a legislature elected by men.

(13) Those persons ought not to make laws who cannot join in enforcing them. Women cannot become soldiers, sailors, or policemen, or take an active part in the maintenance of law and order. They are incapacitated from discharging the ultimate obligations of citizenship.

(14) The intellectual emancipation of women is proceeding, and will continue to do so, without the enjoyment of the political franchise. There is no necessary connection between the two.

(15) No precedent exists for giving women as a class an active share in the Government of a great Country or Empire, and it is not for Great Britain, whose stake is the greatest, and in whose case the results of failure would be the most tremendous, to make the experiment. It would not, indeed, be an experiment, since if the suffrage were once granted, it could never be cancelled or withdrawn.

Printed by the National Press Agency Limited, Whitefriars House Carmelite Street; and Published by the NATIONAL LEAGUE FOR OPPOSING WOMAN SUFFRAGE, Caxton House, Tothill Street, Westminster, S.W.   Price 3s 6d. per 1,000.

THE SUFFRAGETTE THAT KNEW JIU-JITSU.
THE ARREST.

'The Suffragette that Knew Jiu-Jitsu. The Arrest.' By Arthur Wallis Mills, originally published in 1910 in *Punch* magazine.

Oswald Mosley saluting women members of the British Union of Fascists at a rally in Hyde Park, 14 September 1934.

Fascist training in 1934. Mary Richardson, chief organiser of the BUF's women section, is standing at the back.

CHAPTER 9

How the GLC Almost Destroyed Covent Garden

Postcard of Covent Garden from 1925. (Judges Postcards Ltd)

The London premiere for the film of *My Fair Lady* took place at the Warner Theatre in Leicester Square on 21 January 1965. The Pathé newsreel described it as the 'greatest ever musical' and the event couldn't have been anything less than a glamorous occasion. Accompanied by her husband, Mel Ferrer, Audrey Hepburn came wearing a long pale-violet Givenchy gown; Cecil Beaton was there with his sister; Rex Harrison came with Vivien Leigh by his side; and even Colonel Jack Warner himself attended the show. The cinema was only a few hundred yards from Covent Garden, a location featured in the film (albeit a Hollywood studio version) and which in the mid-sixties was still a functioning wholesale fruit, vegetable and flower market. It had been trading officially, in exactly the same place, for almost 300 years ever since the Duke of Bedford in 1670 acquired from Charles II a charter allowing a fruit and vegetable market to take place every day except Sundays and Christmas Day. Alan Jay Lerner's and Frederick Loewe's musical and, of course, George Bernard Shaw's original *Pygmalion*, from which it derived, purposely used an Edwardian Covent Garden to show the contrast of rich and poor Londoners rubbing shoulders in what was then mostly a very poor area of inner-city London. Difficult as it is to imagine these days, in 1965, over half a century after the play, film and musical were set, Covent Garden as a place in which to live and work was still a very run-down and shabby part of the West End.

In April 1964, nine months before the *My Fair Lady* premiere, elections for the new Greater London Council (GLC) took place. The GLC was to replace the old London County Council, which had been expanded to include many outer London boroughs, and there was much surprise when Labour won overwhelming control with sixty-four councillors to thirty-nine. If the result wasn't anticipated in 1964, with hindsight the reasons were relatively obvious. The elections had come towards the end of a deeply unpopular and scandal-plagued Conservative government and the GLC elections were the first big chance for a major part of the country's population to make its opinion felt. Presumably many of these newly elected councillors went to see *My Fair Lady* – after all it was, and is, an extremely popular film. To many watching council officials, however, it made one of the world's most famous markets seem outmoded and an inner-city leftover from a bygone age. Just two months after the film's premiere the new council (although they weren't officially governing until the following year) published the Greater London Development Plan, part of which proposed, astonishingly but as was often the wont in those days, that over two-thirds of the historic Covent Garden area should be razed to the ground.

In 1961 the increasingly anachronistic Covent Garden market had essentially been nationalised by the Conservative government when they created the Covent Garden Market Authority. Soon after, a plan was created to move, in 1972, the overflowing market to Nine Elms in Battersea. In 1966, mindful that the fruit and vegetable market would soon be gone from the West End, three councils, the Labour-controlled GLC, the Tory-run City of Westminster and the Labour-run Borough of Camden, together with Bovis, the Prudential Assurance Company and Taylor Woodrow, worked together on the Covent Garden scheme. In 1968 the team put on an exhibition which allowed the public their first chance to see the plan that would rip out much of the Covent Garden neighbourhood, including the houses around Earlham Street and the terraces of Maiden Lane and Henrietta Street, and replace it with four-lane highways, subterranean walkways and enormous office blocks. The GLC put it a different way, describing the scheme as 'dealing satisfactorily with conditions of bad lay-out and obsolete development'.[1] Essentially, all of the parties were interested in just one thing – a totally comprehensive redevelopment of the ninety-six acres that made up the historic Covent Garden area. In his book *The Changing Life of London* published in 1973, the late George Gardiner, a former journalist and Tory MP who, with Norman Tebbit and Airey Neave, would end up playing an important role in the election of Margaret Thatcher as Conservative Party leader, wrote that when the initial draft plans were presented to the public 'more than 3,500 people attended, and in fact, most of their comments were favourable'.[2] The suggestions from the public that weren't so enthusiastic were taken on board, however, and a revised plan was approved by the GLC in 1970. By now the political landscape had changed and the three London councils involved in the project, the GLC, Westminster and even Camden, were now all Tory-controlled.

The revised Covent Garden redevelopment scheme covered an area bounded by the Strand, Aldwych, High Holborn, Shaftesbury Avenue and Charing Cross Road and it still proposed the large-scale demolition of the great majority of the eighteenth- and nineteenth-century buildings around the historic old market. Gardiner, after rather excitedly describing the Covent Garden scheme as Central London's biggest and most exciting redevelopment project since the Great Fire, wrote of the first phase of the plans, which was originally intended to be built by 1975: 'There would be three new schools in place of the two old ones, open recreational spaces and new shopping facilities, new hotels, and something London at present does not possess at all – an international conference centre. It would also include a new covered road, running roughly along the line of Maiden Lane, parallel with the Strand, carrying eastbound traffic while the Strand is made one-way westwards.'³ No major development plans created in the sixties were ever complete without an international conference centre although this one was designed to completely enclose Covent Garden's famous piazza – the Italian-style arcaded square built by Inigo Jones in the 1630s which had been commissioned by the fourth Earl of Bedford to encourage wealthy Londoners to move to what was then a semi-rural area. It has been said that Inigo Jones's new and exciting designs for Covent Garden made it, as far as London was concerned, the birthplace of modern town planning.

The second phase of the redevelopment proposal was planned to be completed by 1980 and involved the areas from Maiden Lane down to the Strand. The main feature of the second tranche of development was an 'exciting' new upper-level pedestrian street that would link Trafalgar Square and Leicester Square with the conference centre. Beneath the raised walkway a brand-new main road would run from Charing Cross Road to the Aldwych. The third phase involved the area north of the conference centre-cum-piazza and would consist mostly of new housing (much of it built above smaller offices), the new schools and other community facilities. In the same area there was to be, as was the fad in those days, another concrete upper-level pedestrian street that would run from east to west beneath an internal service road that would be linked to various large car parks. At Cambridge Circus there would be a new recreation centre, with a swimming pool and squash courts, and an office building one and a half times the size of Centre Point (infamously empty at the time, with the developer, Harry Hyams, happy to be making money from the rising value of the property rather than letting it out). Covered pedestrian areas would lead to shops, existing theatres, restaurants and pubs, and over at the northern end of Drury Lane there would be a group of pedestrian squares at different levels, surrounded by shops and flats. The third phase of developments was conceived to be completed by 1985.

George Bernard Shaw completed his five-act play *Pygmalion* in 1912, although the idea had first been mentioned by the writer in a letter to the actress Ellen Terry fifteen years previously in 1897. This was the same year that Charles Booth's final volume of *Life and Labour of the People in London* was published, which included surveys of the 1890s exposing the appalling health and living conditions of much of London's urban poor. One extraordinary feature of the study was the maps that illustrated the levels of wealth and poverty found by the research's investigators on a street-by-street basis. In Covent Garden there were areas on roads such as Betterton Street which were described, in Booth's words, as, 'Very poor, casual. Chronic want.' While just off Endell Street on each side of Nottingham Court, Booth described the area as, 'Lowest class. Vicious, semi-criminal.' The Royal Opera House stood not a hundred yards away from Nottingham Court and it's not difficult to see why Shaw chose the area as a place where the rich and the poor lived, worked and played in such close proximity. In 1914, the year after *Pygmalion* premiered at the Hofburg Theatre in Vienna, the Covent Garden Opera House was a major draw for most of the world's top operatic talent. Nellie Melba, Antonia Scotti and Enrico Caruso all sang on stage during that year. On 11 May there was a gala, with the British royal family in attendance, held at the Opera House to mark the state visit of the King and Queen of Denmark. George Bernard Shaw, a supporter of woman's suffrage, would have no doubt approved when halfway through the performance a suffragette stood up in the balcony stalls and shouted, 'King George, women are being tortured in your dominions.' She was quickly seized and roughly handled by the surrounding crowd. Meanwhile other suffragettes seated in the gallery showered leaflets on the audience below. It was noted that King Christian of Denmark caught one of the leaflets, folded it carefully and put it into his pocket.

Four weeks previously *Pygmalion* had opened in London at His Majesty's Theatre to much applause and laughter. At one point in the evening there was a laugh that was said to have lasted 76 seconds when Mrs Patrick Campbell, who was by now a grandmother and perhaps a little old at fifty-one to be playing Eliza Doolittle, used all her experience when she said, with perfect diction and impeccable comic timing, 'Not bloody likely.' After the curtain-fall Sir Herbert Tree made a speech and explained that, unfortunately, there had been so much laughter the playwright had left the theatre in despair.[4] A few days before the first night, Shaw must have had an inkling what was likely to happen when during an interview with the *Daily Telegraph*, and sounding not unlike Professor Higgins, he said, 'Why on earth don't people laugh internally, like old Weller in Pickwick?' He added, 'Loud laughter is merely a bad habit.'[5] No one laughed at all when in April 1971 the Covent Garden Community Association was formed to say, essentially, 'not bloody likely' to what at the time seemed an almost unstoppable radical redevelopment plan. There were other dissenters too: the Labour MP for Vauxhall, George Russell Strauss, was worried about the 'beautiful and elegant' theatres that were now at risk including the Adelphi, the Garrick, the Vaudeville, the Lyceum, the Arts and the Duchess:

What is happening is that the land on which the theatres stand is so valuable that developers are going, or have already gone, to the proprietors and saying they would like to buy them for a large sum of money to enable them to undertake large-scale development and make large profits ... Most of them were built in the latter part of the last century or the first twenty-five years of this. They are beautiful theatres which it would be a tragedy to London to destroy.[6]

In 1962 the Labour MP Anthony Crosland had written a book entitled *The Conservative Enemy*; in it he presciently said:

Excited by speculative gain, the property developers furiously rebuild the urban centres with unplanned and æsthetically tawdry office blocks; so our cities become the just objects of world-wide pity and ridicule for their architectural mediocrity, commercial vulgarity, and lack of civic or historic pride.

Ten years later in June 1972, Crosland, who had entered parliament in 1950 and was now the shadow environment minister, made a passionate and influential speech in the commons attacking the damage to London made by the post-war developers:

I believe with passion that it is now time to call a halt. It is time to stop this piecemeal hacking away at our city. It is time to say to the GLC, to Westminster City Council, to Land Securities Investment Trust, to Town and City Properties, to the lot of them, 'Gentlemen, we've had enough. We, the people of London, now propose to decide for ourselves what sort of city we want to live in' ... People will not have London continuously mutilated in this way for the sake of property development and the private motorist. They will not have an endless number of Centre Points and an endless number of uniform, monolithic, comprehensive redevelopments which break up communities and destroy the historic character of the city.[7]

The pendulum had at last started to swing the other way and in July that year there was a local inquiry into the Covent Garden proposals. Camden Borough Council, which by now had changed from Conservative to Labour control, had also became a formal objector to the plan it had helped work up three and five years previously. To the horror of many people who lived and worked in Covent Garden, it initially looked as though the GLC had won the redevelopment war when in July 1972, a month after Anthony Crosland's speech, the plans were completely upheld by the inquiry inspector in his recommendation to the Conservative Secretary of State for the Environment, Geoffrey Rippon. Within a couple of weeks, however, Lady Dartmouth (the daughter of Barbara Cartland who would later marry the Earl of Spencer and become the stepmother of Princess Diana) resigned from her post as chair of the joint local authority committee which had been overseeing the redevelopment plans. Because of her background it was easy to underestimate her, but as Judy Hillman in *The Guardian* wrote at the time: 'Behind the saccharine image there stands an extremely able politician, a feminine but tough bargainer.'[8] When Lady Dartmouth resigned she said: 'When we are all dead and gone and long forgotten, London will still be there. This is what really matters.' She had been affected by angry protesters who had at one point besieged her house and in her resignation letter she explained:

> I have felt increasingly that our proposals are out of date and out of tune with public opinion, which fears that the area will become a faceless, concrete jungle … I am unable to work for a project in which I no longer believe, and which could do unnecessary and irreparable damage to an historic part of London.

Not everyone had changed their minds and George Gardiner was still typical of many London politicians, and not just Conservatives, when he wrote:

> Any loss of nerve on this [the Covent Garden Development Scheme] by the GLC in face of protest from a small section of London's populace … will go down as a black day in London's history. If the drift of population away from the centre is combined with a retreat from a policy of comprehensive redevelopment in favour of mere site development it is the next generation of Londoners who will be the losers and who will look back on our timid age with scorn.[9]

Most people by now were disagreeing with Gardiner's stance, and the post-war consensus on modernising cities like London, using the bulldozer approach to redevelopment and traffic circulation, was starting to fall apart. In January 1973, nearly five years after the Covent Garden Redevelopment proposal was originally made public and six months after the inquiry inspector had recommended the latest version, Geoffrey Rippon, while ostensibly approving the plan, effectively killed it. He had added 250 buildings to the list of those already protected because of historical and architectural merit. This made comprehensive redevelopment in the Covent Garden area almost impossible.

It was first proposed to the LCC that Covent Garden should be moved from its West End location in January 1914.[10] There were already complaints about traffic problems and the slow speed of handling and it was thought the market would be more suited to a site adjacent to a railway. The idea came to nothing: among other reasons world wars came in the way, but sixty years later in 1974, and two years after it was originally planned, the famous old fruit and vegetable market moved to Nine Elms in Battersea. The market traders had mixed views about the move. George Mole, who in 1977 had worked at Covent Garden, old and new, for forty years thought that work was far easier than in the old days: 'You could work like a beast of burden there, pulling piles of fruit uphill, sometimes with baskets on your head. Here you can use your head to think with.' Many of the traders missed the ballet girls tripping into rehearsals at the Opera House and they also missed the 'sometimes tight' actors and actresses who dropped into the old Covent Garden. Not long after the move to Nine Elms, John McCormack of Yeoward Brothers said: 'In the old place I would sit next to film stars in cafés. I have had a cup of tea with Rita Hayworth. Gilbert Harding was around a lot. Ava Gardner was there with no shoes or stockings … well, she had stockings, but she didn't have shoes.'[11]

King Street, Covent Garden in 1974. (Dave Flett)

Russell Street, Covent Garden in 1974. (Dave Flett)

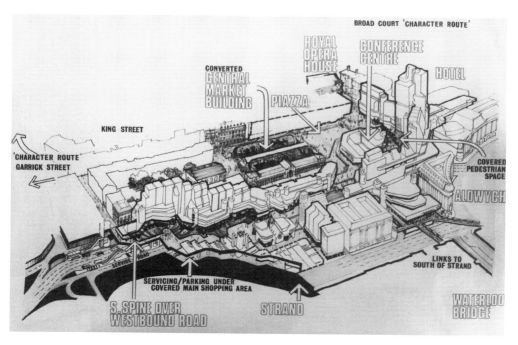

Covent Garden Redevelopment Plan from 1970. (Courtesy of the London Metropolitan Archives)

CHAPTER 10

When Lord Haw-Haw
Met Mr Albert Pierrepoint,
Albeit Briefly

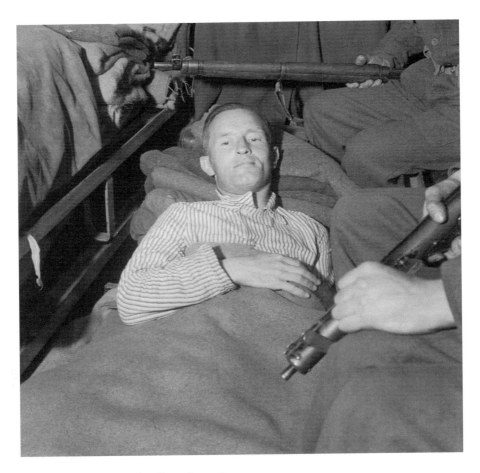

Above: The capture of William Joyce in 1945.

The death penalty never once acted as a deterrent in all the jobs I carried out. And I have executed more people than anyone this century.'[1]

Albert Pierrepoint.

William Joyce, the man with the infamous nickname 'Lord Haw-Haw', is probably Britain's best known traitor, of relatively recent times anyway. He had a catchphrase as famous as any comedian's, and to cap it all he had a facial disfigurement in the form of a terrible scar that marked him as a 'treacherous villain' as if the words themselves were tattooed across his forehead. Saying all that, many people have argued that he shouldn't have been convicted of treason at all, let alone executed for the crime.

On the cold and damp morning of 3 January 1946, a large but orderly crowd had formed outside the grim Victorian prison in Wandsworth, the main gates of which aren't more than a stone's throw from the more salubrious surroundings of Wandsworth Common. Some people had come to protest at what they considered an unjust conviction; others, albeit a handful, came to demonstrate about the use of capital punishment; while some, rather morbidly, wanted to be as close as they could to what came to be the last execution of a person convicted of high treason in Britain.

About 500 miles away, as the crow flies, at Joyce's old school called St Ignatius, in Galway, a mass had taken place. The consecration of the Eucharist had been timed for exactly the moment that Joyce was due to be executed. In the end the planned timing was in vain. It was at one minute to nine, an hour later than initially planned, when the governor of Wandsworth prison entered the condemned man's cell to inform him that his time had come.

William Joyce had woken early that morning. He washed, but didn't shave, and changed from his prison clothes into the blue serge suit he had been wearing at the time of his arrest in Germany. Although he ate no breakfast, he drank a cup of tea. For the last few months Joyce had actually been eating relatively well and while in prison his weight had increased substantially. When he was first brought to Wandsworth in the autumn he weighed 135 pounds (61 kg) but was now 151 pounds (68.5 kg). This wasn't incidental information at the time; the weight gain was of more than passing interest to Albert Pierrepoint, the man who was to be his executioner. The weight of every prisoner for whose death he would be ultimately responsible, he carefully noted in a leather-covered diary or ledger. It carried the details of all the executions for which he had been responsible and contained the dates, ages, heights, weights and, most importantly, the 'drop' for each hanging. Part of the hangman's craft was to calculate the exact length of rope required to instantly kill the condemned man or woman. If the rope was too long, the criminal would be decapitated; too short, and it would be an agonising death of several minutes by strangulation.

Pierrepoint's calculations were worked out from grim advice given in an official 1913 government document called the *Table of Drops*. It had been put together after a series of failed hangings at the end of the nineteenth century, including those of John 'Babbacombe' Lee, also known, not surprisingly, as 'the man they couldn't hang'. Lee survived three attempts to hang him at Exeter Prison in 1885 after which the Home Secretary commuted his death sentence. He was released twenty-two years later in 1905 and died in the USA in 1945. A committee, chaired by Lord Aberdare, was formed in 1886 to discover and report on the most effective manner of hanging, the results of which were published three years later. After a few more unfortunate incidents, a significantly revised edition of the *Table of Drops* was published in 1913.

In 1917, as a twelve-year-old, and twenty-eight years before he came face to face with William Joyce in the cell at Wandsworth, Albert Pierrepoint had been asked at school to compose an essay about his future ambitions. He wrote: 'I would like to be public executioner as my Dad is, because it needs a steady man who is good with his hands like my Dad and my Uncle Tom and I shall be the same.'[2] Young Albert had only found out about his father's macabre profession the year before, although he didn't know that, after carrying out 107 executions, he had been dismissed from his post seven years previously after arriving drunk at Chelmsford prison to carry out a hanging. Albert's Uncle Tom, however, went on to work as a hangman for thirty-seven years before his eventual retirement in 1946 after a dispute over compensation for a cancelled hanging.

In 1931 Albert wrote to the prison commissioners offering his services as an assistant executioner. A few months later, after initially being told that there were no vacancies, he was offered an interview at Strangeways prison in Manchester. After a week-long course at Pentonville prison, Pierrepoint's name was added to the List of Assistant Executioners on 26 September 1932. Pierrepoint's first execution as 'Number One' was of the ex-nightclub owner and gangster Antonio 'Babe' Mancini, at Pentonville on 17 October 1941. Just before the trapdoor was sprung Mancini was heard to utter a muffled 'Cheerio!' Mancini was to be the first of many and Albert Pierrepoint, who took pride in making death by hanging 'as instant and humane a thing as it could ever be', went on to hang 433 men and seventeen women during his lifetime.

Thirteen months older than Albert Pierrepoint, William Joyce had been born in Brooklyn, New York, in April 1906 to an English Protestant mother and an Irish Catholic father. His father had already taken United States citizenship when, three years after the birth, the family returned to Galway, where William went on to attend the St Ignatius Jesuit College from 1915 to 1921. William was precociously politically aware and, like many Irish people at the time, was politicised by the Irish War of Independence. Unlike most in Galway, however, he and his father were Unionists and both openly supported British rule. William hung around the headquarters of the Royal Irish Constabulary at Lenaboy Castle, and later said that he had aided and run with the infamous Black and Tans, the notoriously undisciplined and brutal British auxiliary force sent to Ireland after the First World War in an attempt to help put down Irish nationalism. William essentially hated anyone who held anti-British views, and he was not yet sixteen when he was forced to escape to London after several death threats from the local IRA.

After a short stint in the British Army (he was soon discharged when it was found he had lied about his age), Joyce enrolled at Birkbeck College of the University of London, where he gained a first but also developed an initial interest in Fascism. In 1924, while stewarding at a Conservative Party meeting at the Lambeth Baths in Battersea, a seventeen-year-old Joyce was attacked by a gang in an adjacent alleyway, and received a vicious and deep cut from a razor that sliced across his right cheek from behind the earlobe all the way to the corner of his mouth. He lost a lot of blood and initially his life was in danger, but after two weeks he was released from hospital. It left him with a terrible facial scar. Joyce was convinced that his attackers were 'Jewish communists' and the incident influenced the rest of his life.

In 1933, at the age of twenty-seven, Joyce joined Oswald Mosley's British Union of Fascists. Within a couple of years he was promoted to the BUF's director of propaganda and was responsible for training speakers. He was a gifted orator and was soon deputising for Mosley at major rallies. Once a female heckler shouted, 'You're a right bastard,' to which he replied, 'Thank you, mother.' For a while Joyce became the star of the British fascist movement.

William Joyce was instrumental in moving the union towards overt anti-Semitism, something with which Mosley had been relatively uncomfortable. Joyce's career with the BUF only lasted five years, however, for in 1937, with membership plummeting, a devastated Joyce was sacked from his paid position in the party by Mosley.

In late August 1939, shortly before war was declared, and probably tipped off by a friend in MI5 that he was about to be arrested, Joyce and his wife Margaret fled to Germany. There he struggled to find employment until he met one of his English supporters, the Mosleyite Mrs Frances 'Dorothy' Eckersley, who soon got him recruited for radio announcements and script writing at German radio's English service in Berlin. Crucially, this was at a time when his British passport was still valid. Four years previously the American-born Joyce had, under false pretences, obtained a British passport so that he could accompany Mosley abroad. At the time, a birth certificate was not needed to substantiate statements made on application; an endorsement from a public official was all that was required.

The infamous nickname of 'Lord Haw-Haw', associated with William Joyce to this day, was coined by a *Daily Express* journalist called Jonah Barrington not two weeks into the war. The title was actually meant for someone else completely – almost certainly a man called Norman Baillie-Stewart who had been broadcasting in Germany from just before the war. Barrington's nickname referenced Baillie-Stewart's exaggeratedly aristocratic way of speaking: 'A gent I'd like to meet is moaning periodically from Zeesen [the site near Berlin of the English short-wave transmitter]. He speaks English of the haw-haw, dammit-get-out-of-my-way variety, and his strong suit is gentlemanly indignation.'[3]

Four days later, on 18 September, Barrington started to call the broadcaster from Germany 'Lord Haw-Haw' and wrote in the *Express*: 'Lord Haw-Haw, hard though he pretends to be blue-blooded and British, trips up occasionally, "Sir Winston Churchill," he said recently, and then, "Ach, nein! I mean Mr Winston Churchill."' Barrington also tried to imagine Lord Haw-Haw's appearance: 'From his accent and personality I imagine him with a receding chin, a questing nose, thin, yellow hair brushed back, a monocle, a vacant eye, a gardenia in his buttonhole. Rather like P. G. Wodehouse's Bertie Wooster.'[4]

Baillie-Stewart had already been convicted in the United Kingdom for selling military secrets to Germany in the early thirties, and had the dubious distinction of being the last person in a particularly long line to have been imprisoned for treason in the Tower of London. Late in 1939, when William Joyce had become the more prominent of the Nazi propaganda broadcasters (although at the time no one knew exactly who he was), Barrington swapped the title over and, in April 1941, he announced Lord Haw-Haw's real name. In Germany, Joyce's nickname was 'Froehlich' which means 'Joyful'.

The British public were officially discouraged from listening to the Lord Haw-Haw broadcasts which always began with the infamous words, 'Germany calling, Germany calling.' Just three months into the war, however, the *News Chronicle* reported that Lord Haw-Haw's 'Views on the News' broadcasts were listened to by about 50 per cent of the British public. Cassandra's popular column in the *Daily Mirror* thought the problem was with the BBC's dreary output, saying that it was time to 'get hold of a news-broadcaster with real incisive personality':

> The BBC has never seemed to be able to rid itself of the polite, charming and somewhat effeminate young men who nightly mince through the news. Haw-Haw has ten times the punch of any one of them ... Are they still going to go on lisping their nightly way to defeat on the air. Or is somebody going to get a chance to get in front of the microphone and put over our point of view in accents slightly less reminiscent of well-bred motor salesmen down on their luck.[5]

Lord Haw-Haw's over-the-top and sneering attacks on the British establishment were enjoyed by many, and early in 1940 the *Daily Express* wrote: 'More and more people are tuning in to Nazi broadcasting and laughing their heads off at the preposterous bedtime stories of Lord Haw-Haw.'[6] It wasn't only because the broadcasts were funny that the British public were tuning in: during an era of heavy state censorship and restricted information there was a natural desire by listeners to hear anything Nazi Germany was saying, whatever was said. At the start of the war, simply because there was more to brag about, the German news reports were considered, by some people, to contain slightly more truth than those of the BBC. It was never taken too seriously though, and William Joyce's manner didn't help. The *Daily Express* again: 'Enemy propaganda is taken at its face value by the British people. Our Government has relied upon British common-sense, with the result that the very incredibility of enemy lying destroys its effectiveness. That's comforting.'

As the tide turned towards the Allies in the latter stages of the war, Joyce and his wife moved to Hamburg. On 22 April 1945 he wrote in his diary: 'Has it all been worthwhile? I think not. National Socialism is a fine cause, but most of the Germans, not all, are bloody fools.'[7] Eight days later, and on the very day that Adolf Hitler and Eva Braun committed suicide in their Berlin bunker, Joyce made his last broadcast. He was drunk, and the remains of his Irish accent were heard through his slurring voice. He finished his final broadcast with, 'Heil Hitler! And farewell.' William and his wife Margaret soon fled to Flensburg, a town near the Danish border, and it was there, in a nearby wood, that Joyce was captured by two soldiers. They, like Joyce, were out looking for firewood and when the former Lord Haw-Haw with his distinctive voice stopped to say hello, one of the soldiers asked, 'You wouldn't by any chance be William Joyce, would you?' To 'prove' otherwise, Joyce reached for his false passport and one of the soldiers, thinking he was reaching for a gun, shot him through the buttocks, leaving four wounds.

The soldier who had shot Lord Haw-Haw's bottom was called Geoffrey Perry. He had, however, been born into a German Jewish family as Hourst Pinschewer and had only arrived in England to escape from Hitler's persecution. In the end a German Jew, who had become English, had arrested an Irish-American, who pretended to be English but had become German. It was almost poetic justice.

Back in London, Joyce was charged at Bow Street magistrates' court and in the dock quietly stated, 'I have heard the charge and take cognisance of it.' He was then driven to Brixton prison in a Black Maria and on arrival it is said that he mumbled, 'So this is Brixton.' 'Yes,' retorted his guard, 'not Belsen.' The American writer, journalist and historian William L. Shirer met Joyce in Berlin during the early part of the war and said what he thought had driven him: 'I should say that he has two complexes which have landed him in his present notorious position. He has a titanic hatred for Jews and an equally titanic one for capitalists. These two hatreds have been the mainsprings of his adult life.'[8]

The trial of William Joyce began on 17 September 1945 and for a short period, when his American nationality came to light, it seemed that he might be acquitted. 'How could anyone be convicted of betraying a country that wasn't his own?' his defence lawyers argued. The attorney-general, Sir Hartley Shawcross, however, successfully argued that Joyce's possession of a British passport (even if he had misrepresented himself to get it) entitled him to diplomatic protection in Germany and therefore he owed allegiance to the king at the time he started working for the Germans.

There was a problem, however: the BBC monitoring service could not identify any of his broadcasts before 2 August 1940, and the only evidence came from Detective Inspector Albert Hunt of the Special Branch who had questioned Joyce before the war while he was an active member of the BUF, and who claimed to have recognised his voice while monitoring broadcasts in the autumn of 1939. He couldn't say which station he had been listening to, nor the country from which it came. He couldn't even say whether it was September or early October 1939 when he thought he had heard Joyce's voice.

Until 1945 Inspector Hunt's less than impressive evidence would not have been enough to convict anyone for the grave crime of treason. The Treason Act of 1697, which itself amended the Statute of Treasons of 1351, required either two acts of treason witnessed by one person, or one overt act witnessed by two people. Under these ancient provisions, Joyce would have been acquitted. In June 1945 a new treason act was passed which abolished the special rules of evidence and replaced them with the same rules that were applicable to murder trials. Joyce was kept in Germany until this new act was law, and then brought to Britain the next day to be charged.

On 19 September 1945, almost exactly six years after he had started broadcasting from Germany, William Joyce stood in the dock of the Old Bailey. The judge, in his summing up, quoted a law from 1707 that said the physical presence of a man in the country was not essential to the allegiance he owed to the king. In the end the jury took less than twenty minutes to return with a verdict. *The Manchester Guardian* reported that 'Joyce's nervous twitch twisted into something like a smile' when he heard Mr Justice Tucker pronounce the sentence of death upon him for treason by broadcasting propaganda for the king's enemies. Convicted by virtue of Inspector Hunt's uncorroborated evidence, Joyce, albeit unsuccessfully, appealed to the Court of Criminal Appeal and the House of Lords.

A sizeable minority of the population was uncomfortable with the verdict, mainly because of the nationality issue, but also because he was generally seen as not much more than a figure of fun. On Christmas Day 1945 an accountant named Edgar Bray wrote to King George VI: 'I know nothing about Joyce, and nothing about his Politics. I don't know much about Law either, but I do know enough to be firmly convinced that we are proposing to hang Joyce for the crime of pretending to be an Englishman which crime, so far as I am aware, in no possible case carries a Capital penalty. It happens to be just our bad luck, that Joyce actually WAS an American, (and now IS a German subject), but that is no reason to hang him, because we are annoyed at our bad luck.'[9] The historian A. J. P. Taylor agreed with Mr Bray and once made the point that Joyce was essentially hanged for making a false statement on a passport, the usual penalty for which was the trivial and insignificant fine of just £2.

Fifteen weeks after the Old Bailey trial, the governor of Wandsworth prison, accompanied by Albert Pierrepont and his assistant Alexander Reilly, entered William Joyce's cell. From that point on everything moved so quickly that Joyce would have hardly known what was happening. Pierrepoint was particularly proud of the speed of his executions and they rarely took more than a few seconds after a prisoner had set eyes on him. Pierrepoint had a macabre party piece which he demonstrated to anyone new assisting him during an execution. Before leaving his room to hang anyone, he would sometimes light a cigar and then leave it burning in an ashtray. When he returned to the room after the hanging, he would draw on the cigar and show that it was still alight.

Almost as soon as the three men entered Joyce's cell, Pierrepoint placed a pinioning belt around Joyce's wrists behind his back and then pulled it tight. At the same time a false wall was drawn back and Joyce was led to the adjacent execution chamber a few yards away. With just enough time before they reached the chalked marks on the varnished wood floor, Joyce looked down at his badly trembling knees and smiled. It was noticed by the practised and experienced hangman, who calmly uttered the last words that Joyce ever heard: 'I think we'd better have this on, you know.' While he was speaking he placed a white cap over Joyce's head and subsequently the noose straight after. Pierrepoint heard a familiar click of the belt and buckle as Reilly quickly pinioned Joyce's legs. As soon as this was completed the assistant stood up and flung his arms back in a gesture of completion. At that point Pierrepoint pulled the lever which automatically opened the trap door beneath Joyce's feet. The prisoner's spinal cord was ripped apart between the second and third vertebrae and the man known throughout the country as Lord Haw-Haw was dead.

Not far away a group of smartly dressed men in winter coats stepped away from the main crowd that was waiting outside the Wandsworth prison gates and, behind some nearby bushes, almost surreptitiously, raised their right arms in the 'Heil Hitler!' salute. Within a few minutes of Albert Pierrepoint's expert execution, and with the blood from Joyce's scar that had burst open during the hanging still dripping onto a spreading red stain on the canvas floor, the body was taken to the prison mortuary. The jury that had convicted him was allowed to see the remains and a coroner pronounced that the death was due to 'injury to the brain and spinal cord, consequent upon judicial hanging'.

At eight minutes past nine a prison officer came out and pinned on to the prison gates an official announcement that William Joyce had been hanged. At 1 p.m. the BBC Home Service reported the execution and read out the last, unrepentant pronouncement from the now-dead man: 'In death, as in this life, I defy the Jews who caused this last war, and I defy the power of darkness which they represent. I warn the British people against the crushing imperialism of the Soviet Union. May Britain be great once again and in the hour of the greatest danger in the west may the Swastika be raised from the dust, crowned with the historic words, "You have conquered nevertheless." I am proud to die for my ideals; and I am sorry for the sons of Britain who have died without knowing why.'[10]

There were very specific rules applicable to the burial of executed prisoners at the time, and William Joyce's body was treated the same as any other. He was buried within the Wandsworth prison walls, in an unmarked grave, and was allowed no mourners. In the middle of the night, the body had been dumped, literally unceremoniously, on top of the remains of another man, a murderer called Robert Blaine who had been hanged five days previously. A layer of charcoal, not lime, was used to separate the two bodies.

In total 135 people were hanged at Wandsworth prison during the nineteenth and twentieth centuries, with the final execution taking place when Henryk Niemasz was hanged on 8 September 1961 for the murder of Mr and Mrs Buxton in Brixton. The gallows were not dismantled until 1993, which was twenty-nine years after the last execution in Britain, and twenty-four years after the death penalty was abolished for murder, although the death penalty still existed for treason until 1998. The condemned cell is now used as a television room for prison officers.

Wandsworth prison was not to be the final resting place for William Joyce. His daughter had long thought that he should be buried in a cemetery and not in an unmarked grave in a south London prison yard. After a long campaign and several letters to various home secretaries, she was at last allowed to have her father's body properly buried. On 18 August 1976 the original grave was dug up in the middle of the night and the remains were reburied in the Protestant part of the large Bohermore cemetery in Galway. 'Ireland calling! Ireland calling!' said the *Guardian* and 'Lord Haw-Haw goes home' wrote the *Daily Mail*. Joyce, even thirty years after his execution, had few supporters, whether Irish or British, and the grave was placed in the cemetery some distance from any others. Whether it is because William Joyce has been forgotten or the space at Bohermore is now more of a premium but it is only in the last two or three years that Joyce's grave has been joined by any others.

9. N.HANRAHAN.W.NAUGHTON.FRED.MCEVOY.DES.SHEE,   ?   M.J.SILKE.F.COLGAN.
O'FLAHERTY.B.LYDON.H.SHEE.P.THORNTONN.SHEE.T.CONNEELY.T.HIGGINS.K.GEOGHEGAN.J.SHEA
MARTIN BURKE.MR.O'SHEA. KELLY.H.NAUGHTON.J.DOYLE.W.JOYCE.MR.SCALLON.H.KELLER.P.HIGGINS
(AUSTIN MULLERY   C.NAUGHTON   J.McDONAGH P.MC.DONAGH   .   ?

William Joyce aged thirteen at St Ignatius College in Galway. (Courtesy of Mike Gunnill)

Opposite above: William Joyce sitting on the far right, shortly after joining the British Union of Fascists in 1932. Leader Oswald Mosley is in the centre on the bottom row. (Courtesy of Mike Gunnill)

Opposite below: William Joyce and his wife Margaret in Shoreditch Market shortly before fleeing the United Kingdom for Germany and the start of the Second World War.

Mr and Mrs Pierrepoint in 1952. (© Trinity Mirror/Mirrorpix/Alamy)

Wandsworth prison gates in 2014.

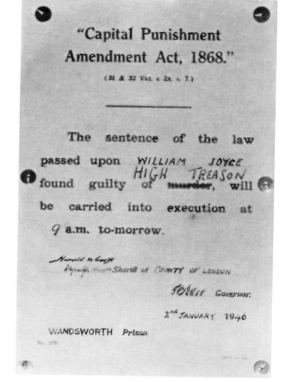

Right: The notice on the gates of Wandsworth prison gates announcing the execution of William Joyce.

Below: Mrs Heather Landol, daughter of William Joyce, at her Kent home. (Mike Gunnill)

CHAPTER 11

Christine Keeler and the Fight at the Flamingo All-Nighter

Georgie Fame at the Flamingo Club in 1963. (Courtesy of EMI Archives)

In March 1962, a month after Billy Fury had dismissed them as his backing band – he felt they were 'too jazzy' – Georgie Fame and the Blue Flames started a three-year residency at The Flamingo Club. It was a sweaty, smoky, scarlet-walled nightclub in the basement at 33–37 Wardour Street, opposite Chinatown's Gerrard Street. It was famous for its weekend all-nighters when it stayed open from midnight until six in the morning. It's not widely known but the Profumo affair, the political scandal that led to the resignation of John Profumo, the secretary of state for war, in October 1963, and ultimately the fall of the Conservative government a year later, was all the fault of Georgie Fame. A slight exaggeration maybe but, if he hadn't occasionally employed the musician Wilfred 'Syco' Gordon to play with the Blue Flames, there was a chance that Britain's political history may have taken a completely different course.

Christine Keeler was a regular visitor to the All-Nighter club at the beginning of the 1960s. She was still working most evenings at Murray's Cabaret Club on Beak Street and had been a showgirl there since 1958 when she was just seventeen. The cabaret, named after its owner Percy 'Pops' Murray, had been in Soho since 1933. In those days, to avoid being caught out by the strict licensing laws that prohibited drinking after 11 p.m., the club was run on a 'bottle party system', where patrons signed a chit which enabled them to drink alcohol that they had previously 'ordered', but not paid for. By the late fifties the club was run by Percy's son David, who was a personal friend of the society osteopath and portrait painter Stephen Ward. It was at Murray's that Ward first got to know Christine Keeler.

Showgirls like Keeler performed two shows a night, essentially walking around topless, wearing not much more than a pair of high-heeled shoes, a tiara and sequins. They were also paid to chat to the customers between shows, encouraging them to buy expensive wine and champagne, for which they received commission and tips. Murray's was Keeler's first regular job, and her starting salary of £8 per week (£175 in 2015) was substantially more than the average woman's wage in those days. Keeler usually finished at Murray's around 3 a.m., which meant that, after a dash down to the southern end of Wardour Street, she still had three hours' dancing at the Flamingo. When Georgie Fame started playing regularly at the club in the spring of 1962, Keeler's infamous affair with John Profumo had been over for four months.

Their relationship had begun on a warm summer's evening the previous July, when Jack Profumo and his wife, Valerie Hobson, were at a dinner party held by Lord Astor at Cliveden House, an Italianate mansion and estate in Taplow, a few miles from Maidenhead. Stephen Ward, who lived in one of the estate cottages, a mile or so along the Thames, asked if he and a few friends could use the swimming pool inside the walled garden that evening. When laughter and splashing were heard by the dinner guests, some wandered down to investigate. Jack Profumo, fatefully, saw a naked Christine Keeler climb out of the pool … For the next few months the minister for war embarked on an affair with the twenty-year-old showgirl. She was, however, also sleeping with the Russian spy Yevgeny Ivanov, the assistant naval attaché at the Soviet embassy. These concurrent affairs mostly took place at Stephen Ward's flat at Wimpole Mews in Marylebone, where Christine was now living.

The Flamingo Club had started in 1952, after a twenty-one-year-old film salesman and occasional '30 shillings a night' pianist called Jeffrey Kruger had dinner at the Mapleton Hotel on Coventry Street. A big jazz fan, Kruger often wondered why every jazz club he visited was always such a dive. He would later say: 'The biggest hold-up to jazz in this country was that it got a bad name. It was associated with dirty cellars, drink and people who had no respect for themselves.'[1] Kruger started talking to Tony Harris, the manager of the hundred-room hotel, and was shown a basement which he saw would be perfect for his idea of a new kind of jazz club. 'Jazz at the Mapleton' opened in August 1952, and people came to hear modernist jazz from musicians such as Ronnie Scott, the Johnny Dankworth Seven, and Kenny Graham's Afro-Cubists. After a few months the club changed its name in honour of Kenny Graham's composition 'Flamingo', and the newly named 'modernist' Flamingo Jazz Club took off. The doorman was Kruger's father, an East End Jewish hairdresser. The Flamingo's owner recalled that there had never been much trouble at the new West End venue and gave the reason: 'Luckily, one of my dad's customers was Jack Spot the biggest mobster in London. My dad shaved him every morning. When I opened the Flamingo, Dad went to see Jack and explained that the Flamingo belonged to his son.' A few years later Kruger explained the strict door policy at the club: 'No man can be admitted without a necktie and no girl is welcomed who looks like a refugee. It is possible and preferable, I think, to be hip and keep a high social standard.'[2] Michael Burke was fifteen in 1954, and remembers his time at the Flamingo in the basement of the Mapleton around then:

It was down a few stairs; (I think it was about 3/6 to get in), into a fairly large, quite well-lit room … No alcohol was sold, only soft drinks; Coca Cola, stuff like that. As far as I can remember it was a white crowd, mostly young men there to meet girls. And the girls were there to dance. The small dance floor was to the left of many rows of chairs facing a raised stage. To the right was another area containing toilets, the drinks counter, and a dressing room for the musicians. Many of the young men wore what was the fashion of the time, charcoal grey draped suits, "Mr. B" (Billy Eckstine) white shirts with roll collars, and skinny "slim-Jim" ties. A few guys wore full Teddy-boy outfits! With those long high waisted 4-button jackets with velvet collars, and pegged pants. A kind of hybrid mix of 18th Century elegance, and American Zoot Suit! The girls wore sleeveless blouses, long calf-length skirts, and their flat shoes had very long straps that were tied around their legs, almost to their knees. I used to get there early, about 7 p.m., before the music even began. Tony Hall, with a very 'mid-Atlantic' accent, was the MC. The groups were often 'mix and match' including Tony Kinsey or Tony Crombie, drums, Bill Le Sage piano, Jack Fallon or Sammy Stokes on drums. Frequent players were Harry Klein, baritone sax, Vic Ash, clarinet, Johnny Dankworth, alto, Ronnie Scott, tenor, and Jimmy Deuchar, trumpet. The core of that era's Bop musicians. One great night had Kenny Graham's Afro-Cubans group which I remember was a knock-out!

In those years the British Musicians Union banned foreign (American) musicians from working in Britain, because they were 'stealing work from the local lads'. So the only Americans who had permits to perform were singers (and their regular piano accompanists). Billie Holiday was somehow persuaded to do a gig at the Flamingo after her concert at the Royal Albert Hall. So she didn't actually appear at the Flamingo until about 11 p.m. I got there early as usual, to ensure a seat, and by the time she arrived the room was filled to capacity. The excitement was great … you could feel the tension in the air. During the wait several well-known entertainers, including singer Marian Ryan, and a gentleman called Cab Kaye who had two black girls who sang a very great version of 'Shine.' Billie finally took the stage. She was still wearing the gold full-length dress she wore for her concert appearance. Her hair was black, but had gold highlights on the top. Several musicians took the stage, including a couple of sax players; I think probably Ronnie Scott and a young alto player, Johnny Rogers. Billie sang 'Willow Weep for Me' and 'Lover Man' with just piano, bass and drums, and then she said 'How about some horns?' but it seemed that the sax players were so bemused by her and intimidated, that they remained sitting at her feet and wouldn't get up to blow. She continued to sing numbers for about an hour before she left the stage to great applause. The crowd left, mostly to catch the last trains and buses home.[3]

A year or so after Billie had performed at the Flamingo, Ronnie Scott held some auditions at the club. His singer, Annie Ross, was ill and he needed a replacement for two weeks. After all the hopefuls had tried out he pointed at a short eighteen-year-old East End girl and said: 'You. Little one. Outside the Mapleton Hotel, Leicester Square. Monday morning. Nine o'clock.' At the time Barbara Windsor couldn't work out why she had been chosen when so many other better, more experienced singers had been auditioned. She ended up singing the hits of the day such as 'Band of Gold' and 'Love and Marriage' with musicians such as Pete King, Benny Green, Tubby Hayes, Les Condon and the drummer Tony Crombie. Ronnie Scott, for some reason or other, always insisted she played the maracas while she sang.[4] A year after Windsor's short stint as a jazz cabaret singer, the Flamingo moved premises to Wardour Street, the location where it made its name.

There was, however, another club night in the basement at the Mapleton (the building is still a hotel but now called the Thistle Piccadilly). It was an all-nighter that began in 1955, and took advantage of a time when American fashion was all the rage and thus was called Club Americana. For ten shillings you got live jazz and a three-course meal – tomato soup, chicken 'n' chips and ice cream. The night club was run by Rik and Johnny Gunnell and attracted black American servicemen who, only a decade after the end of the Second World War, were based in Britain in large numbers. The club was also frequented by members of the growing West Indian community. Club Americana, in 1958, also moved to 33 Wardour Street, and the Gunnell brothers launched the Friday and Saturday All-Nighter that operated at the same premises, but after the pre-midnight Flamingo Jazz Club had closed.

It surprised a lot of people that Jeff Kruger had got permission from the chief constable at the Savile Row police station to run the all-nighter. Kruger explained: 'I told him, if you let me have an all-night licence, all the kids who hang around Soho in the early hours will go there and you'll know where they are. You can put any number of plain-clothes men inside the club, but you've got to promise only to arrest people outside, never inside. There'll be no alcohol, and we'll stay open till the tube starts running so the kids can get home again.'[5] It wasn't just the convenient late hours, however, that brought Christine Keeler to the Flamingo in Wardour Street. She loved the company of the black GIs and the West Indian men who were once going to Club Americana but were now coming along to the new All-Nighter club. 'Syco' Gordon remembered his time at the Flamingo: 'We'd walk in smoking ganja, taking pills and all these beautiful girls were so nice. We'd start making friends with them and start dancing. White and black would mix together. Like brother and sister. We loved dancing. We never had fights down there. All the pimps and the gangsters used to hang out down there and we had a good time. They used to have all the prostitutes you know. When they finished work they'd come down there and pick up the black guys. They just liked the black guys the way we used to dress nice ... they used to pay us, to go with them you know. They'd bring all their money when they finished work.'[6] US Airman Hopkins, in an interview he gave in 1964, said: 'Many girls go there [The Flamingo All-Nighter] and are picked up by the GIs. These girls are usually well dressed and attractive and have wealthy boyfriends – sugar daddies – who provide flats and clothes. Usually these girls come in late at night.'[7]

Val Wilmer, the writer and photographer, described the Wardour Street club in the early sixties – 'The all-nighter at The Flamingo was quite wild. The black influence was strong there and to be honest it was all a bit of a blur. They were playing things like Lord Kitchener's 'Dr Kitch' over the PA and Dexter Gordon and Gene Ammonds and Jack McDuff and then ska and bluebeat. Everybody made an effort. It was stylish hair, nice dress, pencil skirts and pale pink lipstick. That was the thing.'[8] Georgie Fame once recalled: 'It was the only place where black American GIs could hang out, dance and get out of it. By midnight, when the club opened, most of them were out of it. They would have left the base late afternoon, got on the train with a bottle of something and by the time they came into the club they would be raving.'[9]

It's worth being reminded that clubs with a mixed crowd, outside Soho, weren't at all common. The 'colour bar' was still legal and enforced at many British dance halls. Mecca's Locarno Ballroom in Bradford refused admission to a black man in November 1961. After the Musicians' Union told its members not to play there until the situation changed, Mecca executive, and originator of Miss World, Eric Morley responded by saying, 'Why doesn't the MU mind its own business?'[10] The MU's position on the 'colour bar' can be applauded, but their arcane rules about American musicians performing in Britain were still being enforced. Kruger was constantly battling with the Musicians' Union and when he brought over the jazz musician Chet Baker, the American was told that he could sing but not play the trumpet. If he did both he and Kruger risked jail.

At the same address, 33 Wardour Street, and twenty-five years before the All-Nighter at the Flamingo was attracting, as Georgie Fame once put it, 'black American GIs, West Indians, pimps, prostitutes and gangsters',[11] Jack Isow's Shim-Sham Club was, with the exception of black American

GIs, attracting a not dissimilar crowd. There was a large main room on the first floor which consisted of a small, elevated bandstand, a circular bar which displayed non-alcoholic drinks of lemon and orange squash, a 30 by 20-foot space reserved for dancing, and forty tables. A kitchen prepared food such as smoked salmon, mock turtle soup, fried fillet of plaice, lobster mayonnaise, Peach Melba.[12] A twenty-year-old man called Leonard Feather, who would later become the chief jazz critic for the *Los Angeles Times*, wrote an article about the Shim-Sham Club (named after a tap dance performed in Harlem in the early thirties) for the 9 March issue of *Melody Maker* in 1935. It was headed 'Another London Harlem Club' and 'Yeah, Man!'

Feather commented on the striking murals by an artist called 'Sanderson' that depicted 'Negro types' and continued: 'Gradually the walls of the room seemed to shrink as hundreds of people filed in until I thought every jig-chaser in London must be among those present. Near-beer, weeds and lounge suits were the order of the night with many. Eight hours for work, eight hours for sleep, and eight hours at the Shim-Sham. That will be the new daily round for these carefree coloured denizens of London.'

Randolph Dunbar the Guyanese clarinettist also wrote about the club, again in the *Melody Maker*, but a year later in 1936. In an article entitled 'Harlem in London', Dunbar wrote about the dancing of the 'white and coloured people together' but also noticed that the resistance to any racial mixing on the dance floor depended on the makeup of the interracial couple. If the female partner was black, 'and of that irresistible Creole type of loveliness', the couple might provoke admiration. But a black male partner would be looked upon as 'something despicable' and his white partner classed as 'trash'.[13] The Shim-Sham eventually closed down after too many police raids as 'one of the largest Bottle Party establishments running in the West End, and without doubt one of the worst'. A Music Union organiser once said of the Shim-Sham club: 'All sorts mixed there – Mayfair, Soho, boxers and friends of Royalty – a whole cross section of society.'[14] There were boxers at the Flamingo a quarter of a century ago. Georgie Fame remembered one face in the crowd watching him: 'Cassius Clay, as he was then, came down when he first fought Henry Cooper. Cassius would come into town and say "Where do the brothers hang out?" He'd be told they all go down The Flamingo.'[15]

Fame, who was born Clive Powell, was instructed to change his name as part of the Larry Parnes stable (like Billy Fury and Marty Wilde among many others). He often employed black musicians. His trumpeter Eddie Thornton was from Jamaica, as was an occasional accompanist, Wilfred

'Syco' Gordon, who came to London in 1948. Syco often brought to The Flamingo Club his brother Aloysius 'Lucky' Gordon, a drug dealer, and as Christine Keeler would later write, rather dismissively: 'He called himself a blues singer.' He also had a long list of convictions for fraud, assault and shop breaking. Keeler later described Lucky (the nickname came from when his parents won a lottery prize the day he was born) in her autobiography, *The Truth at Last*, as 'just a thug who had been thrown out of the British army for having a go at an officer ... and been in trouble everywhere he went'. Lucky was usually dressed in black: leather jacket, a roll-neck jumper and a beret. Keeler first met him in the spring of 1962 when, at Stephen Ward's behest, she bought some grass at the El Rio café in Notting Hill. She gave him the phone number for Stephen Ward's flat at Wimpole Mews in the hope of future drug-deals, and they became lovers, of a kind. Lucky was particularly possessive, often violently so, and after he was spurned by Keeler she later became so frightened of his continual threats that she bought a Luger to protect herself.

In July of that summer of 1962, a year after Christine Keeler had met John Profumo at Cliveden, the magazine *Queen*, owned by Jocylyn Stevens and mostly aimed at the younger side of the British Establishment, published a column called 'Sentences I'd like to hear the end of'. It was written, as usual, by the Associate Editor of the magazine, Robin Douglas-Home, a nephew of Lord Home, the Foreign Secretary at the time (and later prime minster). He was also part of Princess Margaret's social set. Home, who always kept his ears close to the ground, was exceedingly well placed to hear any society gossip. That month the column included the seemingly innocent words: '... called in MI5 because every time the chauffeur-driven Zil drew up at her front door, out of the back door into a chauffeur-driven Humber slipped ...' It was no more than a fragment of a sentence and utterly incomprehensible and innocuous to most people, but it sent shockwaves through Whitehall and Fleet Street. It was the first time that the security risk of Profumo, the war minister, sleeping with the same woman as a Russian naval attaché, was out in the open.

Meanwhile Georgie Fame and the Blue Flames were leading an exhausting, albeit exhilarating, schedule. As well as often performing at Klooks Kleek at the Railway Hotel in West Hampstead, Ricky Tick's in Windsor, and The Scene in Ham Yard during the week, they would often play outside London on Saturday nights. Fame later remembered: 'We'd be coming in from playing an American air force base somewhere in Suffolk and we'd throw the gear back in the wagon and drive back to London and get back to the all-nighter in time for our set. We did the 1 a.m. and the 4.30

a.m. set. The guys would open the way through the crowd for us and help us carry the shit on to the stage. A stabbing at the Flamingo prompted the American air force authorities to ban servicemen from the nightclub ...'[16]

The man who held the knife in the stabbing incident to which Fame casually referred was called Johnny Edgecombe, a thirty-year-old Antiguan with several past convictions, including living off immoral earnings (for which he received six months' gaol in 1959) and unlawfully possessing drugs. Christine had met him in the summer of 1962, at about the same time as the *Queen* magazine gossip column was published. Edgecombe, who liked to be known as 'the Edge', had told her that he knew 'Lucky' and his fearsome reputation, and that he was willing to offer her protection. On 27 October, despite the likelihood of bumping into Lucky, Keeler and Edgecombe decided to go to the All-Nighter at the Flamingo. As soon as they arrived she saw him: 'Lucky was there as usual, smoking and drinking with his cronies. And mad-eyed ...'

Lucky rushed over and picked up a chair as a weapon and then chased Keeler and Edgecombe through the club. Keeler managed to escape and hide on the crowded dance floor but Lucky caught Johnnie and they squared up to each other. Lucky suddenly made a dash for the exit but the bouncers stopped him at the door. Edgecombe slowly walked over towards a trapped Lucky and then in an instant whipped out a flick-knife. Keeler later recalled: 'The knife flashed and then Lucky's face was pouring with blood. Lucky had his hands to his face. He screamed with rage and pain. The cut ran from his forehead to his chin down the side of his face, and the blood poured into his eyes, blinding him. "You'll go inside for this!" he screamed. "I'll get the law, you'll go inside."'[17]

Edgecombe grabbed hold of Christine's arm and they ran out of the Flamingo as fast as they could. Later that night they dropped into a 'shebeen', an illicit bar, on Powis Terrace in Ladbroke Grove. They were told that they had just missed Lucky Gordon who, accompanied by police officers, was looking for them both. A few days later, after Gordon had been treated for his wound at a local hospital, he sent Christine, in a fit of jealousy, the seventeen used stitches from his face. He warned her that for each stitch he had sent she would get two on her face in return. Meanwhile, Keeler and Edgecombe were in hiding with a friend of his in Brentford. It wasn't long, however, before Keeler became tired of this arrangement and told Edgecombe she was leaving. Brentford was not the sort of place to which she had lately become accustomed.

On 14 December 1962, Keeler went to visit Mandy Rice-Davies, who was now living at the Wimpole Mews flat. Edgecombe, still desperately upset that Christine had left him, called the flat's telephone and by chance Christine answered it. Now he knew where she was, he arrived in a cab within minutes. When Keeler refused to speak to him he angrily shot six bullets at the door of the flat and after she poked her head out to plead with him to go away, one up at the window. No one was hit, but the gunshots were to echo for many months around London. Frightened, Christine called Ward at his surgery and he in turn called the police, who quickly arrived and arrested Edgecombe.

The incident gave the press, who were far more deferential to the Establishment at the time, the chance to explore the Profumo rumours that had been circulating around Fleet Street for months. What seemed a motiveless shooting in a quiet Marylebone side street would normally have attracted little attention, but Edgecombe's appearance at the magistrates' court the following day made the front pages. He was charged not only for the shooting at Wimpole Mews, but also for slashing Lucky's face at the Flamingo.

Three months later Edgecombe, an Antiguan, but described in the newspapers as a Jamaican film extra, was tried at the Old Bailey on 14 March 1963. He told the jury that he had first met 'Miss Keeler' the previous June and they had lived together at three addresses. 'I suppose I was in love with her,' he told the court. Miss Keeler, however, was particularly conspicuous by her absence. She had been whisked off to Spain. Somebody, somewhere thought various people would be badly compromised if she were allowed to talk in the witness box. Because of Keeler's absence, Edgecombe was found not guilty for the attempted murder of his former lover, but also, despite Gordon telling the jury of the fight at the Flamingo and showing them the 5-inch scar caused by Edgecombe's knife, acquitted of wounding Lucky. Edgecombe, however, was found guilty of possession of an illegal firearm, for which he received seven years in gaol but was to serve just over five. Years later the thirty-year-old Antiguan wrote that he thought his trial was racially motivated: 'The Englishmen didn't mind having a black guy for a brother, but they didn't want him as a brother-in-law. The British people wouldn't wear a situation where a government minister was sleeping with the same chick as a black guy. I was an embarrassment to the Government and they had to put me away and shut me up. If I had been a white guy, it would have blown over.'[18]

The next day, only encouraged by the non-appearance of Keeler, the *Daily Express* signalled the gathering political storm by putting the headline 'WAR MINISTER SHOCK' adjacent to a large photograph of

Keeler under the word: 'VANISHED'. The first real public hint of the scandal growing around Jack Profumo came a week later during a late-night Commons debate. George Wigg, with parliamentary privilege, referred to rumours surrounding twenty-one-year-old Miss Keeler, who was then only known as the missing witness in Edgecombe's Old Bailey shooting case, and asked the Home Secretary to deny them.

Profumo was urgently woken from his sleep during the middle of the night, and taken to a meeting with Tory party grandees to work out his next step. Later that day Profumo made a statement to a tense and full House of Commons: 'I have not seen her since December 1961. It is wholly and completely untrue that I am in any way connected with or responsible for her absence from the trial.' Mr Profumo then continued and uttered the fateful words: 'There has been no impropriety whatsoever in my acquaintance with Miss Keeler.'

Profumo left the chamber to the cheers of the Conservative MPs. Meanwhile the prime minister, Harold Macmillan, showed his support by walking alongside him with his hand on the minister's shoulder. Later that evening, confident that it would all soon blow over, Profumo went for a dance at Quaglino's with his wife, the former actress Valerie Hobson. A few days later, during a lunch with Chapman Pincher, the experienced *Daily Express* defence correspondent who was also a friend, Profumo said: 'Look, I love my wife, and she loves me, and that's all that matters. Anyway, who's going to believe the word of this whore against the word of a man who has been in Government for ten years?'[19]

On 1 April 1963 Christine was fined for her non-appearance at Edgecombe's trial while, outside the court, Lucky Gordon was bundled away by the Metropolitan Police, shouting 'I love that girl!' Two months later Gordon was given a three-year prison sentence for supposedly assaulting Keeler. By now details of the story involving Profumo and the Russian attaché/spy Ivanov were emerging, drip by drip. The chain of events that started with the fight of Keeler's jealous ex-lovers at The Flamingo All-Nighter Club eventually caused John Profumo to stand up in the House of Commons on 6 June 1963 and make a statement: 'I have come to realise that, by this deception, I have been guilty of a grave misdemeanour.' The next day, in its leader, the *Daily Mirror* spoke for much of the population: 'What the hell is going on in this country?'

Two days later Stephen Ward was arrested and charged with several counts of living off immoral earnings and of procuring. By now his rich, establishment, society friends were fading away. Ward's trial at the Old Bailey began on 22 July 1963, during which the prosecuting counsel,

Melvyn Griffith-Jones, portrayed Ward as representing 'the very depths of lechery and depravity'. According to Geoffrey Robertson QC, author of *Stephen Ward Was Innocent, OK*, the Judge, Mr Justice Marshall, made repeated improper interventions in the trial while misdirecting the jury on both the evidence and the law – most grievously in the definition of prostitution. Robertson also maintained that the judge's summing up was cruelly biased. He was actually only half way through the summing up and was to continue the following day when, on 30 July, after writing several letters to friends, Ward took a massive overdose of Nembutal. In one of Ward's notes, to Noel Howard-Jones, at whose Chelsea home he had been staying, he wrote: 'Dear Noel, I'm sorry I had to do this here! I do hope I haven't let people down too much. I tried to do my stuff, but after Marshall's summing up I've given up all hope.' Ward added, 'The car needs oil in the gear box, by the way, be happy in it.'[20]

The next day Mr Justice Marshall completed his summing-up, despite the absence of Ward, and after over four hours of deliberating, the jury found Ward guilty. Stephen Ward, essentially, had been unable to prove that Mandy Rice-Davies and Christine Keeler's rent hadn't come from the proceedings of prostitution, and he was convicted on those two counts. The sentence was postponed until Ward was fit to appear, but on 3 August he died without ever regaining consciousness. Keeler's solicitor read out a statement to say that she was 'very distressed by the news of the death of Dr Ward, who has played a central part in her life, and for whom her feelings were very strong. Under these circumstances she does not intend to carry out the plans to take part in a film based on her life, due to commence shooting next week.'

On 6 December 1963, after a drunken tape-recorded confession that she had lied about Gordon assaulting her, Keeler pleaded guilty of perjury and conspiracy to obstruct justice. Her barrister pleaded to the judge before sentencing: 'Ward is dead, Profumo is disgraced. And now I know your lordship will resist the temptation to take what I might call society's pound of flesh.' Lord Denning in his recent report about the Profumo affair had recently interviewed Keeler: 'Let no one judge her too harshly. She was not yet 21. And since the age of 16 she had become enmeshed in a net of wickedness.' It was all to no avail and the judge sentenced Christine Keeler to nine months in jail, which ended what her barrister termed 'the last chapter in this long saga that has been called the Keeler affair'.

At the end of 1963, Georgie Fame and the Blue Flames recorded a live album entitled *Rhythm and Blues at 'The Flamingo'* and it was released in early 1964. Fame was now managed by Rik Gunnell, while the publicity for the record was looked after by Andrew Loog Oldham, who was also the manager of the Rolling Stones. In October of that year, despite a change of leadership, the Conservative government was narrowly defeated by the Labour Party, and Harold Wilson became prime minister. After the much publicised trouble at The Flamingo, American service men were banned from visiting the club. Drawn by the weekend all-nighters and the music policy of black American R & B, soul, and jazz, The Flamingo Club was already the favourite hang-out for London's newest teenager cult, the Mods. But that's a different story...

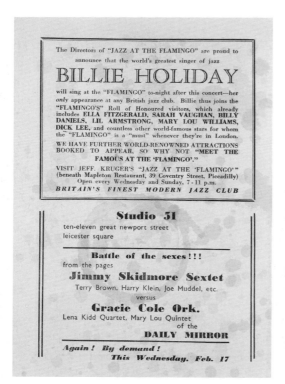

MAPLETON HOTEL, 39, COVENTRY STREET, LONDON, W.1.

Above left: Billie Holiday at the Flamingo.
The ad comes from the Royal Albert Hall programme, February 1954.

Above right: Postcard of the Mapleton Hotel from 1949.

Club Americana in the basement of the Mapleton Hotel, November 1955. (© Keystone Pictures USA/Alamy)

Above: Lucky Gordon and Johnny Edgecombe on their way to see Lord Denning, 10 July 1963. (© Keystone Pictures USA/Alamy)

Left: Christine Keeler outside the Old Bailey, 12 December 1963. (© Keystone Pictures USA/Alamy)

Stephen Ward, Bryanston Mews, 22 June 1963. (© Trinity Mirror/Mirrorpix/Alamy)

CHAPTER 12

The Blind Beggar and the Death of George Cornell by Ronnie Kray

George Cornell's Vauxhall Victor parked outside the Blind Beggar, 11 March 1966. (© Trinity Mirror/Mirrorpix/Alamy)

One hundred and one years after the evangelist William Booth preached his first open air sermon outside the Blind Beggar Public House on the Whitechapel Road – a sermon which ultimately led to the establishment of the Salvation Army – Ronald Kray walked into the very same pub. Or at least it would have been the same pub had it not been rebuilt in 1894 by Mann, Crossman & Paulin's Albion Brewery at the same address. It was 8.30 p.m. on 9 March 1966 and Kray was accompanied by his right-hand man, Ian Barrie, while the driver, John 'Scotch Jack' Dickson, was told to wait outside in his Mark 1 Cortina.

A pub had been on the same spot in Whitechapel since 1673 and it was named after Henry de Montfort, the son of the Earl of Leicester, who was said to have posed as a blind beggar to escape detection after the Battle of Evesham in 1265. Of course Ronald Kray wouldn't have been the first villain, big-time or otherwise, who had found himself in that infamous East End pub. Before the First World War, the Blind Beggar was the meeting-place of a gang of pickpockets and ne'er-do-wells. One of them, called 'Bulldog' Wallis, got into a fight with a Jewish couple and ended up killing the man by pushing the tip of his umbrella through one of his eyes. Wallis was arrested, but the East End code of silence prevailed and he had to be released from police custody through lack of evidence. He returned to the Blind Beggar a hero, and was accompanied by his cheering supporters.

There was no cheering when Ronnie Kray arrived at the Blind Beggar; he and Barrie entered the pub quietly and without a fuss. That is, until Barrie shot two bullets into the ceiling. Kray had been told that George Cornell, a member of the sadistic and ruthless south London Richardsons' gang, was drinking in the pub. Not only was Cornell part of a group of villains that were the Krays' main rivals, he was also particularly disliked by Ronnie, who would write one day: 'In front of a table full of villains, George Cornell called me a "fat poof". He virtually signed his own death warrant.'[1]

There were just five people in the pub: Cornell and two of his friends, Albie Woods and Johnny Dale, who were all at one end of the bar; a seventy-nine-year-old man was sitting at the other end reading a newspaper and half watching the television; and also a barmaid who had been chatting to Cornell while washing glasses. She had just put on 'The Sun Ain't Gonna Shine Anymore' by the Walker Brothers on the pub's record player. The Blind Beggar didn't have a juke box.

George Cornell put down his light ale when he saw Ronnie approaching and said, sarcastically, 'Well, look who's here …' While Woods and Dale were sloping away to hide in the gents, Ronnie walked over to Cornell, took out a 9 mm Mauser from his pocket and shot him through his head at close range. At that point the barmaid dropped the glasses and ran down into the cellar. Kray wrote in the twins' autobiography, *Our Story*: 'He fell forward on to the bar. There was some blood on the counter. That's all that happened. Nothing more.'

Once outside, and according to 'Scotch Jack', the driver, Ronnie was now genuinely excited: 'I actually shot him,' Ronnie said, 'I actually shot him.' He later described his mood at the time: 'I felt fucking marvellous. I have never felt so good, so bloody alive, before or since.'[2] They got back into the Cortina and it was driven back to the Lion pub on Tapp Street, about half a mile away. Reggie was drinking with some of the Firm at the pub and after being told what had happened, jumped up and shouted: 'Drive off the manor. Just drive off the manor.' In various cars, and taking different routes, the Firm ended up in a back room of the Chequers public house on the High Street in Walthamstow. Ronnie's clothes were burnt and the 9 mm Mauser was given to the cat-burglar Charlie Clark to be disposed of. Not particularly well, it seems, as years later the German 9 mm pistol was found in the mud of the River Lee and is now in Scotland Yard's Black Museum.

George Cornell had been left bleeding on the floor of the Blind Beggar. The manager of the pub, a woman called Patsy Quill, called an ambulance and it wasn't long before the dying man was being seen by doctors across the road in the London Hospital. They quickly had the patient transferred to Maida Vale Hospital, which specialised in brain injuries, but at 10.29 p.m., and roughly two hours after he had been shot, Cornell died before any operation took place.

At midnight the Firm gathered round the radio and cheered when the death of George Cornell was announced. 'Always shoot to kill,' said a relieved Ronnie before adding usefully, 'Dead men can't speak.' The police found it impossible to find witnesses to the murder. The two friends of Cornell, Albie Woods and Johnny Dale, had quickly slipped away out the back of the pub, although not before wiping the glasses on the counter to get rid of any fingerprints. The barmaid at the Blind Beggar said she hadn't seen who did it. Nor had the old man. He must have seen something, said the police, and they asked him why he wouldn't help put Ronnie Kray away: 'I hate the sight of blood,' he said, 'particularly my own.'

The police were led by Detective Superintendent Leonard Ernest 'Nipper' Read who had got his nickname during his early days as a very small lightweight boxing champion. Despite interviewing hundreds of people, no one would admit to the police that they knew anything about who had committed the murder, although in reality everyone did. George Cornell's wife Olive certainly knew, and one night she turned up at Vallance Road, the Krays' family home, shouting and screaming threats and even threw a brick through the window. By now anonymous letters were being sent to Scotland Yard by people exasperated by the slow progress of the investigation. This example arrived on 4 August 1966:

> Sir, the two Kray brothers are too clever & tricky for you, certain big people are terrified of these two like everyone else in underworld London. Kray bothers rule and will wangle out-here. They are two clever gang leaders also bullies. They terrify everybody. By one who knows.

Ronnie had now killed someone and thought it was time Reggie did likewise. Jack 'the Hat' McVitie was a nervous and alcoholic small time former member of the Firm who had reneged on a contract to kill Leslie Payne, a former accountant of the Krays. Jack 'The Hat' had been paid in advance, but unwisely had been boasting that he had cheated the twins out of their money. McVitie was lured to 'a party' that was taking place in the basement of 79 Evering Road in Stoke Newington. When he arrived Reggie Kray put a pistol to McVitie's head and pulled the trigger twice, but it just clicked and nothing happened. Ronnie Kray then held McVitie, and Reggie, with a large knife, stabbed him in the face and stomach before driving the blade deep into his neck. One of the gang would later say, 'When Reggie was stabbing Jack, his liver popped out and they had to flush it down the toilet.' McVitie's body has never been found. Gang member Tony Lambrianou, who was responsible for disposing of the body, once said of the twins: 'They were not evil men. They done unto those what they would have done to them, and this involved other villains.' This from the man who placed McVitie's body into a car and had it crushed into a 3-foot cube, which was called 'the Oxo'.

It was to be over two years before the Kray twins were arrested for the two murders which eventually became their downfall. The accountant, Leslie Payne, realised he might as well talk to the police. He had nothing to lose. The code of silence that had protected the twins for so long began to be slowly broken.

Late in the evening of 8 May 1968, a huge team of nearly a hundred armed police officers arrived at Tintagel House in Vauxhall for a final briefing. Tintagel House had been Nipper Read's headquarters, specially chosen to be away from Scotland Yard and any of the Krays' paid informers. At dawn the next day, the team simultaneously arrested the twins and twenty-four other members of the Firm. The twins were found at Braithwaite House in Finsbury where they found Ronnie curled up with a young fair-haired man, and Reggie sleeping with a woman from Walthamstow.

On 6 July 1968 the twins appeared at a hearing in front of the Metropolitan Chief Magistrate, Mr Frank Milton, at Old Street Court. Among the witnesses, at last, was the barmaid from the Blind Beggar – known, as far as the court was concerned, as 'Mrs X'. Although she had been unable to identify the killer of Cornell on the night of the murder, now under police protection she felt safe enough to point out Ronnie and Ian Barrie as the two men who had walked into the bar that evening. There was now enough evidence against the twins and the case was referred for trial at the Old Bailey.

After eight months on remand, the twins went to trial in January 1969. It was the longest and most expensive criminal case in British history and continued for several weeks. Mrs X appeared and after being accused of inventing her evidence by Mr John Platt-Mills, who was representing Ronnie Kray, told him: 'You should have my nightmares about it, then you would know whether I was inventing it or not.' Just after 7 p.m. on the evening of Tuesday 4 March 1969 and after 6 hours 55 minutes of deliberation, the jury unanimously found Ronnie and Reggie Kray guilty of the murders of Cornell and McVitie. Mr Justice Melford sentenced the twins to thirty years in gaol with no chance of parole.

For years the Krays' supporters, of which there were many, maintained that the only people who suffered during their 'reign' were other villains and members of the East End underworld. For the ordinary person, the East End was safer back then. When the broadcaster, photographer and writer Dan Farson once told the Cockney actor Arthur Mullard that the Krays 'only killed their own kind', Mullard responded in his distinctive Cockney, 'Yus, 'uman bein's!'[3]

It has often been written that one of the bullets used to shoot George Cornell ricocheted and hit a juke box while 'The Sun Ain't Gonna Shine Anymore' by the Walker Bothers was playing. The pub didn't have a juke box in 1966, only a record player, but it seems the song was playing when Ronnie Kray walked into the Blind Beggar. No one really knows whether the story is true that, while Cornell lay dying in the pub, a stray bullet made the record jump and left it playing: 'The sun ain't gonna shine anymore, anymore, anymore, anymore, anymore ...'

The interior of the Blind Beggar. George Cornell was sitting on the stool by the cash register when Ronnie Kray walked into the pub, 11 March 1966. (© Trinity Mirror/Mirrorpix/Alamy)

CHAPTER 13

When James Earl Ray Came to Earl's Court

The James Earl Ray FBI wanted poster. At the time it was said to be the FBI's largest and most expensive manhunt.

At 11.15 on the morning of Saturday 8 June 1968, and a few hours before the funeral of Robert Kennedy in New York City 3,500 miles away, a man wearing a beige raincoat and tortoiseshell-rimmed glasses arrived at the passport desk inside the Europa Terminal at Heathrow Airport. It was only thirty-five minutes before his BEA Flight 466 to Brussels was due to take off and he had already checked in his luggage. As he got his passport out of his jacket, Ken Human, the immigration officer, noticed he had a second passport and asked to see them both. The passports were identical except one had the name Sneyd whereas the other, issued in Ottawa, had the man's surname as Sneya.

While the man was explaining that the first passport had accidentally been misspelt and that he had had another one issued while recently in Lisbon, they were suddenly joined by Detective Sgt. Philip Birch. The policeman looked at both the passports and then tapped the man on the shoulder and said: 'I say, old fellow, would you mind stepping over here for a moment? I'd like to have a word with you.' The man who called himself Sneyd offered no protest and followed the policeman into a nearby office. He was searched and found stuffed in his back right pocket was a loaded Japanese-made Liberty Chief revolver, the handle of which was wrapped in black gaffer tape. When Birch asked him why he was carrying a gun, the man replied: 'Well, I'm going to Africa and I felt that I might need it. You know how things are, out there.'

Birch immediately called Scotland Yard and it wasn't long before Detective Chief Superintendent Tommy Butler was travelling towards Heathrow. He was known to the London's criminal fraternity and beyond as 'One Day Tommy' for the time he took apprehending criminals, but also the 'Grey Fox' for his shrewdness. When it came to publicity Butler was not prone to shyness. He was most notable for leading the team that investigated the Great Train Robbery in 1963 and liked to be in the news. When he arrived at London's main airport he knew exactly who he had come to arrest and soon the rest of the world did too.

The suspect was taken to Cannon Row police station, part of the New Scotland Yard building designed by Norman Shaw. At this point he was still claiming that his name was Sneyd and that he was a Canadian citizen, born in Toronto. During the questioning, however, Butler told him: 'We have good reason to believe that you are not a Canadian citizen but an American.' Butler then told the suspect that they believed he was the wanted man known as James Earl Ray and responsible for the murder of Dr Martin Luther King. The man, who until then had been standing, suddenly slumped down on the seat behind him and put his head in his hands and said, 'Oh God.' A few moments later he added, 'I feel so trapped.'

Just over two months earlier on 4 April 1968, Dr King had been leaning over a second-floor balcony at the Lorraine motel in Memphis, talking to his chauffeur, Solomon Jones, who was on the ground floor. A high velocity bullet suddenly hit King in the neck, severing his spinal column, and in less than an hour, at St Joseph's hospital in Memphis, he died. The murder weapon, a Remington hunting rifle, was quickly found not more than a block away from the shooting. From the gun's serial number and some clues in a white Mustang that had been seen leaving the scene, it was quickly established, via a couple of pseudonyms, that the main suspect for the murder was a forty-year-old man called James Earl Ray – at the time still an escapee from the Missouri State Penitentiary, where he had been serving a twenty-year sentence for armed robbery. The *Daily Express*, not inaccurately, would later describe Ray as 'a petty, clumsy, stick-up man whose stupid mistakes had put him behind bars many times'.[1]

Four days after he had fired the lethal bullet from the window of a boarding house across from the Lorraine motel, James Earl Ray had already crossed the border into Canada. It was well known among many American prisoners, and Ray had been a habitual but unsuccessful criminal most of his adult life, that it was ludicrously easy to get a copy of a birth certificate in Ontario. Ray chose the name of a Toronto policeman Ramon George Sneyd, probably at random, in a city directory. After mailing a $2 postal order, he received within a few days a birth certificate with his new name. In an old newspaper in the Toronto library Ray found the maiden name of the original Sneyd's mother and the relevant date of birth. All Ray now had to do was to swear that he was Canadian and ask for a passport. Within twenty-four hours Ray was on a BOAC plane to London and after a day continued on to Lisbon in Portugal.

At the time it was said to be the largest and most expensive investigation in the FBI's history. Due to the amount of clues left behind, they only had one suspect but had no real leads as to where he was. In the meantime, however, Ray was in Lisbon working out what to do. Ray by now probably assumed that people were on his trail and had gone to the Canadian consulate, telling them that his name had been misspelled and asked 'Sneyd' to be changed to 'Sneya'. The Canadian lackadaisical approach to passport issuing continued, and with no questions asked Ray was given a replacement on 16 May. Running out of funds and realising that it would be far easier for him to operate in an English-speaking country, he flew back to London the next day. He soon booked himself into a hotel called Heathfield House at 181–183 Cromwell Road on the outskirts of Earl's Court, for which he paid just over £2 a night (approximately £32 in 2015) for the privilege.

Earl's Court was an area of London known after the war as the 'Danzig Corridor' due to the number of Polish people who had settled there. In the late forties there were 38,000–40,000 Poles living in and around London, then the largest foreign-born community in the capital. Twenty years later Earls Court was more likely to be called 'Kangaroo Valley' because of the large number of transient Australian and New Zealand travellers living there. At the time it was one of the cheapest areas to stay close to central London. There were also hundreds of cheap and seedy hotels and hostels, so it was the perfect part of London to stay relatively anonymous. In 2015 Heathfield House is still a hotel but it is now called the Rockwell and any contemporary assassins needing a single room in 2015 would have to pay around £120 per night.

Ray stayed at Heathfield House for ten nights and after checking out walked down to the New Earl's Court Hotel at 35–37 Penywern Road, less than half a mile away. Penywern Road was a particularly shabby and run-down street in those days and the hotel, like the rest of the terrace, was made of London brick with the rendered parts covered in peeling, dirty white paint. Above the door was a blue awning. The receptionist at the hotel was called Jane Nassau and she remembered Ray staying there: 'He was extremely shy, pathetically shy,' she said. 'He signed in as Canadian. But I thought it was strange. He had this deep southern drawl. He was extremely nervous.' She also remembered explaining the British currency, which had become even more confusing for a foreign traveller as some new 5p and 10p coins had been introduced a month or so before: 'But he was a bit thick. It didn't sink in.'[2]

While Ray was still at the New Earl's Court Hotel, on 1 June, the FBI had a break. At the Bureau's request (they also, of course, were aware of Canada's lax passport rules), the Royal Canadian Mounted Police had been laboriously checking 300,000 passport photos and eventually came across a picture that looked like the only real suspect for Martin Luther King's murder – James Earl Ray.

Three days later, on the afternoon of Tuesday 4 June and exactly two calendar months after Martin Luther King had been shot, Ian Colvin, a journalist in the foreign newsroom of the *Daily Telegraph*, walked in to find a note at his typewriter which read: 'A Mr Sneyd called, will call later.' Ian Colvin as a journalist had begun his career on the *News Chronicle* as a correspondent in Berlin but had been expelled by the Nazis in 1939. During the fifties and sixties he worked as a foreign correspondent for the *Daily Telegraph* in Africa and the Middle East. At the time of his death in 1975, he was the *Telegraph*'s chief leader writer. Ray did call Colvin later and this time the *Telegraph* journalist answered his phone. He heard a nervous voice say: 'This is Ramon Sneyd. I want to join my brother who

has been in Angola.' Ray explained that he was a Canadian and had read
Colvin's articles about mercenaries in Africa. He wanted the telephone
number of Major Alistair Wicks, mentioned by Colvin and who had been
second in command of the so-called 5 Commando Unit ANC, a mercenary
force in the Congo made up of about 300 men, most of whom were from
South Africa.

Ray claimed that his brother was missing and he hoped that Wicks
might put him in touch with a group who could help locate him. Colvin
was wary of giving out any information about Wicks, who would have
had plenty of enemies, and instead offered to pass along Sneyd's number.

After Ray had called Colvin from a payphone a few feet from the desk in
the hotel foyer, he asked Nassau about his bill for the first week. His money
was now running out and he told her that he would have to go to his bank
and make a withdrawal. Not long after this conversation Ray entered the
Trustee Savings Bank at 179 Earls Court Road and less than five minutes'
walk away from his hotel. One of the cashiers looked up to see Ray wearing
a blue suit, large sunglasses and a trilby hat. He pushed a small, pink paper
bag toward her on which he'd written, 'Place all £5-10 pound notes in this
bag.' The cashier noticed a gun between the fingers of one of his hands. She
got £105 out of her drawer and pushed the notes towards him. Ray took
the money and slowly walked out. He accidentally left the bag behind and
later it was discovered it had his right thumbprint on it.

It was easy for Ray to make a quick escape from the area and he must
have casually walked into Earls Court tube station, literally across the road
from the bank. He travelled four stops to Paddington and then came across
a jeweller's at 131 Praed Street called 'Treasures'. The owners, Maurice
and Billie Isaacs, then aged sixty-one and fifty-seven respectively, were just
closing up when Ray walked in. He produced his gun and expected the
middle-aged couple to cower in fright. Instead Mr Isaacs quickly grabbed
the pistol and managed to punch Ray in the face. Shocked, the American
went to leave but not before turning round at the doorway and pointing
his gun at the jewellery shop owners, who ducked behind the counter. The
gun was never fired and Ray returned to his hotel.

Ray decided to check out of the New Earl's Court Hotel and told Jane
Nassau, falsely, that he was leaving for the airport. It was now raining
heavily and clutching his bags Ray went out looking for another room. He
initially tried the nearby YWCA at 118–120 Warwick Way, but although it
did have rooms for men, it was full and he was directed to the nearby Pax
Hotel three doors down the same road at number 126. The Pax Hotel was
then really a private house but its owner, Swedish-born Anna Thomas,

let out several rooms and there was a small sign that simply read 'Hotel' hanging down from a small first-floor balcony. The building is now called the Bakers Hotel and a single room there in 2015 is around £85 per night.

When Thomas opened the door of her hotel Ray was standing there, dripping wet in a beige raincoat, a suitcase in one hand and books and newspapers under his other arm. He introduced himself as Sneyd and said that he would take a room. Two days after the first call to Colvin, Ray called the journalist again, complaining that he had not heard from Wicks. He let Colvin know that he had moved again and now he was at Hotel Pax. Colvin had passed on the message to Wicks but Wicks hadn't recognised the name and not surprisingly, considering the world he moved in, had decided not to return the call. This time, however, Colvin questioned the caller and Ray admitted that his brother was not really missing but that he actually wanted to become a mercenary himself.

The call was continually being interrupted because Ray, unused to the British public phones was struggling to insert coins at the right moment. Colvin managed to tell him, however, that it wasn't a good time to join any mercenary group and told him that both the British and Africans frowned on them these days. Colvin also told Ray that the place to get any information wasn't London but Brussels. Although at the time Colvin found the stranger who kept calling him 'overwrought and somewhat incoherent', he nonetheless sent a postcard to Pax Hotel suggesting that Sneyd contact the Belgian embassy.

At 9.30 a.m. on Saturday 8 June, Anna Thomas knocked on 'Ramon Sneyd's' room and found that her tenant had packed up and disappeared. The room had been left clean except for a newspaper that featured Robert Kennedy's assassination that had taken place two days before. The day after Martin Luther King had died, Robert Kennedy made a speech where he said 'no martyr's cause had ever been stilled by an assassin's bullet'. Ray had also left behind a Cold War spy thriller called *Assignment Tangier* by Cameron Rougvie. The bright, lurid cover featured a cross-legged woman in a yellow bikini, the top of which was draped undone. The blurb talked of 'international intrigue, Mafia villainy and free-booting contrabandists, helped by the lovely Sandra Grant'. Inside the back of the book was a mass of figures where Ray had tried to compare the value of dollars to pounds. In the sink, crammed down the spout, was a plastic syringe.

Thomas would later say that she was quite glad to see Ray leave: 'He was so neurotic, such a strange fellow. I felt sorry for him but he was so obviously a troubled man that he gave me the creeps.'[3] As Thomas cleaned the room, Ray was making his way to Heathrow Airport, probably via the BEA terminal on the Cromwell Road, where he could also check in his luggage before being taken by coach to the Europa Terminal at Heathrow ...

James Earl Ray was held under heavy guard at Cannon Row, where the security extended to sealing off the roads Cannon Row and Derby Gate. He was charged under the name Sneyd for possessing a forged passport and carrying a firearm without a permit. It wasn't until 18 July, forty days after his arrest at Heathrow airport, that the Home Secretary, James Callaghan, was able to sign a Warrant of Surrender that authorised James Earl Ray's extradition to the United States. Ray was taken to the United States Air Force base at Lakenheath in Suffolk and from there he was flown back to the USA at 12.38 a.m. on Friday 19 July 1968.

On 10 March 1969 (his forty-first birthday), at a hearing that lasted just 150 minutes, James Earl Ray confessed to the assassination and pleaded guilty to save himself from the electric chair. Three days later he wrote a letter to the court asking that his plea be set aside (the judge refused the request) and he was sentenced to ninety-nine years in prison.

In 1981 Ray was stabbed twenty times by a group of his fellow prisoners. After losing a lot of blood, he contracted hepatitis during the subsequent blood transfusions. It was the hepatitis that eventually killed him. Ray died in prison in Nashville, Tennessee, on 23 April 1998, just over thirty years after he had killed Dr Martin Luther King.

Heathrow, Oceanic Terminal in 1968. (R. B. Reed)

'Ramon George Sneyd'
passport photo.

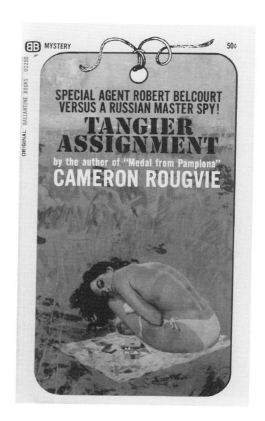

Assignment Tangier by Cameron
Rougvie, published by Ballantine
in 1965 and left behind at the Pax
Hotel by James Earl Ray.

Left: Pax Hotel at 126 Warwick Way in 1968.

Below left: New Earl's Court Hotel on Penywern Road in 1968.

Below right: Room 54 door key, New Earl's Court Hotel.

Earl's Court Road in 1968. (Bill Holmes)

CHAPTER 14

The Death of Benny Hill and the Windmill Theatre in Soho

Benny Hill in his kitchen at his flat at 1–2 Queensgate in May 1969. (© Trinity Mirror/ Mirrorpix/Alamy)

On Easter Sunday morning in 1992, just two hours after he had been speaking to a television producer about yet another comeback, and five days after being released from hospital after a heart-scare, seventy-five-year-old Frankie Howerd collapsed and died. Benny Hill, seven years younger than Howerd, was quoted in the press as being 'very upset' and saying, 'We were great, great friends.' Indeed they had been friends, but Hill hadn't given a quote about his fellow comedian, he hadn't even been asked for one – he couldn't have been – because he was already dead.

The quote about Howerd had actually come from Hill's friend, former producer and unofficial press agent Dennis Kirkland, who hadn't been able to get in contact with Hill and was starting to worry. It wasn't until the 20th, the day after Howerd had died, that a neighbour noticed an unpleasant smell coming from Flat 7 of Fairwater House on the Twickenham Road in Teddington.

The neighbour contacted Kirkland, who was a regular visitor to the Teddington apartment block, and it wasn't long before the television producer was climbing a ladder and peering through the window of Hill's second-floor flat. Inside he saw his friend surrounded by dirty plates, glasses, videotapes and piles of papers, slumped on the sofa in front of the TV. The body was blue, bloated and distended and there was a dried trickle of blood that had seeped from one of his ears. Hill had been dead for two days. He had only been seen in public a few days before when he had sat in the audience of *Me & My Girl* at London's Adelphi Theatre. Benny had gone along to see Louise English, an ex-Hill's Angel who was appearing with Les Dennis. On the same evening, having recovered from heart trouble himself just a few months earlier, Benny had sent Frankie a telegram: 'Stop stealing my act – I do the heart attack jokes.'[1]

During the summer of 1940 and during the height of the Blitz, Alfred Hawthorne Hill or, as he was usually known, Alfie arrived at Waterloo on a Southampton train. He was just seventeen. He'd given up his Eastleigh milk round, which really did have a horse and a cart, and he had sold his drum kit for £6 to finance the next part of his life. There was almost nothing in this Max Miller fan's head but an ambition to succeed as a comic performer – show business was in the family's blood; both his father and his grandfather had once been circus clowns. He had with him the addresses of three variety theatres in his pocket, but after a week of sleeping rough in a Streatham bomb shelter, it was luck rather than judgement that enabled the naive Hampshire boy to get a dogsbody job from a kindly agent. Hill remembered this time in 1955: 'At the Chiswick Empire they did not want to know about Alf Hill. I had much the same reception at the "Met", but at the Chelsea Palace I was lucky enough to arrange to see Harry Benet at his office the next morning.'[2] Hill turned up at Benet's office in Beak Street and was offered £3 per week to be an assistant stage manager (with small parts) for a new revue called *Follow the Fan*. For years after Hill would often joke that although he was no longer an ASM, he still had small parts.

Twelve months or so later Hill, now eighteen, had become eligible for conscription but by now he was having the time of his life. He naively thought that by travelling around the country (he was now with *Send Them Victorious*, another revue) he could pretend he had never received the OHMS manila envelope ordering him to enlist. The ruse worked until November 1942, when the revue was at the New Theatre in Cardiff for the last engagement before the pantomime season. Two military policemen presented themselves at the theatre stage door and Alfie Hill was 'advised' to give himself up. He couldn't drive and he knew nothing about engines, but within a month Hill found himself a private in the Royal Electrical and Mechanical Engineers as a driver and mechanic. Not surprisingly, considering his lack of knowledge or interest in engines, Alfie Hill played no useful part in the war. Although he was taught to drive in the army he would subsequently never own a car or drive in his civilian life. Not long after VE Day, and when he was in London on leave, he applied to be part of the services' touring revue called *Stars in Battledress*.

There was one problem: Hill didn't have 'an act', and he had just twenty-four hours to create one. For inspiration he walked to the Windmill Theatre on Great Windmill Street in Soho – he knew that it was the one place in London where you could see comedians during the day. He noticed one Windmill turn in particular, a man called Peter Waring whose scripts were written by Frank Muir, who at that time was still attached to the RAF. Hill would later say: 'Waring was the biggest influence on my life. He was delicate, highly strung and sensitive…when I saw him I thought, "My God, it's so easy. You don't have to come on shouting, 'Ere, 'ere, missus! Got the music 'Arry? Now missus, don't get your knickers in a twist!' You can come on like Waring and say, 'Not many in tonight. There's enough room at the back to play rugby. My God, they are playing rugby.'"'

Waring, the ex-conjuror turned comic, had been performing at an ENSA concert at RAF Henlow when he met Frank Muir. ENSA, an organisation set up in 1939 to provide entertainment for British armed forces personnel during the Second World War, stood for the Entertainments National Service Association but many made the joke that it stood for 'Every Night Something Awful'. Muir, like Benny Hill a few months later, was immediately attracted to Waring's style of humour and he later described him in his autobiography as 'one of the new "class" acts, a slim, good-looking thirty-something, with the shiny, slightly wavy black hair then much admired, a good dinner jacket and a cork-tipped cigarette, which he held a little awkwardly because of a badly wounded right arm'.[3] The ENSA programme notes said that Peter Waring's real name was Commander Peter Roderick-Mainwaring DSO RN, who had been invalided out of the navy after he had been severely injured by an enemy shell on the Murmansk convoy run.

After the war Frank Muir wrote a BBC radio series for Waring called *Heigh-Ho!* It was popular and went down well, but Muir could never understand why it wasn't commissioned for another series. He later found out that Commander Peter Roderick-Mainwaring DSO RN had never existed and Peter Waring was just a conman, albeit a very funny one. His badly injured arm was not caused by a Nazi shell in the Arctic but by a burn when Waring had leant against a hot water pipe on a cross-Channel ferry. It was reported a few years later that influential Waring went to prison for fraud, eventually hanging himself in a cell in Blackpool.

The Windmill Theatre on the corner of Great Windmill Street and Archer Street, just off Shaftesbury Avenue, was a magnet to many of the new wave ex-servicemen comedians, of whom there were many. The theatre was infamous for its risqué dancing girls and nude tableaux, but the shows also featured a small resident ballet company, a singer or two and some brand-new comedians usually at the start of their career. It was a tough crowd for the comedians – not too many patrons were there for the jokes.

The theatre had been bought in 1930 by a seventy-year-old 'white-haired, bright-eyed little woman in mink' called Mrs Laura Henderson whose late husband 'had been something in Jute'. At the time it was a run-down old cinema called the Palais de Luxe (actually one of the first in London) but she had the building extensively rebuilt, glamorously faced with glazed white terracotta and renamed the Windmill Theatre. Under the careful guidance of her manager Vivian Van Damme, a small neat man who more often than not would be smoking a cigar, the theatre slowly became a success. The 'Mill', as it became known in its heyday, started to present a non-stop type of revue that had a terrible title which assimilated the word 'nude' and 'revue' and was called Revudeville.

Van Damme, amusingly known as VD to everyone backstage, had an astute judgement of both English sexual taste and of what the Lord Chamberlain – the national theatre censor – would allow. 'It's all right to be nude, but if it moves, it's rude,' said Rowland Thomas Baring, 2nd Earl of Cromer, who was the Lord Chamberlain at the time. On the Sunday night before any new show opened Van Damme would invite the Earl of Cromer to a special performance. To make the censor's mood amenable to what he was about to see, VD made sure there was generous hospitality before the curtain was raised. It was said that the Lord Chamberlain never delegated his responsibilities on these occasions.

At the beginning of the war the government ordered compulsory closure of all the theatres in the West End – a stricture that, due to many protests, ended less than two weeks later. The Windmill re-opened immediately and stayed open throughout the rest of the war with five or six performances a day. The shows started at 11 a.m. and continued until 10.35 p.m. at night. During the worst of the Blitz it was sometimes too dangerous to expect people to get home safely and the stagehands and performers often slept in the lower two floors underground. Around 1943 the theatre created its famous motto – 'We never closed' – although wags quickly changed this to 'We never clothed'. In fact the 'Mill' became a semi-cherished institution and garnered a reputation of defiance. This, together with Van Damme's tasteful 'girl-next-door' version of English femininity, made the Windmill Theatre a major symbol for London's 'Blitz Spirit' all around the world. This indestructible gesture of defiance was summed up at the theatre when one naked young woman broke the 'no moving' rule by brazenly raising her hand to give a V-sign at a V1 bomb that had exploded nearby. She earned herself a standing ovation.

Once the audience arrived in the morning some of them would stay and watch all the six shows throughout the evening and night. Des O'Connor, just one of the comedians who got an early break at the Windmill, was on his fifth show of the day when he completely dried up. Somebody, who had been at all the previous shows that day, shouted out: 'You do the one about the parrot next!' During the later performances the audience that were sitting in the back of the stalls would wait for those in the front rows to get up and leave. When they did, the men at the back would quickly leap over the seats to get to the front – a daily event that became known as the 'Windmill Steeplechase'.

Benny Hill, who by now had changed his name – he thought Alfie Hill made him sound like a cheap barrow boy and Jack Benny was one of his favourite comedians – had two auditions at the Windmill. On both occasions, and after barely finishing his first gag, he got a dreaded 'Thank you, next please' from Van Damm somewhere in the darkness of the stalls. He certainly wasn't the only comedian who would later go on to become a huge star but was rejected by the Windmill Theatre. Both Bob Monkhouse and Norman Wisdom also failed to get past the one-man Van Damm judging panel. The list of comics who did perform at the Windmill is extraordinary, however, and included Jimmy Edwards, Tony Hancock, Arthur English, Harry Secombe, Peter Sellers, Michael Bentine, Bruce Forsyth, Dave Allen, Alfred Marks, Max Bygraves, Tommy Cooper and Barry Cryer. There was a comedy revolution taking place and performers who, in a sense, had wasted years of their young adulthood on the war, were desperate to make up for lost time. They had seen the best of humanity and, of course, the worst. They had a connection with each other like no generation since.

For Hill, after failing his second audition at the Windmill, it was back to the working men's clubs in parts of London like Streatham, Tottenham and Harlesden. In those days the Soho agents never actually mentioned money and used to show the amount that was to be paid by laying fingers on the lapels of their jackets. One finger meant £1 while two fingers meant double. It was nearly always the former for Benny back then. As the months went by his act was getting more and more polished and in 1948, in a rehearsal room across the road from the Windmill, he had an audition as Reg Varney's straight-man in a revue called *Gaytime*. There were only two people auditioning for the part and Hill had performed an English calypso (this would have been pretty rare just after the war), which he sang to his own guitar accompaniment:

> We have two Bev'ns in our Cabinet/Aneurin's the one with the gift of the gab in it/The other Bev'n's the taciturnist/He knows the importance of being Ernest!

After he had performed his musical comedy turn, Hill was told by Hedley Claxton, an impresario who specialised in seaside shows, that he had got the job. The other contender for the role that afternoon in 1948 was a young impressionist from Camden called Peter Sellers. Later that year Peter Sellers secured a six-month booking at the Windmill performing in sketches or sometimes as an impersonator. It wasn't his first appearance at the Windmill. As a child he had performed in a show with his mother Peg, who was a burlesque dancer at the theatre not long after it opened.

Hill and Reg Varney's double act was generally a success, and they were signed up for three seasons of *Gaytime* and subsequently a touring version of a London Palladium revue called *Sky High*. The weakest spots in the shows were Hill's solo performances – he found it difficult to engage with the audiences, especially in the north of England. When the revue opened at the Sunderland Empire the local newspaper wrote: 'I thought Reg Varney's personality pleasing and warming, but was not so "taken" with some of his comedy.' Presumably out of kindness there was no mention of his comic partner. Hill had completely died in his own solo spot and it had ended after the audience started giving him a slow handclap.[4] By this time Hill had already appeared on BBC radio a few times but struggled to make his mark. A particularly damning BBC report on Benny Hill, dated 10 October 1947, said:

Ronald Waldman: The only trouble with him was that he didn't make me laugh at all – and for a comedian that's not very good. It's a mixture of lack of comedy personality and lack of comedy material.

Harry Pepper: I find him without personality and very dully unfunny.

In 1950, at a time when only one in twenty households owned a television, Hill, unlike many performers and agents who either feared it or thought it a flash in the pan, realised that television would be huge and all-consuming. He understood that it would gobble up comic material and that it was already ending the career of variety artists who had successfully performed the same act all their lives. Comic writers started to be as important as the performers, perhaps even more so, and Hill started to write literally hundreds and hundreds of sketches, eventually submitting great numbers of them to the BBC. The head of Light Entertainment was now Ronald Waldman, who three years previously had criticised Hill's lack of comedy material and the ability to make him laugh at all. This time, however, Waldman was more than impressed and offered Benny Hill his own show right there and then.

Hi There was transmitted on the BBC on the evening of 20 August 1951 and the 45-minute one-off show, featuring a series of sketches wholly written by Benny Hill, was relatively well-received. It wasn't until four years later that Hill got his own BBC series when in January 1955 the first ever *The Benny Hill Show* was broadcast. Hill was always a relatively uncomfortable performer on stage. Roy Hudd once wrote: 'I saw him several times live and he never seemed totally at home with an audience.' Dennis Kirkland later wrote that 'He made no secret of his hatred for live theatre. It made him sweat; literally shake with nerves.'

The new medium of television utterly suited Hill with his 'conspiratorial glances and anticipatory smirks' to camera. After a shaky first episode the rest of the series was a big success and in some ways set a new standard for British television comedy. Hill used all the expertise of the studio make-up department to great effect, and also utilised new technology enabling him to include recorded inserts in his sketches and use split screen trickery, for instance, to play all the panellists in parodies of programmes such as *What's My Line* and *Juke Box Jury*. All this, to people watching at home, made old routines seem brand new.

Benny Hill never looked back and was a mainstay of British television for the next thirty-five years. Initially his shows appeared on the BBC but from 1969, when the new London weekday ITV franchise needed some high-profile signings, on Thames Television. The 'cherub sent by the devil', as Michael Caine once described Hill, eventually became a big star all over the world. It seemed at one point, just as many in the UK were starting to find his comedy rather old-fashioned and sexist, that the rest of the world thought Benny Hill WAS British comedy.

Towards the end of the eighties Colin Shaw of the Broadcasting Standards Council issued a mandate: 'Although the half undressed woman has been a staple element in farce and light entertainment shows, the convention is becoming increasingly offensive to a growing number of people and should be used only sparingly … It's not as funny as it was to have half-naked girls chased across the screen by a dirty old man. Attitudes have changed.'

Benny Hill was very confused about the accusations of sexism in the latter part of his career. He felt that over the years his comedy hadn't really changed and he'd been doing almost the same thing for decades. This was true; he literally had been telling the same jokes throughout his career and he was always happy to recycle his own material and others. Society around him had moved on, however, and an elderly man surrounded or chased by scantily-clad women made for uncomfortable viewing.

There is no doubt that Benny Hill had an odd relationship with women and it appears that Benny Hill never really had a proper relationship during his lifetime. In 1955, just as his career was taking off at the BBC, he was interviewed by Jane Dexter in the *Daily Mirror*. He was surrounded by dozens of girls, 'not all overdressed,' said Dexter, 'so why did he find it so difficult to find a girlfriend or wife?' Benny explained:

> It's like working in a chocolate factory. You see so many chocolates you don't bother to take a closer look. Besides I don't want a glamour girl. I'd like a girl who works in an office or a factory or a shop. That's where the pretty ones with common sense hide – and that's where I'm looking.[5]

In fact the closest he got to marriage was a couple of years later, with a dancer from the Windmill Theatre called Doris Deal. He took her for meals in the West End, they held hands, and it was assumed they were seeing each other. When Hill procrastinated a little too long and told her he wasn't ready for marriage, she promptly left him. There were other close, albeit non-romantic, relationships with women through the years including a young Australian actress called Annette André (she went on to appear in *Randall and Hopkirk (Deceased)*). He even proposed to Annette once although, to be polite, she pretended not to notice.

It seems that Benny Hill, famous throughout the world by surrounding himself with young women, either was scared of intimate sexual intercourse or, as some un-named sources have implied, he was impotent or gay. Before the war some gay dancers he was working with asked a naive Alfie whether he was 'queer'. Not understanding the question, he answered, 'Not really, but I've got my funny little ways ...' Mark Lewisohn, in his Benny Hill biography *Funny, Peculiar*, recounts a conversation Bob Monkhouse once had with Benny Hill in a cafe in Shaftesbury Avenue: 'He wanted his women to be more naive than he was, women who would look up to him. He also said it was fellatio he wanted, or masturbation. "But Bob, I get a thrill when they're kneeling there, between my knees and they're looking up at me. And I want them to call me Mr Hill, not Benny. 'Is that all right for you, Mr Hill?' That's lovely, that is, I really like that," I asked him why and he said, "Well, it's respectful..."'

In 1989, twenty years after Benny Hill made his first series for Thames Television, their new Head of Light Entertainment, John Howard Davies, invited him into the offices for a chat. Howard Davies had played the title role in David Lean's *Oliver Twist* as a nine-year-old in 1948, but as an adult at the BBC had worked on *Steptoe and Son*, *Monty Python*, *Fawlty Towers* (it was his idea to cast Prunella Scales as Sybil) and produced all four series of *The Good Life*. Having just returned from a triumphant Cannes Television Festival, Hill, not surprisingly, assumed that they were meeting to discuss the details of some new *Benny Hill Shows*. The former child-star thanked him for all the series he had made for Thames but then promptly sacked him. Howard Davies would later say, 'It's very dangerous to have a show on ITV that doesn't appeal to women, because they hold the purse strings, in a sense.'[6]

The following year, in 1990, *The Benny Hill Show* was broadcast in ninety-seven countries around the world, except, ironically, in Britain. Benny Hill never really recovered from the shock of the meeting with Howard Davies and he was certainly treated badly. It was only three years later that Kirkland found him dead in his apartment, just a stone's throw from the Thames Television studios in Teddington. The worldwide success of his shows made Hill very rich and he left over £7 million pounds in his will. Unfortunately it hadn't been updated since 1961 and all the beneficiaries, his mum, dad, brother and sister, had also all died. The money went to nieces and nephews he hardly knew.

> When I was a lad and crazy to get into showbiz I used to dream of being a comic in a touring revue. They were extraordinary, wonderful shows. There were jugglers and acrobats and singers and comics, and most important of all were the girl dancers. My shows are probably the nearest thing there is on TV to those old revues.
>
> Benny Hill, 1991[7]

Wartime portrait of Alf Hill – he changed his name to Benny soon after the war.

Left: Fine Fettle opened at the Palace Theatre on Shaftesbury Avenue for seven months from 6 August 1959. The *Daily Mirror* described it as 'very much a seaside show masquerading as a West End one', and that's exactly why the audience loved it and it ran for seven months. Hill never enjoyed performing live and *Fine Fettle* was his second and last proper stage show.

Below: Windmill dancers Doreen Lord and Beryl Catlin up on the roof of the Windmill Theatre and looking down on Great Windmill Street with Shaftesbury Avenue in the distance, *c.* 1950. (Courtesy of Jill Shapiro)

By the stairs up to the roof, Windmill dancers Mellonie Whymark, Anita D'Ray and Annette Gibson, *c.* 1950.

Above left: Revudeville programme cover from 1946.

Above: Benny advertising oatmeal stout from the Stockwell-based Hammerton Brewery, 1955.

Left: The Windmill Theatre in 2012. (Rob Baker)

CHAPTER 15

When Fifty Hoxton Schoolchildren Met Charlie Chaplin at the Ritz

Charlie Chaplin and the children from Hoxton in the comedian's suite at the Ritz, 17 September 1921.

Charlie Chaplin was woken up on the morning of 17 September 1921 while in his bed at the Ritz Hotel on Piccadilly. 'Visitors from Hoxton,' he was told through the door, and from outside the window he could hear children singing a song over and over again:

> When the moon shines bright on Charlie Chaplin
> His boots are cracking, for want of blacking
> And his little baggy trousers need mending
> Before we send him to the Dardanelles.

The song, written to the tune of 'Red Wing', was not one of Charlie's favourites. It had been written in protest at Chaplin not enlisting during the First World War and had originally 'scared the daylights'[1] out of him when he had first heard it. In March 1916 the Mutual Film Corporation had signed Chaplin at a fee of $10,000 per week with a bonus on signing of $150,000. Mutual's initial publicity boasted that: 'Next to the war in Europe Chaplin is the most expensive item in contemporaneous history.'[2] This may have gone down well in the US but of course in most of Europe it was a different matter. The *Daily Mail* soon let its readers know that there was a clause in the Mutual contract that forbade Chaplin to return to Britain during hostilities so as not to risk his being conscripted into the British armed forces. A year later, in June 1917, Lord Northcliffe wrote in an editorial of the *Weekly Dispatch*: 'Charles Chaplin, although slightly built, is very firm on his feet, as is evidenced by his screen acrobatics. The way he is able to mount stairs suggest the alacrity with which he would go over the top when the whistle blew.'[3] It was eventually reported that Chaplin *had* gone to a recruiting office but at 5 feet 4 inches tall and not more than 126 pounds he was turned down by the doctors for being underweight. Chaplin, however, went on to receive letters containing white feathers for many years to come.

By 1921 'The Moon Shines Bright on Charlie Chaplin' had lost its original connotations or at least it had to the group of fifty children from the Hoxton School that had walked across London to see him. To much publicity, Chaplin had arrived in England from America only a week earlier, disembarking at Southampton after a pleasant and sunny voyage. He had sailed across the Atlantic on the RMS *Olympic*, the elder sister ship of the *Titanic*, luxuriously re-fitted after life as a troopship during First World War and now, of course, complete with the requisite number of lifeboats. Chaplin particularly enjoyed the ornate splendour of the Ritz-Carlton restaurant, where he fed himself on un-Californian food such as pheasant, grouse and wild duck. 'For the first time,' he later wrote, 'I felt the elegant gentleman, the man of means.'[4] The comedian had returned to Europe mainly to promote his new and first full-length (six-reeler) film called *The Kid* – already a huge success in America and eventually becoming the second highest grossing movie of 1921. Much of the success of the film was due to little Jackie Coogan's extraordinary performance as the 'Kid'. Chaplin wasn't alone in realising that the overwhelming response to Jackie was because he symbolised the countless orphans left after the recent World War.

Although Chaplin was looking forward to his first premiere in England, he also badly needed a holiday. He had just recovered from a bad dose of influenza and in the last seven years he had made seventy-one films. He was exhausted and was desperate to get away: 'Away from Hollywood, the cinema colony, away from scenarios, away from contracts, press notices, cutting rooms, crowds, bathing beauties, custard pies, big shoes, and little moustaches.'[5] *The Manchester Guardian*, in rather a gushing style, although not that dissimilar to other newspapers covering the event, wrote of the first glimpse of the homecoming Hollywood star, 'Mr Chaplin just bubbled over with good nature and good humour. He poured out smiles and laughter and merry jokes in bumper measure, and all with the utmost simplicity and perfect freedom from affectation.'[6]

The Mayor of Southampton greeted Chaplin and began speaking rather nervously, with an apology about the weather, 'It does not always rain in England ...' Chaplin quickly interrupted, 'I am an Englishman, Mr Mayor,' he said, 'and English weather, whatever it is, is good to see. It was raining, I remember, when I went away nine years ago.'[7]

Chaplin was now an incredibly rich man but his childhood in Walworth had been a desperately poor one. Both his parents, Charles and Hannah Chaplin, were music hall performers but of no great talent or fame. When Charlie was just three, Charles Snr left the family home after his wife gave birth to a boy whose father was Leo Dryden – another music hall performer and who would become known as the 'Kipling of the Halls' for his patriotic songs. In 1893, six months after the birth, Dryden visited Hannah and forcibly took their child, Charlie's half-brother, away from her. By most accounts Dryden was an aggressive man, married three times, and gave all his wives an unpleasant and rough time.

Struggling financially, Hannah Chaplin had a breakdown soon after and the following year, along with Charlie and his brother Sydney, entered the Lambeth Workhouse. Within a few weeks, however, the two boys were sent to Hanwell School for Orphans and Destitute Children. In 1903, after further breakdowns, Hannah was placed in the Cane Hill Lunatic Asylum in Surrey. Chaplin later wrote about a visit to see her in 1912, just before he left to live in America: 'It was a depressing day, for she was not well. She had just got over an obstreperous phase of singing hymns, and had been confined to a padded room. The nurse had warned us of this beforehand. Sydney saw her, but I had not the courage, so I waited. He came back upset, and said that she had been given shock treatment of icy cold showers and that her face was quite blue. That made us decide to put her into a private institution – we could afford it now.'[8] The brothers took their mother from Cane Hill and placed her at Peckham House – a private asylum in south London that cost 30 shillings a week. Not an inconsiderable sum in 1912.

Chaplin had been performing to audiences from the age of five. It was said that he was literally pushed on to a stage when a tough Aldershot crowd of mostly soldiers started jeering when, half way through a song, his mother suddenly lost her voice. Chaplin would later say that his first performance was his mother's last. Charlie started to sing a song made famous the year before by the Coster performer Gus Elen called "E Dunno Where 'E Are' about a Coster called Jack Jones who had 'come into a little bit of splosh' and developed unpleasant airs and graces in front of his old friends.

> Jack Jones is well known to everybody,
> Round about the market, don't yer see
> I've no fault to find wiv Jack at all
> When 'e's as 'e used to be
> But somehow, since 'e's 'ad the bullion
> Left 'e 'as altered for the wust
> When I see the way 'e treats old pals
> I am filled wiv nothing but disgust
> 'E sez as 'ow we isn't class enuf
> 'E sez we ain't upon a par
> Wiv 'im just because 'e's better off
> Won't smoke a pipe, must take on a cigar

Right from the start audiences loved Charlie Chaplin, and the appreciative Aldershot crowd threw coins up on the stage for him. After the five-year-old Charlie declared that the performance would only continue after he had retrieved all the coins, they laughed and threw even more. In the end his mother came back on and had to carry him off stage. By the age of nineteen Chaplin had become a member of Fred Karno's prestigious music hall troupe, and it was with them that he first took a trip to America in 1910. (One of the other members of Karno's company was Stanley Jefferson, who would later become known as Stan Laurel.) On a second visit in 1912 Chaplin caught the eye of Mack Sennett, and he began to work in the still very young movie business. Within a few years he had appeared in more than sixty films, most of which he had directed himself. By 1918 Charlie Chaplin was one of the most famous men on the planet.

When the train bringing Chaplin to London started to slow down as it approached Waterloo station, he was pleased to spot his Uncle Spencer's old pub, the Queen's Head on Broad Street,[9] just past Vauxhall station. When he alighted onto platform 14 at Waterloo, just a mile or so away from where he had grown up as a child, he was visibly shocked at the thousands and thousands of people waiting ready to greet him. *The Times* wrote: 'At Waterloo the stage might have been set for the homecoming of Julius Caesar, Napoleon, and Lord Haig rolled into one.'[10] David Robinson, Chaplin's biographer wrote: 'His homecoming was a triumph hardly parallelled in the twentieth century outside a few great royal or national events.'[11]

The police managed to get Chaplin down to the street. 'Hooray!' 'Charlie! Charlie!' 'Here he is!' 'Good luck, Charlie!' 'Well done, Charlie!' 'God bless you. God love you!' shouted the adoring crowd of all ages, some waving handkerchiefs and others raising their hats. Chaplin was almost pushed and lifted into a waiting car, which then drove down to the Ritz on Piccadilly. Another enormous crowd was waiting there and, 'Everybody – including the police – went mad,' reported *The Manchester Guardian*. A tanned Chaplin, with dishevelled hair, dressed immaculately in a grey overcoat, stood up in his open top car and shouted above the noise: 'Thank you very much, for this generous, kind and affectionate welcome. This is a great moment for me. I cannot say much. Words are absolutely inadequate.'[12] The police were almost overpowered by the boisterous and excited crowd and there was a struggle on the steps of the hotel before they managed to get Chaplin inside. The crowd continued cheering until he appeared at a first-floor window, where he broke up a huge bunch of carnations and threw them down to the crowd. A few days later he received a letter (one of tens of thousands, many of them begging, including 671 from 'relatives'): 'My boy, tried to get one of your carnations and his hat was smashed. I enclose you a bill of 7s. 6d. for a new one.'[13]

Chaplin told the waiting reporters desperate for an interview, that he was tired and needed to rest, but actually soon slipped out of the Arlington Street service entrance at the back of the hotel. On his own he took a taxi across Westminster Bridge. On the south-east side of the Thames he smiled when he saw the new London County Council building, which was almost complete (and would open the following year). The sight of it had amused him as its construction had started ten years previously, even before he had left London. He was surprised to see a Bible-reading beggar under the arches by the Canterbury Music Hall who had also been there in the same spot the last time he had passed. Chaplin then directed the taxi past Christ Church on Westminster Bridge Road. When he was a child, but working as a lather boy at a barber's in Chester Street, the vicar ran a magic lantern 'gaff' at Baxter's Hall next door. Chaplin once told a friend that the place had special memories for him; 'It meant warmth and companionship; it meant adventure and novelty; it meant food ... you could get a cup of coffee and a piece of cake there, and see the Crucifixion of Christ all that the same time, and for the modest charge of one penny.'[14] After Christ Church came the Kennington Baths, the 'reason for many a day's hookey', where he had once gone swimming, second class, for three pence (but only if you brought your own swimming trunks). The taxi then took him up Brook Street, which Chaplin described at the time as, 'The upper Bohemian quarter, where third-rate music-hall artists appear.'[15]

Then he got out of the taxi and walked to Lambeth Walk, an old haunt of his childhood. It smelt the same to him; the fish and chip smell, blended with the odour from spluttering naphtha lamps, brought back many memories. A slight woman with a young child came up to him, excited and out of breath, and said, 'Charlie, don't you know me?' He did; she was once a servant girl who waited at a cheap lodging house where he had one stayed. She had lost her job in disgrace, after she had fallen pregnant. He later wrote of her: 'I could detect a certain savage gloriousness in her. She was carrying on with all odds against her. Hers is the supreme battle of our age. May she and all others of her kind meet a kindly fate.'[16] He gave the woman some money for her child and then hurried on his way.

Chaplin noticed by now that his smart, expensive clothing had made him conspicuous. Some people had noticed him and although at a respectful distance of five yards or so, a growing crowd had begun to follow. He asked a policeman for help, who reassured him, 'That's alright, Charlie. These people won't hurt you. They are the best people in the world.' While the policeman was hailing a cab the crowd started to surround him; 'Hello Charlie!' 'God bless you, Charlie!' 'Good luck to you, lad!'[17]

The hailed taxi took him away past Kennington Gate towards Brixton Road, where he saw Glenshore Mansions, where he lived at the beginning of his prosperity. He asked the taxi to pull up at the Horns Tavern, where he drank a ginger beer for old time's sake. Chaplin was soon recognised again and he rushed back into his taxi. On the way back to the Ritz it took him past Kennington Cross where, as a young lad, he remembered hearing a harmonica and clarinet play 'The Honeysuckle and the Bee', which introduced to him for the first time 'what melody really was. My first awakening to music.'[18] As a boy he learned the words to the song the next day, so enamoured was he with the tune.

> You are the honey, honeysuckle. I am the bee:
> I'd like to sip the honey, dear, from those red lips. You see
> I love you dearie, dearie, and I want you to love me.
> You are my honey, honeysuckle. I am your bee.

The taxi travelled back across Westminster Bridge and back to the Ritz for dinner, but not before Chaplin noticed Sharps the photographers on Westminster Bridge Road. He went inside and asked if he could have prints of some photographs the company took of him when he was in Casey's Court Circus about fifteen years before. The assistant told him that the negatives would have been destroyed. Chaplin pointed at a picture of Dan Leno in the window, who had died seventeen years before. Chaplin wrote of the visit the following year: 'Have you destroyed Mr Leno's negative? I asked him. "No," was the reply, "but Mr Leno is a famous comedian." Such is fame.'[19]

A few days later, after a meal at the Embassy Club on Old Bond Street, Chaplin, in the company of a few friends, decided to take another trip to south London. Although it was after ten in the evening, he decided to visit 3 Pownall Terrace in Kennington (the street was demolished in 1968), where he had lived in a little room at the top of the house. It was now occupied by a Mrs Reynolds. 'Were you asleep?' Chaplin asked. The old war widow replied that she'd been awake listening to the newsboys outside, shouting the result of the British Heavyweight contest[20] that evening. 'Many's the time I've banged my head on that sloping ceiling,' Chaplin said to her after she had taken him to see his old room, 'and got thrashed for it.' Carlyle Robinson, described as Chaplin's manager by the *Daily Mirror*, told the newspaper in an interview in 1921 that the attic scenes in *The Kid* were based on a replica of that room in Charlie's old 'diggings' in Kennington.

Back at the Ritz on the morning of 17 September, Chaplin got dressed and walked into the sitting room of his suite to meet the young visitors from Hoxton. He found fifty excited boys and girls from the Hoxton School. One boy, called Charles Loughton, stepped forward and handed him a box of cigars and a letter. It read: 'You were one of us. You are now famous over the world. But we like to think you were once a poor boy in London as we are. You are now a gentleman, and all gentlemen smoke cigars. So we have chosen a box as a little gift to "Our Charlie".' Then a young girl, Lettie Westbrook aged thirteen, gave Charlie a bouquet with a note saying, 'With our thanks for all the fun you give to us.'[21]

After Chaplin had given each child a packet of sweets, he impersonated an old man in a picture gallery. By a skilful use of his overcoat, hat, and stick, he appeared to grow gradually to a height of some nine feet in order to look at the highest pictures, and the children screamed with laughter. Three weeks after Chaplin met the boys and girls from Hoxton School, and after a weekend spent with H. G. Wells and his family, Charlie left London, via Waterloo, for New York on the RMS *Olympic* again.

Charlie, along with his brother Sydney, had brought their mother to California a few months before his trip to England. After a particularly harsh and tragic life, much of which had been spent in workhouses and mental institutions, Hannah Chaplin was at last being properly looked after in a bungalow near the sea in Los Angeles. She was relatively normal for long periods and would talk to guests about her old music hall days but also the Zeppelin raids on London. One visitor, Wyn Ray Evans, once pointed out a strange mark on Hannah's arm. Chaplin's mother quickly withdrew it and then started hiding bread about her person. After Hannah had left the room the nurse explained that the mark was a tattoo from the workhouse and that it brought back days when she had nothing to eat and would hide bread for Sydney and Charlie.[22]

It was while Hannah was in Los Angeles that she was reunited with her son who had been cruelly snatched away from her by his father thirty years before. He was now called Leo Dryden Wheeler, and when the time came for Wheeler to meet his mother he asked her dramatically, 'Do you know who I am?' 'Of course I do,' Hannah replied pleasantly. 'You're my son. Sit down and have a cup of tea.'[23]

Chaplin's mother, the woman on whose life he had based so many of his female characters, and who had probably been suffering from the symptoms of syphilis for over twenty years, fell seriously ill with an infected gall bladder and was taken to the Physicians' and Surgeons' Hospital in Glendale in August 1928. Chaplin had always found visiting his mother difficult but in the last week of her life he visited her every day. During her final hours, not long after nurses had heard them both laughing, Chaplin tried to reassure her she was getting better. Hannah quietly said 'Perhaps' and then fell unconscious, never to wake up.

Charlie Chaplin and Jackie Coogan in a publicity still from *The Kid*, Chaplin's first full-length film.

Above: Portrait of Charlie Chaplin Senior.

Opposite above: The waiting crowds for Chaplin as he arrives at the Ritz, 11 September 1921.

Opposite below: Charlie Chaplin in a cab on the Brixton Road while exploring his old haunts in south London, October 1921.

The sheet music cover for Leo Dryden's very popular ballad 'The Miner's Dream of Home' from 1891. Dryden claimed that Francis, Day & Hunter paid £20 for the song, the most they had paid up to that time. The lyrics were particularly apt for Chaplin's homecoming exactly thirty years later:

It is ten weary years since I left England's shore,
In a far distant country to roam,
How I long to return to my own native land,
To my friends and the old folks at home!

Above: The Waterloo area in
c. 1921.

Right: Hannah Chaplin in
1927.

CHAPTER 16

The Rise and Fall of Colin Wilson and how he Met Marilyn Monroe

Colin Wilson and his girlfriend Joy in their flat in Notting Hill in 1957. (© Keystone Pictures USA/Alamy)

The writer Colin Wilson once said: 'I had taken it for granted that I was a man of genius since I was about thirteen.' For a few short months after the publication of his first book, called *The Outsider*, in 1956, it seemed that the rest of the world thought so too. *The Outsider* was a collection of essays that explored the philosophical idea of 'the outsider' in literature, including that of Kafka, Camus, Hesse, Sartre and Nietzsche. It was an impressive collection of modern writers but it seems almost extraordinary today that, within a few days of publication, the twenty-four-year-old Wilson was rocketed into celebrity orbit for what was essentially a book of existential literary criticism. It was a good way, for many of the tens of thousands who bought *The Outsider*, of making an acquaintance with intellectual foreign authors without the laborious obligation of actually having to read any of their books. Incredibly, Gollancz, the publishers, sold out their initial print run of 5,000 copies on the very first day of publication.

Britain's two main literary critics were both extremely effusive in their reviews of the book. Philip Toynbee in *The Observer* asked, 'Who is Colin Wilson? How did he have the time?' before describing the book as 'an exhaustive and luminously intelligent study of a representative theme of our time' and a 'real contribution to our understanding of our deepest predicament'. An equally ebullient Cyril Connolly in the *Sunday Times* pronounced it as 'extraordinary' that 'a young man of twenty-four has produced one of the most remarkable first books I have read for a long time'. Connolly didn't stop there: 'He has a quick, dry intelligence, a power of logical analysis which he applies to those states of consciousness that generally defy it.' Extravagant praise from a man who would later admit that he hadn't actually read the book.[1] The two Sunday newspaper heavyweight critics were certainly not alone with the compliments, however, and Kenneth Walker in the *Listener* described *The Outsider* as 'The most remarkable book on which the reviewer has ever had to pass judgement.' One cautionary note came from Kingsley Amis, who wrote in the *Spectator*, 'One of the prime indications of the sickness of mankind in the mid-twentieth century is that so much excited attention is paid to books about the sickness of mankind in the mid-twentieth century.'

After the celebratory reviews in the *Sunday Times* and the *Observer*, the less highbrow newspapers were now following the Colin Wilson story. Dan Farson, one of Britain's first television stars, but then writing for the *Daily Mail*, wrote: 'I have just met my first genius. His name is Colin Wilson.' At this stage no one seemed to notice that Wilson was agreeing, far too readily, with the 'genius' part of his description. In his journal

Wilson wrote: 'This book will be the *Waste Land* of the fifties, and should be the most important book of its generation.'[2]

The literary world were shocked that *The Outsider* had been written by a man who seemed to have come from nowhere – he hadn't even been to university, red brick or otherwise. Wilson was a working class lad from Leicester and had left school a few weeks before he was sixteen. After reading Sir James Jeans' *The Mysterious Universe* at the age of twelve, he initially decided, not without confidence, to become a scientist – 'My daydream had been to become Einstein's successor.' Two years later he had precociously put together a work of essays covering all aspects of science called *A Manual of General Science*. A developing interest in literature and poetry made him change his mind about scientific study, and after two unfulfilling jobs – one of which was a laboratory assistant at his old school – he drifted into the Civil Service. He quickly became bored and in the autumn of 1949, as part of his National Service, he joined the Royal Air Force. After just six months and numerous clashes with authority, Wilson attempted to feign homosexuality in order to be dismissed. An RAF medical board, assuming that Wilson was only pretending, and certainly not inexperienced with this ruse, was particularly tough with its questioning. The young writer-to-be, however, managed to get the better of them with his acting: 'I put on a show of mild hysterics, and accused them of treating homosexuals like criminals, and they had no alternative but to discharge me.'[3] A succession of menial jobs followed before he decided to travel around Europe. He returned to Leicester in 1951 where he married his first wife, Betty Troop, and they both moved to London, where their son was born. The marriage soon disintegrated and again he drifted in and out of many unrewarding jobs. During this traumatic period, Wilson was continually working and reworking the novel that was eventually published as *Ritual in the Dark* in 1960.

He met his girlfriend Joy on one of his numerous short-term jobs – he was a Christmas shop assistant at Peter Robinson on Oxford Circus and she was in charge of the cash registers. He fell for her immediately, partly because he was impressed with her middle-class background: 'When I heard Joy, I thought, "Oh marvellous, that's what I want." And when I asked her, "What books have you got on your shelf?" she said she'd got Yeats and Ulysses, and Proust in French, I thought, "My God, that's the girl I really want!" Betty didn't read at all.'[4]

While Wilson was working as a labourer in a plastics factory at Whetstone, he got into an argument with a foreman about his timekeeping, for which he got the sack. During the same week his landlady gave him notice on his flat. With next to no money, Wilson realised that if he bought a tent and a sleeping bag he could avoid paying any rent, and started sleeping on a golf course on the outskirts of London. It wasn't long before he realised that putting a tent up and down was not only time consuming but attracted unwanted attention. He started sleeping rough with only his waterproof sleeping bag for protection. After about a month he started to spend the night more centrally on Hampstead Heath. This was conveniently close to his girlfriend's lodgings and also to the British Museum, where he had now started writing. His day would start with breakfast at a café near Chalk Farm station, where he could get a cup of tea and two thick slices of bread with dripping for 7d (approximately 3p). He would then cycle to the British Museum where every day, despite the attendant threatening to complain about him, he would leave his rucksack with his sleeping bag at the cloakroom.

By the end of 1954 Wilson was writing at the museum during the day and working in the evening at a large café on Haymarket. It was brand new with an interior designed by Antoine Acket, and was part of a small chain called The Coffee House. He was a kitchen porter initially, but after a while started serving the customers, which he enjoyed. He got on with many of the fellow employees, who were mostly drama and art students. He wrote in his diary on 4 February 1955: 'The Coffee House job in the evenings suits me well enough – not tiresome yet, and needn't become so if I discipline myself not to let time drag. They give me sandwiches to bring home and I eat them all day and so save myself buying food ...'[5]

Now, with a steady job, there was no need to sleep rough, and for a short while Wilson rented a room in New Cross. Soon his bohemian manageress at the Coffee House, through a friend of hers, found him a room on Baker Street. On Christmas Day, 1954, alone in his room, he started missing his family and even felt cut off from society. He wrote about this time twenty years later:

> An inner compulsion had forced me into this position of isolation. I began writing about it in my journal, trying to pin it down. And then, quite suddenly, I saw that I had the makings of a book. I turned to the back of my journal and wrote at the head of the page: 'Notes for a book *The Outsider in Literature* ...'[6]

In a second-hand bookshop one day, Wilson noticed a book called *A Year of Grace* – an anthology of mysticism by the publisher Victor Gollancz. He realised that Gollancz might possibly be interested in his *The Outsider*.

He had by now written a third of it, but quickly wrote an introduction and sent what he had to the Gollancz office in Covent Garden. Ten days later he received a letter from Gollancz which said that he had read the typescript and that he would like to publish it. It was mid-June 1955, and now Wilson had to write half a book and deliver it by September. Without the time to write the rest in longhand and subsequently typing it out slowly afterwards, he asked a young woman from the Coffee House to help him. She could type and take short hand and when they met up Wilson tried out this new method of writing. He began by saying to her: 'This is chapter seven, and it is to be called "The Great Synthesis". Put that in capitals and follow it with a row of dots.' Wilson had meant the dots to go underneath but she had typed 'The Great Synthesis ...' The mistake was never rectified and every edition of *The Outsider* still has the three leader dots to this day. Wilson soon realised she wasn't helping him work any faster and he started writing directly using the typewriter. It was how he wrote for the rest of his life.

After the manuscript was delivered, Gollancz took Wilson out for the first expensive restaurant meal that he had ever eaten. They ate smoked salmon and drank red wine. After the lunch Wilson wrote to his mother that Gollancz had told him: 'I think it possible that you may be a man of genius.' Wilson later wrote, 'It was a conclusion that I had reached years before, but it was pleasant to hear it confirmed.'[7]

The excited British press thought that Britain, at last, had its own existentialist intellectual to compete with the Continental sophisticates. What made it even better was that Wilson wore sandals, a ubiquitous oatmeal polo-neck jumper, and a pair of studious spectacles. The myth that surrounded Colin Wilson really started, however, when David Wainwright in the *Evening News* revealed that the author had saved money by writing *The Outsider* in the British Museum by day, but sleeping rough on Hampstead Heath during the night, with only the protection of a water-proof sleeping bag, during the night: 'The wind in my face was lovely and when I did go back inside to live I found it very hard to sleep. But towards the end I was getting very depressed, carrying around this great sack of books.'[8]

With relish Wilson quickly threw himself into his new celebrity status and found himself invited to glamorous parties throughout the capital. One night he was standing at the urinals of the Athenaeum Club in Pall Mall and found himself next to the tall and almost blind Aldous Huxley. 'I never thought I'd be having a pee at the side of Aldous Huxley,' said Wilson. 'Yes, that's what I thought when I was standing beside George V,' retorted the famous author. On 12 October 1956, Wilson went to a Faber & Faber party where he had hoped to meet T. S. Eliot. He was introduced to William Golding and Laurie Lee, both virtually unknown at that time, but when Eliot hadn't turned up Wilson decided to make his way home. Still slightly drunk from champagne, Wilson noticed huge crowds outside the Comedy Theatre situated just off the Haymarket. Intrigued, he asked the taxi driver to drop him off nearby and he went to investigate.

Hundreds of people were outside the theatre, hoping to get a glance of Marilyn Monroe, who was currently in London to appear in the film version of Terrence Rattigan's play *The Sleeping Prince*. It was being directed by, and co-starring, Laurence Oliver and eventually would become known as *The Prince and the Showgirl*. Marilyn and her husband, Arthur Miller, had arrived in Britain three months previously in July 1956 after going through a tumultuous few weeks. Not only had they just got married, but Miller had also recently appeared, three years after his play *The Crucible* had first been staged, in front of the House Un-American Activities Committee, accused of communist sympathies. At one point the committee brought up a revue scene on which Miller had collaborated in 1939. It portrayed the committee as a mad Star Chamber where witnesses were gagged, bound and tortured. After reading it out, the committee's attorney triumphantly turned to the playwright and asked: 'Well Mr Miller?' After a long ruminating suck at his pipe, Miller replied: 'But – that was meant to be a farce ...'[9]

Miller had been subpoenaed after applying for a passport to accompany his new wife to London. He had refused, in front of the committee, to inform on his friends and fellow writers, and was cited for contempt of Congress – the trial for which would take place the following year. Monroe, against a lot of advice, had publicly supported Miller through these hearings. There was, however, huge worldwide support for the acclaimed playwright. Wary of hurting American credibility abroad, the US State Department ignored the committee's advice and issued Miller with a passport which enabled him to travel with his new wife to London.

While Marilyn was filming with Laurence Oliver at Pinewood, Miller decided to put on a rewritten version of his latest play called *View From the Bridge*. It was to be directed by Peter Brook, and it was the premiere of this play at the Comedy Theatre in Panton Street that had attracted the huge crowd that had made Colin Wilson stop his taxi.

The British public were fascinated with Marilyn Monroe and Arthur Miller. *The Observer*, in a piece about the couple, wrote:

English faces fell at the match. Intellectual weds glamour puss they smirked: how transient, how bizarre! People in New York who are acquainted with both partners unite in acclaiming Miller's physical attractiveness and his wife's instinctive intelligence. 'How wonderful it would be,' cried one of their friends (reversing Shaw's famous reply to Isadora Duncan's proposal) 'if their first child had his looks, and her brains!'[10]

Arthur Miller was no fan of the 'trivial, voguish theatre' of the West End, considering it, not entirely unfairly, as 'slanted to please the upper middle class'. When the auditions started for *A View From A Bridge* in London, he asked the director Peter Brook why all the actors had such cut-glass accents. 'Doesn't a grocer's son ever want to become an actor?' he asked. Brook replied, 'These ARE all grocer's sons.' Ironically, at the end of the auditions, a Rugby-educated lawyer's son called Anthony Quayle came closest to portraying a working-class American accent and he was chosen to play the main part of Eddie, the New York docker. At the opening night, Quayle in Peter Brook's 'brilliantly effective production' was given a standing ovation. Robert Tee in the *Daily Express* wrote: 'I saw Arthur Miller's wife and his play at the Comedy Theatre last night... and his *A View from the Bridge* was every bit as good as my view of Marilyn Monroe from the stalls.'[11]

Colin Wilson had recently become a slight acquaintance of Anthony Quayle, after meeting him at one of his numerous parties; and after pushing through the crowds and two lines of policemen, he got to the stage-door and confidently said: 'Mr Quayle's dressing room?' 'Down the corridor and on the left,' said the doorman. Wilson saw Marilyn standing alone in front of a mirror, where she was trying to pull up what the *Daily Mirror* described the next day as 'a shimmering gown of red satin'. Wilson noted that, despite her best efforts, the dress 'was slipping down towards her nipples' and not wasting the chance of a lifetime, he went to introduce himself – 'I had been told she was bookish,' he remembered. According to Wilson there was a definite 'connection' with Marilyn and she actually grasped his hand as they made their way through the waiting throng to the cars outside.

A gossip columnist buttonholed Wilson before he left the theatre and asked what he was doing there. Wilson said that he had spent the evening hoping to talk to T. S. Eliot and ended up meeting Marilyn Monroe. The next morning the columnist duly wrote about the young author meeting Marilyn at the premiere, but added that Wilson, while there, had been asked to write a play for Olivier. It was publicity like this that made his supporters question whether he really was a serious writer. The *New York Times* had written about his almost over-night ascendancy – 'He walked into literature like a man walks into his own house.' It is, of course, just as easy to walk out of your own house, and Wilson's fall from grace was almost as quick as his initial success. The tabloid backlash began in December 1956 when a story in the *Sunday Pictorial* informed the public that Wilson had a wife and a five-year-old son but was living with 'a mistress' – his girlfriend Joy – in Notting Hill. Around this time, Joy's father came across Wilson's journals and was shocked to read what he took to be horrific pornographic fantasies about his daughter (in reality, according to Wilson, they were notes for his novel he was currently writing). Joy's father, along with her mother, sister and brother, arrived at the front door of the flat that she and Wilson shared, intent on rescuing her.

Incredibly, the story became front page news for days; even *Time* magazine in America wrote about the incident involving their favourite 'English Egghead':

> Without warning, the door of the book-glutted flat was suddenly flung open and in burst Joy's enraged father. 'Aha, Wilson! The game is up!' roared accountant John Stewart, 58, brandishing a horsewhip. Beside Father Stewart stood his wife, bearing a sturdy umbrella … with no further pleasantries, Mrs Stewart fell to pummelling Philosophy Collector Wilson with her weapon, while the others tried to drag Joy from the villain's premises. They screamed at Joy: 'You will go to hell!' Their efforts were futile. Wilson was unbruised, Joy unbound, when bobbies swooped down on the domestic scene. Crimson with anger, John Stewart offered Wilson's diary as proof that the rapscallion was 'not a genius' but 'just plain mad'. Rasped Stewart: 'He thinks he's God!'[12]

The members of the British literary establishment looked down at the young working-class author they had originally fêted, utterly aghast. Philip Toynbee, in his books of the year article in the *Observer*, got the backlash rolling, writing: 'I doubt whether this interesting and extremely promising book quite deserved the furore which it seems to have caused.' By now *The Outsider* had earned around £20,000 (approximately £430,000 in 2015) for Wilson, and the critical reappraisal by many of his former supporters may well have been driven, not a little, by a touch of envy. There can't be many second books that have been set up so beautifully for an author's reputation to be critically destroyed. Sure enough, Wilson's next book, *Religion and the Rebel*, published in September 1957, was witheringly and disparagingly panned – 'half-baked Nietzsche' wrote the *Sunday Times*, a 'vulgarising rubbish bin' wrote Philip Toynbee, who was now remembering *The Outsider* as 'clumsily written and still more clumsily composed'.

Harry Richie in *The Guardian* described why the reviews for *The Outsider* were initially so good:

> Significantly, Wilson's most prominent enthusiasts were all ... younger members or descendants of the Bloomsbury group, upper-middle-class and upper-middle-aged, high priests of high art who worshipped at the altar of modernism and all things sophisticated and French. Wilson dropped all the right names – foreign, highbrow, impressively daunting on both counts – and, with his vague proclamations about the spiritual crisis in modern society and the alienation of his genius Outsiders, pressed all the right buttons.[13]

Wilson and his girlfriend Joy fled to Cornwall to avoid the still-frenzied press. At one point his journals, which he had been writing since the age of sixteen, were stolen and given to the *Daily Mail*, who gleefully printed excerpts including, 'The day must come when I am hailed as a major prophet,' and 'I must live on, longer than anyone else has ever lived ... to be eventually Plato's ideal sage and king...' Not to be outdone, the *Daily Express* had Wilson musing that death could be avoided by those with a sufficient intellect:

> Where there is a grim tremendous urge to live, death becomes almost impossible. Where there is a great battle to be fought, people do not die. Neither do civilisations. People die because they want to. There are exceptions but on the whole the rule is good. And why do people die? Out of laziness, lack of purpose or direction.[14]

Colin Wilson died in December 2013, caused by the aftermath of a stroke. It certainly wasn't laziness or lack of purpose that had anything to do with it – Wilson wrote every day and had 140 books published in his lifetime. It is his first – *The Outsider* – for which he will always be remembered. Within weeks of its initial publication it went into a second, third and fourth printing. It was then published in America and became a bestseller there and was subsequently translated into a dozen languages. Sixty years after sleeping rough on Hampstead Heath and cycling to the British Museum to write it, *The Outsider* is still in print.

Cover of the programme for Miller's *A View From the Bridge* at the Comedy Theatre (now the Harold Pinter Theatre). The New Watergate Theatre Club was a ruse to get past the Lord Chamberlain censoring the play because it featured homosexuality. The *Picture Post* wrote that the Lord Chamberlain had failed in his 'pious attempt ... to spare London the shock of this play – a play New Yorkers withstood without pain for some months'.

The premiere of *A View From the Bridge* at the Comedy Theatre, 11 October 1956. Marilyn Monroe and Arthur Miller both look happy, Vivien Leigh and Sir Laurence Olivier less so. (© Keystone Pictures USA/Alamy)

CHAPTER 17

David Hemmings, Blow-Up and the Red Buildings on Stockwell Road

David Hemmings driving along the Stockwell Road in *Blow-Up*.

Stockwell Road isn't the most exciting and handsome of roads. It may have been once, but the Luftwaffe and typically unimaginative post-war redevelopment put paid to that. It's got a skateboard park, if that's your thing, and David Bowie was born in a road just off it, but even he moved to Bromley when he was six. And that's about it; to most people, even if they live there, it's just a road that joins up Stockwell and Brixton.

If you walk towards the Brixton end, however, and you stop and look carefully at the end of a terrace, you can see a tiny bit of maroon-ish red paint showing through some peeling cream emulsion. It's the remnants of a lot of red paint and a clue that in the winter of 1966 this road made a glamorous appearance, alongside David Hemmings, the model Veruschka, and Vanessa Redgrave, in THE swinging Sixties film – Michelangelo Antonioni's *Blow-Up*. It was the Italian director's first film in English (he had just signed a lucrative deal to make three English-language pictures for Italian producer Carlo Ponti), and it was David Hemmings' first major film role.

On stage, however, Hemmings had already been a star, of sorts. In 1954, thirteen years before *Blow-Up* was released, a twelve-year-old Hemmings had appeared, as a boy soprano, in Benjamin Britten's opera *The Turn of the Screw*. To prepare for the role of Miles, in the as yet uncompleted opera, Hemmings had left school and his home in Tolworth, a south-west suburb of London, and had gone to live with Benjamin Britten at Crag House in Aldeburgh in Suffolk. 'It was one of the most wonderful times of my entire life,' Hemmings remembered: 'We all gathered round the piano – Peter Pears, Jennifer Vyvyan, Joan Cross, Arda Mandikian, Olive Dyer and me … He really constructed the opera round our voices.'[1] Hemmings throughout his life never wavered from saying that Britten's conduct with him was beyond reproach, at all times. 'He was not only a father to me, but a friend – and you couldn't have had a better father, or a better friend. He was generous and kind, and I was very lucky. I loved him dearly, I really did – I absolutely adored him. I didn't fancy him, I did go to bed with him, but I didn't go to bed with him in that way.'[2]

Just five weeks after Britten had completed the opera, the British premiere took place on 6 October 1954 with the Sadler's Wells Opera. It took place against a backdrop of increasing police antipathy to homosexuality. The situation was not helped by the fervently anti-homosexual and moralistic Home Secretary Sir David Maxwell Fyfe. In 1951, the defection to the Soviet Union of Guy Burgess, who was as close to openly gay as you could be in those days, and the (almost certainly) bisexual Donald Maclean had also stoked up public hostility.

Prosecutions for 'gross indecency' were increasing and there had been several highly publicised arrests, such as Lord Montagu and John Gielgud. Britten was also interviewed by police officers in 1953 – he had been at school with Maclean and one of Guy Burgess's boyfriends had lived at Britten's Hallam Street flat in the 1940s – but nothing came of it. At one point, however, Britten discussed the possibility that his partner Peter Pears might have to enter into a sham marriage.[3]

Hemmings' opera career with Britten came to a particularly abrupt end. The English Opera Group had taken *The Turn of the Screw* to the Théâtre des Champs-Elysées in Paris. It was 1956 and Hemmings was now fifteen. In the middle of Miles' main aria, 'Malo', Hemmings' voice suddenly broke. Britten was utterly horrified and stopped the orchestra immediately. He waved his baton in anger at the now ex-soprano, and the curtain slowly lowered. Britten did not speak to, or even acknowledge Hemmings ever again.

Ten years later Antonioni chose Hemmings for the role in *Blow-Up* because he wanted a fresh young actor who had no self-conscious acting style. The Italian director detested 'Method' acting, and in *The Passenger*, filmed in London in 1974 and the third of Ponti's English language films, Antonioni kept on saying to Nicholson, 'Jack, less twitching.' Antonioni once said: 'Actors feel somewhat uncomfortable with me. They have the feeling that they've been excluded from my work. And, as a matter of fact, they have been.' He first saw Hemmings act in an adaptation of Dylan Thomas's *Adventures in the Skin Trade*, at a small theatre in Hampstead. A few days later, at the first audition for *Blow-Up* held at the Savoy hotel, and before the young actor had said a word, Antonioni told Hemmings, 'You look wrong. You're too young.' Hemmings replied, 'Oh no. I can look older. I've done it before. You can trust me on this. I am an actor.'

After one more audition, Antonioni did trust him, and Hemmings went on to play his most famous role. The 'swinging', hip fashion photographer, who discovers by accident that some photos he took seem to reveal a murder, was purposely based on David Bailey, who in the mid-sixties was at the height of his fame. Even a scene where Hemmings buys a large old propellor in a junk shop was based on Bailey doing exactly that. At £8 they even got the price right, much to Bailey's shock when he was watching the film in New York with his new wife, Catherine Deneuve. Bailey was once asked whether his photo sessions ever got as sexy as the one between Hemmings and Veruschka. 'When I was lucky,' he replied.

The shoot for the film began in April 1966 and wherever the filmmakers went they left their mark on London. Antonioni thought the roads were a bit grey in Woolwich and had them painted black, and it was said that even pigeons were dyed so they were just the right sort of pigeons. The Rolls-Royce, once owned by Jimmy Savile, was originally white and the director had that re-sprayed to black. Antonioni once talked of his fastidious attention to detail: 'When I was making *Blow-Up* there was a lot of discussion about the fact that I had a road and a building painted. Antonioni paints the grass, people said. To some degree, all directors paint and arrange or change things on a location, and it amused me that so much was made of it in my case.'[4] Most people thought that Antonioni was only up to his old particular ways when they watched Hemmings drive his Rolls-Royce down a long terrace of Victorian and Edwardian buildings, all painted entirely red. The buildings, however, really were that colour and were made up of dozens of properties all owned by the motorcycle spares company Pride & Clarke, and every one painted red.

The company was founded in 1920 by John Pride and Alfred Clarke and was based on the Stockwell Road for over sixty years. In its heyday the showrooms of 'Snide & Shark', as they were occasionally called, took up a huge stretch of the road and if the *Guinness Book of Records* had ever been interested in motorbike spares counters, they would have featured Pride & Clarke's because it was the longest in the world. With about 2,000 new motorbikes on display plus a good selection of traded-in second hand machines in their showrooms, on a Saturday afternoon, around the time *Blow-Up* was being made, thousands of bikers from all over the country would congregate outside the bright red Pride & Clarke shopfronts.

The contemporary press releases for *Blow-Up* made sure that attention was made to 'the swinging world of fashion, dolly girls, pop groups, beat clubs, models and parties' and one of the best lines in the film is when David Hemmings says to Veruschka at a party: 'I thought you were meant to be in Paris!' to which she stonily replies, 'I am in Paris.' The twenty-six-year-old Veruschka, or Countess Vera Gottliebe Anna Gräfin von Lehndorff-Steinort, to give her full name, was an extremely tall German model, born just before the start of the war in East Prussia. Her father was said to have fainted when the extraordinarily long baby was born, but Veruschka hardly got to know him, as he was executed five years later for his part in the July Assassination Plot against Hitler in 1944. Around the time the film was released she told the press that she now wanted to be a proper actress: 'I should like now to go into the movies,' she said, 'but it is difficult – the men are so small.'[5] The experience of working with Hemmings must have scarred; he was 8 or 9 inches shorter than her 6 feet 4 inches.

The party scene was shot in a house next to the Thames on Cheyne Walk. Owned by the designer Christopher Gibbs, it was full of Moroccan cushions and medieval tapestries. Antonioni paid beautiful people to be extras at £30 each (easily over an average week's wage in 1966),[6] essentially just to get trashed. Paul McCartney once said, 'I remember the word around town was, "There's this guy who's paying money for people to come and get stoned at some place in Chelsea." And of course in our crowd that spread like wildfire ... Everyone was being paid, like blood donors, to smoke pot.'[7]

Kieran Fogarty, in Jonathan Green's *Days In The Life*, remembered the filming of the party scene in *Blow-Up*: 'I was flung into this bedroom in Cheyne Walk ... plonked on the front of this bed with about another nine people on it and Antonioni tossed a couple of kilo bags of grass on the bed and said, "Right, get on with it." It took five days. It just went on and on ... people would stumble out going, "Yeeeaahhh," and go gibbering back. Most of swinging London was there, every deb that was halfway decent looking, and wild they were too. Outrageously dressed, superheavy make-up ...'

One of the reasons the party scene took so long to film was that Veruschka, most of the time, really was in Paris. She would phone the house every few hours saying, 'Tell Michelangelo that my taxi crash ...' Whoever picked up the phone would wander around the house saying, 'It's Veruschka! Her taxi's crashed, she'll be here in five or six hours.' Despite the camera running for almost a week, the scene at the party ended up just 30 seconds long.

Michelangelo Antonioni, who in 1960 won the Special Jury Prize at Cannes with his film *L'Avventura*, wrote an article in that year's December edition of *Films and Filming* entitled 'Eroticism – The Disease of Our Age'. He asked, 'Why are literature and the entertainment arts so thick with eroticism today? It is the more obvious symptom of an emotional sickness.' Six years later, after deciding to take no notice of himself whatsoever, *Blow-Up* became known as the first British mainstream film to show pubic hair, not to mention naked teenage models (including the nineteen-year-old wife of John Barry, Jane Birkin). Not that anyone noticed particularly, as all around the country the public were treated to a 'censored' version of the film, not because the British Board of Film Censors or the local authorities were trying to protect the public's morals, but because the brief moments of nudity, in those more sheltered days, were being trimmed out by projectionists to add to their private collections.

The film was released in March 1967, just as most people, especially in the capital, were getting rather bored with the idea of 'swinging London'. The result of this was mostly bad reviews from the critics in Britain – Peter Evans in the *Daily Express*, after describing Hemmings, aptly, as 'a depraved choirboy', wrote: 'What many people believed was to be some kind of tribute to the vibrant pace-setters turns out to be no less than an epitaph.' He finished by describing the film as 'an unpleasant orgy of self-glorification'.[8] In Europe and America it was often a different story. Richard Schickel in *Life* magazine wrote: 'This movie seems to me one of the finest, most intelligent, least hysterical expositions of the modern existential agony we have yet had on film.' Most of the contemporary reviews talked about the nudity, but none about how Hemmings' photographer treated the women he encountered. Much of it is uncomfortable to watch these days. But it is an enjoyable museum piece that, at least, gives us a good glimpse of groovy sixties London from the eye of an outsider. Additionally, if you want to stop the film at the right moments, you can see, briefly, Michael Palin and a young Janet Street-Porter dancing in stripy Carnaby Street trousers during the Yardbirds nightclub scene.

Four months after *Blow-Up* was premiered at the London Pavilion, the Sexual Offences Act was made law in July 1967. It decriminalised homosexual acts in private between two men, both of whom had to have attained the age of twenty-one. The comments of Roy Jenkins, the Home Secretary at the time, captured the government's attitude: 'Those who suffer from this disability carry a great weight of shame all their lives.' Lord Arran, one of the original proposers of the bill, tried to minimise criticisms by making the qualification to what he called an 'historic' milestone: 'I ask those [homosexuals] to show their thanks by comporting themselves quietly and with dignity ... any form of ostentatious behaviour now or in the future or any form of public flaunting would be utterly distasteful ...'[9]

A few years later the motorcycle business started to change and during the seventies Japanese motorcycle companies such as Suzuki, Honda and Kawasaki took over from the old British and European marques. Alfred Clarke was an astute businessman (the nickname 'shark' wasn't gained for nothing) and the Pride & Clarke firm was sold to Inchcape for about £3 million in 1979. Before the company and the red paint were whitewashed from history, however, the striking red buildings of the Pride & Clarke showrooms had one more brush with fame. In 1977, the former Montrose vocalist Sammy Hagar was in London to record his second solo album at Abbey Road. Known to his fans, but to no one else, as the 'Red Rocker', someone at Capitol Records had the bright idea that the Pride & Clarke shops on the Stockwell Road were perfect for the cover of the so called *Red Album*. So as not to look too downmarket, he was told to stand next to an expensive American car, also coloured red. There is no record of what Sammy Hagar made of the Stockwell Road and there's no record left of the ubiquitous Pride & Clarke shops. Unless you look very, very closely.

David Hemmings astride Veruschka in *Blow-Up*.

Tenor Peter Pears as Quint and child soprano David Hemmings as Miles in the English Opera Group's production of Benjamin Britten's *The Turn Of The Screw*, 13 October 1954. (Denis De Marney/Hulton Archive/Getty Images)

Pride & Clark's Tom Delaney clinches a deal with a mother and her new motorcyclist son, *c.* 1965. (Courtesy of Mortons Archive)

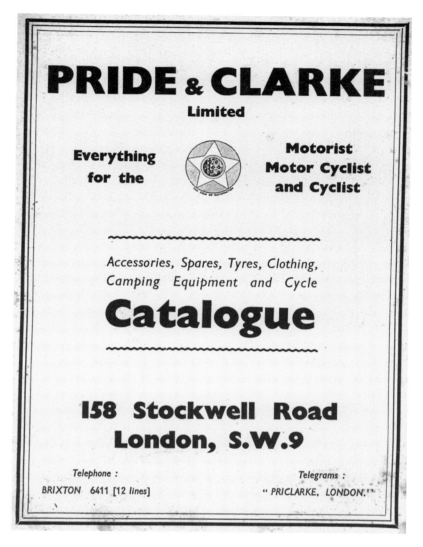

A Pride & Clarke's catalogue cover from 1937.

Sammy Hagar's *Red Album* released by Capitol Records in 1977 and featuring some Pride & Clark red buildings on the Stockwell Road. In 2015 the buildings on the east side of the road visible on the album cover have now been demolished.

CHAPTER 18

Two 'Perfect' Women – Prunella Stack and Gertrud Scholtz-Klink

Just like old friends, Lady Douglas-Hamilton (formerly Prunella Stack) and Gertrud Scholtz-Klink the day after the leader of the Nazi Women's Union had arrived in London, 8 March 1939.

A few months before the beginning of the Second World War, and just nine days before Germany invaded Czechoslovakia, a Focke-Wulf FW 200 Condor landed at Croydon Aerodrome on 7 March 1939. A woman called Gertrud Scholtz-Klink climbed down the aircraft's steps and was greeted warmly by Frau von Dirksen, the wife of the German ambassador. She was dressed almost entirely in black: black halo hat, black coat and skirt, black silk stockings and a pair of low-heeled black shoes. The ensemble was finished with a black cloak which, reported the *Daily Mirror*, 'hid her Swastika badge'. The *Daily Mail*, however, wasn't impressed and thought she could have been mistaken for 'a recently widowed hausfrau from some small German suburb'.[1] Scholtz-Klink spoke to no one and hurried into a waiting German embassy car, which pulled off at great speed out of the aerodrome. Or it would have done if one of the tyres hadn't embarrassingly punctured at the gate. During the fifteen minutes it took to mend, Scholtz-Klink refused to answer any questions fired at her by the waiting press.

At the time Gertrud Scholtz-Klink was considered to be the most important woman in Germany and was the head of the National Socialist Women's Union. Most of the British press covering the visit reported that Hitler had once described the tall, blonde mother of four as the 'perfect Nazi woman'. The *Daily Mail* had been far more complimentary about her during a visit in 1936, calling her a 'brilliant extempore speaker' and describing her as: 'Small and fair, dressed in putty coloured coat and skirt with a school-girlish collar and tie, her face innocent of powder and her almost straight hair braided casually round the back of her head.'[2] The year before, Reuters news agency wrote that Frau Scholtz-Klink fulfilled all the ideals of Nazi womanhood because: 'She's blonde. She's as determined as the most ardent male Nazi. Contends that the twentieth century emancipation of women should yield to the party program: and holds that women should return to the kitchen. She is alone, under forty years old, and wears her abundant hair in Germanic braided plaits.'[3]

Four years later, and a few hours after Scholtz-Klink had landed in south London (Croydon was London's main airport before the war), she was introduced to Lady David Douglas-Hamilton, better known to most people at the time as Prunella Stack, the leader of the 200,000-strong Women's League of Health and Beauty. In 1939, the twenty-five-year-old Prunella was one of the most famous women in Britain and, coincidentally, another 'perfect' woman, as the press often called her 'Britain's Perfect Girl'. The *Daily Mail*, slightly more specifically, described her as 'the most physically perfect girl in the world'. Which was presumably why *Life* magazine reported that year that Prunella Stack had the most photographed legs in Britain.

Scholtz-Klink was introduced to Prunella Stack at a dinner in Claridge's organised by the Anglo-German Fellowship. The organisation had invited Scholtz-Klink over to London, ostensibly, 'for her to study the work done by and for English women' but in reality, despite an almost certain war approaching, the intention of the visit was to remind the British public of the many connections and similarities that existed between the two nations. The AGF had been established in September 1935 after Edward, the Prince of Wales, had made a speech calling for closer understanding of Germany, in an attempt to help safeguard peace in Europe. Lord Mount Temple became chairman, and historian Philip Conwell-Evans and merchant banker Ernest Tennant became the Fellowship's secretaries. Tennant was actually a friend of Joachim von Ribbentrop, the German ambassador to Britain at the time. (Ribbentrop became Hitler's foreign minister in 1938 and was replaced by Von Dirksen). Ribbentrop hated the British with a passion and to many in Britain the feeling was completely mutual. Once in 1937 he greeted King George VI with a Nazi salute. The gesture was completely unexpected and nearly knocked over the king who had moved forward, expecting to shake his hand.[4]

Although Lord Mount Temple stated publicly that belonging to the Fellowship did not assume support for Nazism or anti-Semitism, a lot of people thought otherwise, and the organisation was certainly at times an apologist for both. Companies including Unilever, Price Waterhouse, Dunlop Rubber, Thomas Cook and the Midland Bank had taken out corporate membership, as well as many MPs and members of the House of Lords. The Governor of the Bank of England, Montagu Norman, was also a member. Prunella Stack's husband, Lord David Douglas-Hamilton (they had married in Glasgow five months previously), and her brother-in-law, Douglas Douglas-Hamilton MP, were members of the AGF and both were present that evening in Claridge's. Incidentally, Malcolm, another of the Douglas-Hamilton brothers, although not present that night, was married to Pamela Bowes-Lyon, a cousin of the queen. It's worth noting that this particular dinner celebrating the friendship and similarities between Britain and Germany was held five months after Kristallnacht, the Night of Broken Glass, when during the night of 10/11 November 1938, and with sickening violence, the Nazis burnt over 1,000 synagogues and destroyed 7,000 Jewish businesses throughout Germany and Austria. Ninety-one people were killed by the Stormtroopers and for the first time Jews were arrested on a massive scale, and about 30,000 Jewish men were sent to the Buchenwald, Dachau, and Sachsenhausen concentration camps. *The Times*, despite its editor Geoffrey Dawson being a notable 'appeaser' and a member of the AGF, wrote the day after Kristallnacht under the heading 'A Black Day for Germany': 'No foreign propagandist bent upon blackening Germany before the world could outdo the tale of burnings and beatings, of blackguardly assaults on defenceless and innocent people, which disgraced that country yesterday.'[5]

As head of the National Socialist Women's Union, Gertrud Scholtz-Klink's main task was to promote both male superiority and the importance of childbearing and child-rearing to the 40 million German and Austrian women of whom she was in charge. She once wrote: 'Woman has her place, and man his place. The mannish woman is undesirable in the new Germany nor do we want women to take men's places except in a very few professions where the great sensitiveness and sympathy of woman enables her to do what man cannot do.' The photo-journalist Lorna Hay, writing in the *Daily Mirror* in 1939, described the women she had recently met in Nazi Germany: 'They acquire a married look as soon as they acquire a husband – a sort of umbrella-carrying, pram-pushing, resigned look which has very little of the "Radiant Motherhood" aura about it.'[6] At the meal Frau Scholtz-Klink spoke in German about her responsibilities, and the work done by women in the Reich, while Prunella Stack in replying spoke about the British women's organisations devoted to physical fitness. The Fellowship was utterly unembarrassed by the presence of a leading Nazi, and Scholtz-Klink was made particularly welcome over the next few days. The following evening she again met the twenty-five-year-old Prunella Stack who, with photographers present, was taking an evening class of the Women's League of Health and Beauty at their headquarters at the Mortimer Halls in Great Portland Street. During the remainder of her three-day stay, the German woman leader visited the headquarters of the Mothercraft Training Society at Highgate, the Lapswood Training School for girls at Sydenham Hill and the South London Hospital for Women near Clapham Common. Twelve members of the Women's Committee for Peace and Democracy, however, were not so welcoming and protested against the visit of Hitler's 'Reichsführerin' and walked in single file from Tottenham Court Road to the German embassy in Carlton House Terrace. Some of the posters they carried read: 'Clear Out Scholtz-Klink,' 'Hitler Wants War, We Want Peace,' 'No Nazi Klink for British Women.' One in German read 'Freedom for the Women in Hitler's Concentration Camps.'

The Women's League of Health and Beauty had started life in 1930 led by Prunella Stack's mother – Mary Bagot Stack, usually known as Mollie – a First World War widow who believed, not unreasonably, that rigorous exercise would help get the nation fitter. At the time the word 'league' was in vogue; there was a League of Nations, an Overseas League and a League of Health and Strength for men. Mary once wrote how she had started each day at 6.45 a.m.: 'I jumped out of bed, said my prayers, had a cold bath, opened my windows, stripped off my clothes, and set going on my gramophone the gayest jazz tune I could find, and I exercised around my bedroom in physical bliss. This "skin-airing" should be practised daily with nothing on. I like the goal of beauty, and beauty is unself-conscious.'[7] The league's motto was 'Movement is Life' and its aim was 'Racial Health' (later changed, in 1936, to the more specific 'racial health leading to peace'). Prunella would later maintain that the league wasn't concerned with racial purity or superiority, but with a harmony between 'beauty and peace'. The phrase, however, betrayed an imperialist and racist outlook of the organisation. In the league's prospectus of 1932 it read: 'Women are either the Race-makers, or the Race-breakers. Every human being has started life under some woman's care; they are the "architects of the future"; on them devolves the immense responsibility of racial health.' The 'classlessness' of the league was stressed at all times and not long after the National Government was formed in 1931, Mollie wrote to her members: 'As salaries are down, and prices cut, and the future is in some people's estimation hazardous, it is more than ever necessary for us women to stand together, and prove that all is well, business is as usual, and we fear nothing.' Members' equality was also emphasised by members exercising in the same uniform of rather daring satin knickers and a sleeveless white blouse. Members were advised to shave under their arms, use a deodorant, and to have 'made sure they always had a clean handkerchief stuffed up their left knicker leg'.

To attract publicity, especially as by now Mollie Bagot Stack's health was fading, the league purposely developed and cultivated her daughter as a star and more than encouraged fan-worship for Prunella. The league started to produce gramophone records with music and exercise instructions, but also began performing at public events, including mass exercise demonstrations in Hyde Park and at the Albert Hall; in 1935, the WLHB held a rally at Olympia less than a year after Oswald Moseley's British Union of Fascists had their infamous rally at the same location (where the violent behaviour of the BUF stewards had caused Lord Rothermere and the *Daily Mail* to drop support of the party). In that same year Mollie died of cancer and Prunella, who was still only twenty, took over the organisation. Within three years, and nine months before Gertrud Scholtz-Klink's visit to London, Prunella was leading the league's biggest-ever exhibition of 5,000 enthusiastic members of the Women's League of

Health and Beauty at the Empire Stadium in Wembley. The venue, at that time, was only fifteen years old. It had no roof and was built by Sir Robert McAlpine in 1923 for the British Empire Exhibition that took place the following year. It had been planned that the end of the league's Empire Pageant was going to feature an impressive Greek-influenced athletic dance, with women in white tunics carrying swords, shields and javelins. As soon as the dancers were in place for the finale, chariots emerged from the Wembley tunnel drawn by horses that were supposed to turn right and left and gallop around the cinder athletic track that surrounded the famous turf. The horses, unfortunately, charged straight across the pitch, scattering women in every direction. The careful choreography of the event turned into chaos. Realising that flaming torches were involved, Mr Herbert, Wembley's overweight manager, stood with arms outstretched shouting, 'For God's sake, Ladies! For God sake, take care!' Order was eventually restored and Prunella Stack climbed to the top of a 30-foot-high column and raised her burning torch high above her head. On the pitch below, utterly in awe, the 5,000 rank and file members of the League of Health and Beauty looked up at her, and waves of applause started to echo around the fifteen-year-old stadium.

The seventy-year-old journalist and ex-editor of the *Sunday Express* James Douglas was watching from the uncovered stands. Douglas was infamous at the time for his occasional idealised paeans to British womanhood, but also for his moral stance on lesbianism. He was partly responsible for the banning of D. H. Lawrence's *The Rainbow* and Radclyffe Hall's novel *The Well of Loneliness*, about which he wrote: 'I would rather give a healthy boy or a healthy girl a phial of prussic acid than this novel.' At Wembley Stadium, Douglas was almost overwhelmed by the sight of the healthy Miss Stack: 'The queen of this wonderful spectacle was Miss Prunella Stack. Nothing more exquisite could be imagined than her beauty and her glamour – beyond the dreams of Hollywood.' If Douglas was impressed with the young leader, Tom Driberg, writing anonymously in his *Daily Express* 'William Hickey' column, was not so enamoured. On 1 April 1938 he wrote about a performance at the Albert Hall and described the Women's Health and Beauty dancers as 'Stormtroops' and Prunella Stack as – 'a radiant, strapping, 23-year-old Nordic, with excellent teeth'. Hickey continued, playfully writing: 'She studied new methods of physical training last year in Berlin and "she's frightfully keen on anything German" I was told.'

A worrying government report in 1935 had estimated that over 90 per cent of boys between fourteen and eighteen years of age had never engaged in any form of physical activity whatsoever. After a very disappointing performance in the Berlin Olympics, a delegation from the Board of Education had gone to Germany to have a look at how physical education was being taught there. The delegates particularly admired the 'excellent work' of the Kraft durch Freude (Strength Through Joy) movement. The KdF had started in 1933 and was begun with the aim of breaking down the class divide by making middle-class pursuits available to the masses. This wasn't too far from the aims of Mollie Bagot Stack at around the same time. The KdF provided affordable leisure activities such as concerts, plays, day-trips and holidays and huge specially built cruise ships, such as the *Wilhelm Gustloff* (named after the assassinated Swiss Nazi leader whose wife was once Hitler's secretary), were built specifically for them. What impressed the Board of Education party, however, was the provision of free or cheap physical education and gymnastic classes. After their trip the British delegation concluded that the KdF was: 'Certainly the most agreeable and possibly the most instructive phenomenon of the Third Reich.' Following their return, Neville Chamberlain, then Chancellor of the Exchequer, said: 'In the matter of attention to physical development we may surely learn something from others. Nothing made a stronger impression on visitors to the Olympic games in Germany this year than the splendid condition of German youth.' In 1937, Prunella had been invited to join the board of the National Fitness Council, which had been put together to oversee the government's Physical Training and Recreation Act that was intended to transform the non-splendid condition of British youth, and 'to make Britain an A1 nation'. A 'Keep Fit' campaign was a low-key, relatively cheap attempt by the government to prepare discreetly for a war that they knew, even if the Anglo-German Fellowship hoped otherwise, was certainly approaching.

On 15 October 1938, Prunella married a Scottish laird, Lord David Douglas-Hamilton, the youngest son of the 13th Duke of Hamilton. At their first meeting, at the opening of a swimming pool, he impressed on her that he was keen to start a fitness summer school in the Highlands. As he said goodbye, he took her hand and examined her fingernails. 'I'm glad you don't paint them,' he said. 'I hate artificiality.' Douglas Hamilton had German and Austrian friends (his best man was Prince Ernst August of Hanover) and before their wedding the couple went on holiday in Austria. It was just days after the 8th Army of the German Wehrmacht had marched into the country to be greeted by cheering Austrians, Nazi flags and salutes. Prunella, in her autobiography, described the bands of Hitler Youth marching through the streets shouting 'Jeder Deutsche stimmt mit "ja". Nur ein Schwein stimmt mit "Nein"'. (Every German votes with 'yes'. Only a swine votes with 'no'.) Prunella also visited Germany that summer of 1938, after the league had been invited to participate in a Physical Education Congress sponsored by Kraft durch Freude. It was reported in the British press that at one point she gave a Nazi salute. Prunella and the rest of the League women stayed on the Kraft durch Freude ocean cruise ship *Wilhelm Gustloff*, from which they watched mass demonstrations of German physical culture and folk-dancing. The British Women's League of Health and Beauty performed twice – 'their neat black and white uniforms and slim figures contrasted with the generous build of the blonde German girls', Prunella wrote later. On the ship she was introduced to the Reichsportsführer, Herr von Tschammer und Osten, Dr Ley – the leader of Kraft durch Freude – and even Himmler. In Germany, Prunella concluded that the German girl is encouraged to be an athlete but is not 'figure-conscious'.

A few months after the Anglo-German dinner at Claridge's, Germany invaded Poland, and the Second World War began. In September it was reported in the British press that Scholtz-Klink had recently said to her 40 million charges that: 'German women must now deny themselves all luxury and enjoyment.' Hilde Merchant, in the *Daily Express,* joined the propaganda war and suggested that the Nazi women leader should be taken on a shopping tour of the West End to show her the contrasting way the British women were responding to the war:

> Frau Scholtz-Klink would have seen women at the cosmetics counter spending twenty minutes choosing a new shade of lipstick. A customer was balancing one of the high Hussar felts on the top of her curls. It made her chuckle – 'Well that's a tonic anyway. Even Hitler would be enchanted.' One of the customers in a green, yellow and petunia check suit was swinging round in front of the glass. She turned to the saleswoman and said: 'Bit bright, isn't it? Still, no sense in being gloomy.'[8]

The league's impressive pre-war membership – it had reached 177,000 women in 1937 – started to plummet when many of its women were either called up or had no time for classes. Now pregnant, Prunella moved to Dorset, while her husband, as had all his brothers, joined the RAF. In May 1941 Rudolf Hess, the deputy Nazi leader, flew to Scotland in the supposed hope that he could broker an amazing diplomatic victory by securing peace between Germany and Britain. After parachuting from his plane, and having been captured by a local farmer, Hess said he had come to meet the Duke of Hamilton – the former Anglo-German Fellowship member –

whom, he insisted, he had met in Berlin in 1936. Indeed Douglas, Prunella Stack's brother-in-law, who would have only just become the duke after his father had died, had been in Berlin during the summer Olympics as part of a multi-party parliamentary group. While in Berlin, Douglas-Hamilton had met Hitler and Göring at a grand dinner hosted by Von Ribbentrop – the German ambassador to Britain. The Duke of Hamilton always said that he had never personally met Hess, and indeed threatened to sue anyone who suggested otherwise.

On 30 January 1945 the German ship *Wilhelm Gustloff,* by now a floating army barracks, was sunk in the Baltic Sea by three Soviet torpedoes. Her days as a luxurious cruise-liner had long gone, and as a troop ship she had been bringing back refugees, military personnel and Nazi officials from East Prussia after they had been surrounded by the Red Army. It has been estimated that 9,400 men, women and children died after the ship sank in just forty-five minutes, making it the worst maritime disaster ever. The previous year in 1944, Prunella's husband Lord David Douglas-Hamilton died after his Mosquito plane crashed with engine failure, just short of the runway at RAF Benson. Like her mother, Prunella was widowed at the age of just thirty. After the war she remarried and moved to South Africa with her second husband but returned for Queen Elizabeth's coronation in 1953, accompanied by a controversial (in South Africa) multi-racial group of league members. Three years later she returned to London with her two sons for good.

At end of the war, in the summer of 1945, Scholtz-Klink was briefly detained in a Soviet prisoner of war camp but quickly escaped. With her third husband, SS officer August Heissmeyer, she went into hiding but almost three years later in February 1948, the *Daily Express* reported that Princess Pauline of Wurttemberg-Baden 'once famous for smoking strong cigars, has been arrested by the Americans for harbouring Nazis. Hitler's 'Perfect Woman' Gertrud Scholtz-Klink was arrested on one of her estates'.[9] A French military court sentenced Scholz-Klink to just eighteen months on the charge of forging documents. In May 1950 a review sentenced her for an additional thirty months. She was released in 1953 and then had forty-six years of freedom and died, aged ninety-seven, in 1999. She remained all her life an avid supporter of the National Socialist ideology.

The Women's League of Health and Beauty continues to this day, although now with the more modern sounding name of the Fitness League. Prunella died in December 2010 at the age of ninety-six, outlasting by seven years the old Wembley Stadium where she had performed with her Women's League of Health and Beauty so memorably sixty-five years before.

Prunella coaching at a
Women's League of Health
and Beauty class at the
Mortimer Halls on Great
Portland Street, April 1939.

Mary Bagot Stack,
Prunella's mother and
founder of the Women's
League of Health and
Beauty.

Above: A Women's League of Health and Beauty rally in Hyde Park, May 1932.

Right: Prunella Stack at a Hyde Park rally in 1935. (Courtesy of Sarah Moss)

Left: A member of the Women's League of Health and Beauty practicing her exercises in the garden, May 1935. (Courtesy of Sarah Moss)

Below: Sunbathing on the deck of the *Wilhelm Gustloff* in 1938, the year that Prunella Stack stayed on board along with her Women's League delegation. The liner had been built the previous year for the Nazi Kraft durch Freude (Strength Through Joy) organisation. The ship was originally intended to be named *Adolf Hitler* but was named after Wilhelm Gustloff, a leader of the National Socialist Party's Swiss branch, who had been assassinated in 1936.

CHAPTER 19

Mary Quant, the Mini-Skirt and the Chelsea Palace on the King's Road

Mary Quant and Alexander Plunket Green, 1965. (© Pictorial Press Ltd/Alamy)

These days the King's Road looks not unlike many other high streets across the country, albeit a bit posher. If you stroll down the road you'll see, just like anywhere else, Boots, McDonald's and the ubiquitous coffee-shop chains. In fact, always a trend-setter, the King's Road was where Starbucks chose to open its first ever British coffee shop in 1998. But the King's Road has earned its notoriety for setting rather more exciting trends than over-priced milky coffee, of course, and it was here that perhaps the most celebrated fashion statement of the last century really took off – the mini-skirt.

Everybody knows that Mary Quant invented the mini-skirt. Except that she didn't. In reality nobody really knows for sure who first produced the diminutive garment. Some say it was John Bates, famous for memorably dressing Diana Rigg in *The Avengers*. Others say it was the French designer André Courrèges, although Quant would later write: 'Maybe Courrèges did do mini-skirts first, but if he did, no one wore them.' There is no doubt that skirts were getting shorter each year in the early to mid-sixties, but this was almost certainly to do with technological advances that enabled tights to be produced relatively cheaply rather than anything else. When Quant started to produce her short, sharp mini-skirts cut in the hipster style, she realised that the traditional stocking manufacturers didn't have the right machinery. Initially she had to get theatrical clothing manufacturers to make her bespoke tights (or 'stocking-tights' as she was still calling them in 1967). By 1965 Quant got the London-based Swaren Singh Curry to make tights for her company, as he was prepared to buy the special, expensive pantyhose machinery from America to produce them for her. Within ten years of the mini-skirt becoming ubiquitous on the King's Road, tights came to completely dominate the hosiery market and forced the many stockings producers who failed to respond to changing fashions out of the market. Quant later said that: 'It was the girls on the King's Road who invented the mini. I was making easy, youthful, simple clothes, in which you could move, in which you could run and jump and we would make them the length the customer wanted. I wore them very short and the customers would say, "Shorter, shorter."'[1] It is also often said that Quant invented the word 'mini-skirt' by naming her version of the short skirt after her favourite car – the Mini. Even this isn't exactly true, and again no one really knows the beginning of the word but it's interesting to note that in Quant's first autobiography *Quant by Quant*, published in 1966, the word 'mini-skirt' isn't even mentioned.

Although it was the first British Starbucks that opened at 128 King's Road in 1998, it wasn't the first coffee shop on the premises. This was the

Fantasie coffee bar, which opened at the beginning of 1955, a year or so after Italian actress Gina Lollobrigida opened the Moka Bar in Frith Street, which was the first coffee house in London to install the revolutionary Gaggia espresso machine. The Fantasie, however, was still one of the first new-style coffee bars in London, and certainly outside Soho. The newly 'invented' teenager, too young for pubs, loved the new coffee bars. The author John Sutherland once wrote: 'The Gaggia machine, a great burbling, wheezing, spluttering monster, would grudgingly excrete some bitter caffeinated essence. It would be swamped with steamed-milk foam and dusted with chocolate to form its "cappuccino" hood ... Glass cups and brown sugar (lots of it) were de rigueur. Frankly, 50s espresso was no taste thrill. But it felt smart as hell.'[2]

The Fantasie coffee bar was owned by an ex-solicitor called Archie McNair who lived above the café. There was also a photographic studio in the property used by a young team of photographers, one of whom was the young Anthony Armstrong-Jones later, of course, to become Lord Snowdon, the husband of Princess Margaret ('Inigo Jones, out-'e-come Snowdon', as he once said). It was at the Fantasie that McNair and his close friends, Mary Quant and her boyfriend Alexander Plunket Greene, who he had met drinking at Finch's on the Fulham Road, worked on a plan to open a boutique on the King's Road. Quant described the proposed shop in *Quant by Quant*: 'It was to be a bouillabaisse of clothes and accessories ... sweaters, scarves, shifts, hats, jewellery and peculiar odds and ends.' Initially McNair had asked Quant and Plunket Greene to help him start up Fantasie but they both declined, thinking that coffee bars were to be a flash in the pan. It was a decision they'd soon regret, as this particular coffee bar became crowded every night with a large group of young people who would become known as the Chelsea Set. In the evening vodka and whisky was occasionally (and illegally) added to the drinks, and a local Chelsea-based band called the Chas McDevitt Skiffle Group regularly played, both of which, in their different ways, contributed to the big success of the café. Quant wrote about the 'Chelsea Set' of the time as a bohemian world of 'painters, photographers, architects, writers, socialites, actors, con-men, and superior tarts', although the author Len Deighton held a different opinion, describing the same people as 'a nasty and roaring offshoot of the deb world'. The Chelsea Set, at least as described by Quant, was not exactly new and the King's Road had long been peopled by an unconventional and free-spirited crowd: 'long-haired Chelsea', E. M. Forster had called them back in 1910. Deighton was more upset about how the new moneyed crowd ended up replacing 'an amiable mixture of arty rich and bohemian poor', most of whom were eventually forced to move out of the best parts of Chelsea beyond World's End and even to, God forbid, Fulham. Deighton wasn't the first to make this complaint about Chelsea. In the 1920s some of the working-class streets were being demolished for expensive new flats, and many of the mews stables were being converted into 'perverted coachmen's homes' at 'a quite aristocratic rent' wrote H. G. Wells in 1925.[3] In 1955 McNair and Plunket Greene managed to buy the basement and ground-floor of Markham House on the corner of Markham Square and the King's Road. It was next door to a pub called the Markham Arms that had seen better days (it has long since closed and in 2015 is a Santander bank) but was where the Soviet spies Anthony Blunt and Kim Philby re-established contact after a three-year wait following the flight of Guy Burgess and Donald Maclean to the Soviet Union in 1951.

With the help of £5,000 recently inherited by APG, a sum matched by McNair, they paid just £8,000 for the freehold. The shop, which they called Bazaar, opened in November 1955 and it was an almost immediate success. Within ten days they hardly had any merchandise left. 'It was almost a violent success,' Quant remembered. 'People were sort of three-deep outside the window. The Royal Court Theatre people were mad about what we were doing. And it was very much the men who were bringing their girlfriends around and saying, "This is terrific. You must have some of this!"' This quick popularity was partly to do with naively selling their clothes and accessories too cheaply, thus not only losing money on everything they sold but also upsetting the local shops and their wholesalers by undercutting the fixed retail prices. Initially they made next to no money – Quant was still buying her material from Harrods, not realising there were such things as wholesalers. It wasn't long, however, before the trio of entrepreneurs realised that almost by luck they were on to a huge thing: 'We were in at the beginning of a tremendous renaissance in fashion. It was not happening because of us. It was simply that, as things turned out, we were a part of it.' Ernestine Carter, an authoritative and influential fashion journalist and women's editor of the *Sunday Times*, once wrote: 'It is given to a fortunate few to be born at the right time, in the right place, with the right talents. In recent fashion there are three: Chanel, Dior, and Mary Quant.' A fashion writer for the *Daily Express* wrote, 'Suddenly someone had invented a style of dressing which we realised we had wanted for ages. Comfortable, simple, no waists, good colours and simple fabrics. It gave anyone wearing them a sense of identity with youth and adventure and brightness.'[4]

Quant may have been born in the right place and at the right time, but Mary Quant and APG both worked incredibly hard. Mary once said, 'Business is my whole life. While I'm working I keep going on black coffee and cornflakes. Then I go to bed and sleep for three days.'[5] They had also opened a restaurant in the basement of Markham House called Alexander's, and it didn't take long before it became the place to be seen in Chelsea. Incredibly, at this point they were still both twenty-one. Despite the hard work, according to Quant, the couple always found time to visit the music hall shows at the Chelsea Palace theatre down the road from Bazaar. The shows were often slightly risqué in nature and in 1955 the theatre was putting on shows with titles such as, *Fanny Get your Fun*, *Folies Can-Can* and *Paris After Dark*. One of the shows put on in 1955, the year that Bazaar opened, was called *Burlesque* and was produced by Paul Raymond at the beginning of his career. It featured twenty separate acts such as *Galaxy of Glamour,* which featured Miss Blandish and Her Famous Moving Nudes, and *Mambo Mexicana*, which involved Billy and Brian Denis with June, Kenny Noble, The Sex-Appeal Girls, and The Glamorous Nudes and Ensemble. Towards the end of the show were *Stars of Sex-Appeal*, which included 'Simone Silva's Nude Pose, from the waist upwards, with Robert Mitchum'; 'Hedy Lamarr's Pose from the film *Ecstasy*'; and 'Marilyn Monroe's Internationally Known Calendar Pose'. In case any of the audience would actually think internationally famous movie actresses would be posing semi-nude at the worn out old Chelsea Palace, each of these acts came with a warning that 'These are not intended to depict or impersonate the Films Stars themselves'. At the end of the programme, in bold lettering, it stated, 'In the interest of Public Health, this Theatre is disinfected throughout with JEYE'S FLUID'. 'We went once a week,' said Mary, 'the Chelsea Palace chorus girls wore very naughty fur bikini knickers.'

The terracotta-clad Chelsea Palace of Varieties was situated at numbers 232–242 King's Road, on the corner of Sydney Street, and was originally a music hall designed by the noted theatre designers Oswald Wilson and Charles Long in 1903. By 1923 it started to be used as a cinema as well as showing straight plays and ballets but within two years, in 1925, it was taken over by Variety Theatres Consolidated, and from then on it presented mostly live theatre. During the latter part of 1956, the Chelsea Palace ran a Radio Luxembourg talent competition and it was won for four weeks in a row by the Fantasie coffee shop regulars – the Chas McDevitt Skiffle Group. McDevitt described his flat in Chelsea at the time: 'The flat I had on the King's Road was an ideal pad in an ideal position. It provided a haven for many an itinerant jazzer, visiting American folkies, and unsuspecting embryo groupies.'

During the Chelsea Palace talent contests McDevitt met a twenty-year-old Glaswegian singer called Anne Wilson, whose stage name was Nancy Whiskey. Within six months Nancy Whiskey and McDevitt's skiffle group had recorded a single called 'Freight Train'. To much amazement, not least by the people who made the record, it actually ended up in the charts on both sides of the Atlantic. They even appeared on the *Ed Sullivan Show* in the US alongside the Everly Brothers, six years before the Beatles' famous appearance. With his new success, Chas McDevitt opened his own coffee bar in Berwick Street in Soho which he called, of course, the Freight Train Coffee Bar.

In 1956 the Chelsea Palace was struggling and at the end of November, after fifty-three years, its life as a music hall came to an end. Not long before it closed, and while his wife Mary Ure was in rehearsals for Arthur Miller's *A View From the Bridge*, which would open at the Comedy Theatre in October, John Osborne decided to go to the Palace and see Max Wall, who was headlining a variety bill. He was just in time to catch an act lower on the bill performing an impression of Charles Laughton in his famous role as Quasimodo. Osborne later wrote about the experience: 'A smokey green light swirled over the stage and awesome banality prevailed for some theatrical seconds, the drama and poetry, the belt and braces of music hall holding up an epic.'[6] Osborne saw a sort of odd heroic nobility in the awful talentless performer who came on stage night after night to almost certain derision. The visit to the Chelsea Palace that evening inspired *The Entertainer*, his play about Archie Rice, the failing music hall artiste. When Laurence Oliver had been chosen for the role, Osborne decided to take him on a tour of the music halls in London, or what was left of them. Osborne hadn't realised that when he was writing his play about the dying music hall, places like the Met in Edgware Road and Collins' in Islington were actually all about to be closed. Osborne took Olivier to Collins' where he had wanted him to see a Scottish comedian called Jack Radcliffe who performed a death-bed scene. Taking Britain's greatest classical actor to watch a sketch about death by a 'dying' comic in front of a gloomy, melancholic audience would, he thought, be excellent research for Olivier, who, to put it in Osborne's words, 'could hardly have witnessed such a farewell to hope and dignity'. Radcliffe wasn't performing that night but they did, however, catch a Scottish performer called Scott Sanders who, Osborne once recalled, sang: '"Rolling round the world, waiting for the sunshine and hoping things will turn out right," which he played on a series of pots and pans hanging on a barrow. He was loud, brisk, seldom funny and looked as if he knew it.'[7] Sanders told jokes such as: 'I was in pictures once, at Elstree. The picture was *The Way of All Flesh*, I played a Rissole.' He would speed through his act as fast as he could before retreating to the pub next door. In 1956 an H. G. Dove wrote to *The Stage* describing one of Sanders' performances at Collins' in 1939: 'Making his entrance to gentle rising to boisterous reception from the top shelf, downed tools or (tinker barrow) centre stage, and let 'em have it. "I'm not here for the price of a kip. At the Palladium in a fortnight's time." He then walked off.'[8]

The Entertainer opened the following year at the Royal Court Theatre. Osborne always thought that Laurence Olivier had overshadowed the original production and seventeen years later decided to produce the play himself; this time he cast Max Wall, who he had gone to see all those years ago at the Chelsea Palace. At that time, in 1974, Max Wall was bankrupt and living in a bedsit. His wife, twenty-six years his junior, had just left him, leaving a note that said, 'You will end up in one room, alone, with nothing.' Wall's performance opened to mixed reviews and in *Tatler*, Sheridan Morley wrote that the production was 'a massive disappointment, rather like seeing King Lear played by a real old king. Mr Wall contrived to be … too great a comedian, so one could never understand what he was doing in a tatty nudie show'. The *Daily Mail*'s Roderick Gilchrist completely disagreed and considered that this made the casting all the more apt: 'Max Wall, with those sad, bloodhound eyes and face like a well-hammered coconut, is not merely acting – but living again experiences from his own life.'

In 1957, while *The Entertainer* was still on at the Royal Court, the Chelsea Palace was renamed the Chelsea Granada and was to become a cinema. However, almost immediately, the building was leased to Granada Television, within the same company, and the stalls in the theatre were replaced by a studio floor. To augment Granada's specially built studio complex in Manchester, it became Studio 10 for the next eight years. Sidney Bernstein, who with his brother Cecil owned Granada, which had recently won the franchise license to broadcast commercial television in the north west of England, numbered their studios with just even numbers, simply so it appeared that they owned more studios than they did. The Chelsea Palace, or Studio 10 as it was now called, was actually the last of the London theatres to be converted into a TV studio. The Shepherd's Bush Empire was already a BBC studio, while Associated Television had already converted the Hackney Empire and the Wood Green Empire.

Incidentally, it was at the Wood Green Empire, in 1918, that the Chinese magician known as Chung Ling Soo was tragically shot and fatally injured while performing his infamous act that involved catching a bullet between his teeth. His last words were: 'Oh my God. Something's happened. Lower the curtain.' It shocked everyone. Not so much that he had been shot, but that he wasn't Chinese and spoke perfect English.

Studio 10 was used for the long-running and extremely popular comedy series *The Army Game*, which ran for five years from 1957. An incredible 154 episodes were broadcast, and the cast included many that would become household names for decades to come. Alfie Bass, Geoffrey Palmer, Bill Fraser, Dick Emery and Bernard Bresslaw were all regulars, while the writers included a young John Junkin, Marty Feldman and Barry Took. Another very popular show that came from Granada's King's Road studio was the variety show called *Chelsea at Nine*. It ran for three series and purposely took advantage of the studio's location in the capital to feature artists that were appearing in the West End. This meant that occasionally you would get one of the finest jazz musicians on earth coming straight on after a comedian who would struggle to get on the end of a bill in Skegness. Ella Fitzgerald once had to introduce an act, which was appearing after her on the show, as 'the world's greatest song-and-dance spoons man'.[9] Every time she tried the link she started to laugh and simply couldn't do it.

Although not exactly in the tradition of the risqué burlesque shows at the Chelsea Palace, *Chelsea at Nine* became the first television programme to feature bare breasts on British television, albeit accidentally. The African dance group called the Ballets Africains had rehearsed earlier in the day fully clothed and no one checked what they were going to be wearing for their actual performance. Bruce Grimes, an art director on the show, was in the control room at the time and remembered that, 'Suddenly all the cameras started pointing at the floor or on odd bits of scenery: The director was tearing his hair out, and the cameraman said, "Well, they've got nothing on, they've got bare tits." The producer was there, and the director just said, "What do we do? Do you pull it, or what?" And the producer, you know, he had seconds to make up his mind, said, "Well, we'll call it 'ethnic'. Go for it." So the director said, "Alright, lift the cameras up, show what's going on." And it went out. There was a hell of a fuss, you know.'[10]

On 23 February 1959 a very gaunt and very unsteady Billie Holiday was helped up on stage and performed three songs for *Chelsea at Nine*: 'Strange Fruit', 'Please Don't Talk About Me When I'm Gone' and 'I Loves You Porgy'. The performance proved to be among the last she ever made and she died just five months later of cirrhosis of the liver while, courtesy of the New York police, handcuffed to a hospital bed in New York on 17 July. Luckily for us the shows were by then being 'Ampex-ed' by Granada but unfortunately only 'Strange Fruit' and 'I Loves You Porgy' still survive. The Chelsea Palace was demolished by developers in 1966, soon after Granada had vacated the premises. 'A squalid block of shops replaced it,' said John Osborne years later. One of which, although not particularly squalid, was a branch of Heal's. From 2015, however, the building has become a Metro Bank.

'Don't clap too loud, we're all in a very old building,' said Archie Rice in *The Entertainer*, but the Chelsea Palace was only sixty-three years old when it was demolished in 1966. London, and especially the King's Road, was a very different place ten years after John Osborne went to see Max Wall and Mary Quant had opened Bazaar. At about the same time as the wrecking ball started demolishing the old music hall, the mini-skirt was ubiquitous on the King's Road, and soon pretty well everywhere else. In the ten years since she and APG had opened her shop, Mary Quant had become an international success and was now making upwards of £5 million a year. By the mid-sixties much of the King's Road was now full of trendy clothes boutiques with names that made Bazaar sound rather conservative. The old bootmakers, butchers and greengrocers that had been there for a century or so were now shops called Blast Off, Clobber, Granny Takes a Trip, Ad Hoc, Gloryhole, Forbidden Fruit and Mr Freedom.

In 1967 Loudon Wainwright, father of Loudon Wainwright III and grandfather to Rufus and Martha, was working in London for *Life* magazine. In his column called 'The View From Here' he wrote:

> Until very recently one of my least crucial handicaps has been a sort of built-in propriety which, for example has forced me to avert my eyes whenever I say that a lady was going to have difficulty with her skirt. By difficulty I mean that the skirt was threatening to go up too high – in a chair, in the wind, as its owner disembarked from a taxi. I'm not sure how this propriety has survived the miniskirt fashions ... but a few days of lovely spring weather in London have abolished it forever. The balmy sunshine there brought out the miniskirts in mind-reeling profusion ...[11]

Although Bazaar has now long gone, the next time you're shopping for clothes on the King's Road and you feel like a cup of coffee, nip into the Starbucks, have a good look round, and remind yourself that you're in the building where the Swinging Sixties once started. Albeit in 1955.

The Fantasie coffee bar at 128 King's Road, the later location of the UK's first Starbucks. Screengrab from *Food for a Blush* (or *Food for a Blluuusssshhhhh!*, as the on-screen title puts it). It was shot mostly in 1955 but not completed until 1959 and directed by Elizabeth Russell.

Postcard of the Chelsea Palace, *c.* 1905.

In late 1956, while recording the song 'Freight Train' for Oriole Records, the studio owner Bill Varley suggested to Chas McDevitt that they should add a female singer. The folk singer Nancy Whiskey was invited to join the group, and they re-recorded the song with her vocals. The record was a hit in the UK in 1957 and reached number 5 in the UK Singles Chart.

The Chelsea Palace in 1955. (John Bignell, courtesy of the Royal Borough of Kensington and Chelsea, Family and Children's Service)

A show at the Chelsea Palace in 1955, maybe one of Paul Raymond's. (John Bignell, courtesy of the Royal Borough of Kensington and Chelsea, Family and Children's Service)

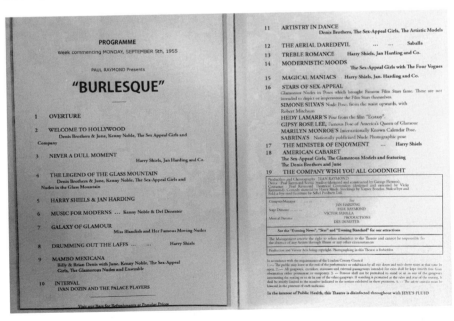

Programme for Paul Raymond's burlesque show at the Chelsea Palace, September 1955.

Right: Heals on the King's Road in 2013. The shop has also now gone, but the building is where the Chelsea Palace once stood opposite Chelsea Town Hall.

Below: The King's Road in 2013 showing where Mary Quant's Bazaar was once situated and, next door, the Markham Arms.

CHAPTER 20

Winifred Atwell – The Honky Tonk Woman

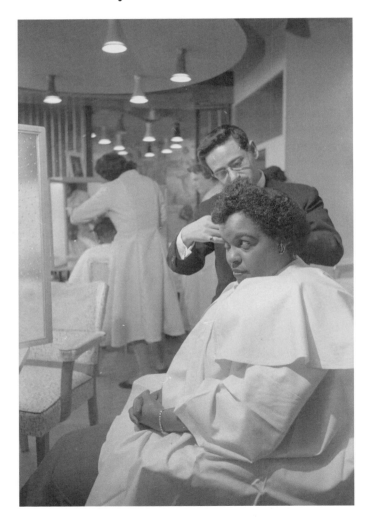

Winifred Atwell in her salon in Brixton, April 1957. (Lee Tracey/BIPs/Getty Images)

At around eight o'clock on the Saturday evening of 14 April 1981, a Molotov cocktail was thrown through a window of The George Hotel on the corner of Effra Parade and Railton Road in Brixton. It was the second night of the Brixton riots and it had been no coincidence that the pub had been targeted – the landlord was infamous in the sixties and seventies for his treatment of local black people and he had been reported to the Race Relations Board for his behaviour. In the 1970s the pub had been the subject of several local marches, and *The South London Press*, not usually known to be at the vanguard of progressive racial politics at that time, wrote that the arson was 'undoubtedly an act of revenge for years of racial discrimination'. It was relatively unnoticed that down from The George on the other side of Effra Parade most of the properties in a small block of shops on Railton Road were also destroyed during the rioting. This included a plumber's merchants at 82A Railton Road, on the corner of Chaucer Road. The building all but burnt down during the night and would eventually be demolished.

Tension in Brixton had heightened earlier that April mainly as a reaction to Operation Swamp 81 – a particularly heavy-handed Metropolitan Police operation designed to reduce crime in the locality. Within six days, mainly through the heavy use of the 'Sus' law (actually a very old law and officially known as the 1824 Vagrancy Act), over a thousand people had been stopped and searched and eighty-two arrested. The operation, presumably intentionally by the Met, was named after a word Margaret Thatcher uttered during a 1978 *World in Action* interview about immigration: 'If there is any fear that it [Britain] might be swamped, people are going to react and be rather hostile to those coming in.' To be fair, and this is not often remembered, she also said in the interview, albeit patronisingly maybe, that 'in many ways [minorities] add to the richness and variety of this country'. It certainly isn't remembered now, and it's doubtful if it was noticed in 1981, but the building at 82A Railton Road that burnt down that night once housed possibly the first black women's hairdressers in London. Situated opposite the drinking club The Glass Bucket, it had opened in 1956 and was called The Winifred Atwell Salon.

In the mid-1950s Winifred Atwell was undoubtedly one of Britain's most popular entertainers. Trinidadian-born, her undisguised cheerful personality and well-played honky-tonk ragtime music brightened up many a 'knees up' in those pre-rock 'n' roll days. In fact when Atwell reached number one in 1954 with 'Let's Have Another Party', she became the first black musician in this country to sell a million records. Between 1952 and 1959 when 'Piano Party' reached number ten, she had eleven top-ten hits and is still the most successful female instrumentalist to have ever featured in the British pop charts. At the peak of her popularity her hands were seen as so valuable that they were insured for £40,000, and it was said – and how many of us would like to sign a legal document like this – that there was a clause in the insurance contract stipulating that she must never wash the dishes.

Atwell was born in Tunapuna, near Port of Spain, in Trinidad around 1914 (most sources say that year but according to her marriage certificate it was 1915 and on her grave it says 1910). She had been playing Chopin recitals since the age of six. After the war she went to study music in New York under the pianist Alexander Borovsky, but arrived in London in 1946 to study classical music piano at the Royal Academy of Music. In the evenings she supported herself by playing ragtime and boogie-woogie at clubs and hotels around London. She had learnt this genre of music playing for servicemen during the war in Trinidad. A year after Atwell arrived in England she married Reginald 'Lew' Levisohn, who gave up his stage career as a variety comedian and became her manager. She was almost groomed for stardom by him and he encouraged her to play her piano more and more in the rollicking upbeat honk-tonk style that was almost completely her own.

In 1948 Winifred was booked at a Sunday charity concert at the London Casino (originally, and now once again, called the Prince Edward Theatre) in Old Compton Street in place of the glamorous actress and singer Carole Lynne, who had been feeling unwell. The impresario Bernard Delfont, who was married to Lynne, had heard from the agent Keith Devon about a 'coloured girl, a pianist, who has the makings of a star'. Winifred Atwell, to huge applause, ended up taking several curtain calls that night and was immediately signed up by Delfont to a long-term contract. In 1951 she signed a record contract with Decca, and the following year she was playing in front of the new Queen Elizabeth at the 1952 Royal Variety Performance. Winifred completed her act that evening with 'Britannia Rag' – a piece of music she had written specially for the occasion. It received a rapturous reception, not least from the Queen, and it was to be her first big hit, reaching number five over Christmas and into the New Year.

During her live performances Atwell brought together the two worlds of her piano playing and would usually open her act with a piece of classical music played on a grand piano, but after a short while would then change over to what she and her audiences came to know as her 'other piano' – a beaten up and specially de-tuned upright that had been bought by her husband in a Battersea junk-shop for just 30 shillings. The small journey across the stage between the two pianos encapsulated perfectly how she managed to turn her career from a trained European classical piano player to the more, despite being Trinidadian, 'authentic' black American rhythmic music for which she was now famous. In 1953 a piano tuner at Blackpool's Hippodrome Theatre came across Atwell's old battered piano and 'kindly' tuned it to play perfectly. To much consternation, no one could be found to de-tune it and when Atwell performed that evening on a perfectly tuned upright piano, the story, literally, became front page news.[1]

The writer and economist C. B. Purdom once wrote that London in the fifties was 'dulled by such extensive drabness, monotony, ignorance and wretchedness that one is overcome by distress'.[2] It isn't particularly difficult to see why Winifred Atwell became so popular at that time. The very successful record producer, lyricist and A&R manager Norman Newell once wrote: 'Winnie was around at the right time. Immediately after the war there was a feeling of depression and unhappiness, and she made you feel happy. She had this unique way of making every note she played sound a happy note. She was always smiling and joking. When you were with her you felt you were at a party, and that was the reason for the success of her records.'[3]

In March 1956, and now at the height of her fame, Atwell had her second number one with 'Poor People of Paris'. A few months later she was due to make her second appearance at the Royal Variety Performance, which traditionally took place on the first Monday of November. Four hours before the curtain rose, and to the shock of the still-rehearsing all-star cast which included Laurence Olivier and Vivien Leigh, but also Sabrina backed by the Nitwits, the show was suddenly cancelled. The day before, on Sunday 4 November, the *Observer* had written about the Suez Crisis, declaring that the action against Egypt had 'endangered the American Alliance and NATO, split the Commonwealth, flouted the United Nations, shocked the overwhelming majority of world opinion and dishonoured the name of Britain'. Later that Sunday afternoon, at a huge rally at Trafalgar Square, attended by 10,000 people or more who were demonstrating under the banner 'Law not War', Aneurin Bevan told the crowd: 'We are stronger than Egypt but there are other countries stronger than us. Are we prepared to accept for ourselves the logic we are applying to Egypt?' To the crowd, who were now loudly applauding, he continued: 'If Sir Anthony is sincere in what he says – and he may be – then he is too stupid to be Prime Minister.'[4] After the speech many of the crowd started streaming down Whitehall towards the prime minister's residence, all the while chanting: 'Eden Must Go, Eden Must Go.' The crowd were met with a ring of police protecting Downing Street, and many demonstrators became bottled in and had nowhere to go. In the confusion, some mounted police charged down Whitehall and rode right into the demonstrators, scattering them everywhere.

The next day the royal family were advised that it was for the best that the Variety Show was cancelled. Bernard Delfont wrote in his autobiography that after the cast were informed: 'Winifred Atwell gave an impromptu party in an attempt to lift our spirits.'[5] Whether the Queen's spirits also needed lifting we don't know, but Winifred performed later at a private performance for the Queen and Princess Margaret at Buckingham Palace where she played 'Roll Out the Barrel' and other royal favourites.

In 1956 Winifred opened her hairdressing salon on Railton Road in Brixton. She had initially lived nearby although by now she lived with Lew in the more salubrious Hampstead, but Atwell still kept property in Brixton and a very young Sharon Osbourne, then Sharon Arden, along with her father Don 'Mr Big' Arden – subsequent manager of The Small Faces, ELO, and Black Sabbath, among others – lived in a house rented from her at 68 Angell Road. Osborne wrote about the property as being typical of the area: 'Our house was large and old, with six steps leading up from the pavement and pillars on either side. At one time it must have been quite grand, but by the fifties the plaster was peeling off, and once you got inside everywhere was dingy, drafty and damp.'[6] Sharon's mother was renting the house as theatrical digs and had met Don when he was a singer and had come to stay in 1950. Six weeks later they were married. Sharon talks of the Brixton she knew as a child in her autobiography:

> In the fifties and early sixties, Brixton was where all the variety artists lived, comedians, singers, ventriloquists, acrobats, entertainers. Pre-TV, variety was the only entertainment there was for ordinary people, and with the Brixton Empress and the Camberwell Palace being less than a mile away, Brixton was the hub. Over the road from us were the fire-eater and a juggler. A dog act, a man called Reg, lived in a caravan in a bombsite behind our road and I used to play with his little girl.[7]

Isabelle Lucas was a Canadian actress originally, who performed in many National Theatre productions, and is remembered as Norman Beaton's wife in *The Fosters* and also for two separate roles in *Eastenders*. Isabelle once spoke about Atwell:

> In those days there were no black salons for black women in this country.

Black women styled their hair in their kitchens. I needed advice on how to straighten and style my hair, but I didn't know any black women in Britain. I had only heard about Winifred Atwell. So one day I looked her up in the London telephone directory and found her listed! I rang her, and to my great surprise she answered! I explained my predicament, and she invited me to her home in Hampstead. It was as easy as that! I met her lovely parents, whom she brought to this country from Trinidad, and Winifred gave me some hair straightening irons.[8]

Now at the height of her career, Winifred Atwell was one of Britain's favourite performers. She had her own series on ATV in 1956, and in the following year another series, this time for the BBC. For a black woman of that era this was nothing short of extraordinary, although unfortunately nothing remains of this mid-fifties TV history and, if any of the shows were recorded, they have long been wiped. By the late fifties, however, tastes in music were rapidly changing, and Winifred Atwell had her last top ten hit in 1959. Her manic style either sounded old-fashioned – the era of rock 'n' roll was now a few years old and not going away – or for people who still liked her style of music, Russ Conway had taken up her baton and would have six top ten hits in 1959 and 1960. Winifred Atwell first toured Australia in 1958 and was particularly popular there. When record sales started to fall in Britain, she spent more and more time in the southern hemisphere. She only started returning to Britain for club bookings and the odd television appearance. By 1961 her hairdressing salon in Railton Road had been sold and the premises became A. C. Skinner & Co. builder's merchants.

In 1961, Sir Robert Menzies, Australia's longest serving prime minister, helpfully defined the difference between apartheid and his 'White Australia' policy, a policy which, at his own admission, kept most 'coloured immigrants out of the country'. Apartheid, he said, 'is a discriminatory policy in respect of people already resident' whereas the 'White Australia' policy was 'discrimination in the admission of persons for permanent residence'.[9] It was in the same year, during a long eighteen-month tour of Australasia, and despite the attitudes of the Australian government at the time, which were nothing short of overt racial discrimination, Atwell realised that she wanted to live permanently in Australia. It was during that long tour, however, that she started to notice how badly Aborigines were being treated. At a concert in Moree in New South Wales she saw that they had been forced to sit apart from white listeners on hard wooden benches. *The Manchester Guardian* also reported at the time that in Rowen in North Queensland, 'Aboriginals had been refused admittance to the theatre when she appeared.

At her request the management had finally left the doors of the theatre open so that the aboriginals could watch and listen from outside.'[10] Ten years later in 1971, Atwell was at last granted permission to stay in the country that she had begun to love. The *Sunday Mirror* reported the news: 'Pianist Winifred Atwell has been given permission to settle down in Australia as an immigrant. She has been told this officially in spite of the country's "White Australia" policy. An Australian immigration official said yesterday that she had been granted residence because she was "of good character and had special qualifications". The immigration minister Mr Phillip Lynch said: "We will not stand in the way of an international artist of such repute."'[11]

Seven years later, in 1978, Atwell's husband Lew died and she never really recovered from the loss. Except for playing the organ every Sunday at her local church she became a virtual recluse in her seafront flat a few miles north of Sydney. In 1981, at around the same time as the flaming bottle of petrol was thrown through the window of what used to be her hair salon on the Railton Road, she was finally granted full Australian citizenship. She died just two years later from a heart attack in Sydney on 27 February 1983.

Above: Winifred Atwell performed at the Pigalle Club on Piccadilly in 1961. She was already spending much of her time in Australia by now.

Opposite: Winifred Atwell in her salon in Brixton, April 1957. (Lee Tracey/BIPs/ Getty Images)

The aftermath of the Brixton Riots, 13 April 1981. The photograph features the remains of what was the Winifred Atwell Salon on the corner of Chaucer Road and Railton Road with the George pub in the distance. (David Stevens/Associated Newspapers/REX)

Winifred Atwell and her poodle Nino at her home, *c.* 1954.

CHAPTER 21

Kempton Bunton and Britain's Greatest Art Heist

Family photograph of Kempton Bunton *c.* 1965. (Courtesy of Chris Bunton)

On Thursday 5 December 1963 the *Daily Express* reported that on the previous evening twenty-four distinguished men had sat down for a traditional English dinner of sole and saddle of lamb at the Royal Academy on Piccadilly. It was to celebrate the opening of 'The Great Goya Exhibition' and masterpieces from the Spanish master had come from all over Europe. Most importantly, and carefully concealed in a tomato train, eleven paintings had travelled from Franco's Spain and had arrived in London the previous week.

With the priceless *Taddei Tondo*, the only marble sculpture by Michelangelo in Britain, looking down on them, the great and the good of the art world were present that night. Except one, Dr Consuelo Sanz-Pastor, the Inspector of Museums in Spain. Dr Sanz-Pastor, who had actually accompanied the Prado pictures to Britain and had also played a major part in arranging the exhibition, was absent because she was a woman and, as the *Daily Express* stated rather casually in the article, the Royal Academy 'never breaks with its all-male tradition'.[1]

One person who was at the dinner was Gerald Wellesley, the seventy-eight-year-old 7th Duke of Wellington. His famous predecessor the 1st Duke, while on service in the 1812 Peninsular War, had had his portrait painted by Goya. In 1963, to the general public in Britain at least, it was possibly Goya's most famous painting. It wasn't part of the prestigious exhibition, however, because it had been stolen.

On 21 August 1961, in the middle of the night and seemingly under the noses of five security guards, Goya's portrait of the Duke of Wellington had been taken from the National Gallery. The guards initially assumed it to have been removed by the gallery authorities as there was no sign of a break-in or forced entry. It was several hours before the painting was reported missing. When the important men of the art world sat down for the Royal Academy dinner two and a half years later, and despite a considerable £5,000 reward, there was still no clue to the painting's whereabouts.

The disappearance of the Goya shocked and embarrassed the esteemed National Gallery. Shocked because it was their first ever theft, and embarrassed because the painting had been taken not three weeks after it had first been put on display. The director offered his resignation and the robbery led to an official inquiry into security at Britain's national galleries and museums. It was initially thought by the authorities, perhaps not surprisingly, to be some outrageous copycat stunt. The Goya theft took place exactly fifty years to the day after the *Mona Lisa* had been stolen from the Louvre in 1911.

A few months before the Goya's appropriation, the New York oil magnate, collector and trustee of the Metropolitan Museum Charles Wrightsman had bought the painting through an auction at Sotheby's for £140,000 (over £2,500,000 in 2015). It had been sold by the Duke of Leeds, but there was widespread protest and questions asked in Parliament about how such a prestigious and patriotic work of art could possibly leave the country. Wrightsman kindly offered it to the National Gallery for the price he had paid. A charitable organisation called the Wolfson Foundation offered £100,000, which embarrassed the government into providing a further Treasury grant of £40,000. With almost indecent haste, on 2 August 1961, the painting was put on display in a proud, prominent position at the top of the National Gallery's central stairs.

A year before the theft, on 20 April 1960, and almost as far away from the rarefied metropolitan art-world as you can get, a fifty-five-year-old retired lorry driver called Kempton Bunton was fined £2 for not having a television licence at Newcastle's Magistrate's Court. He was given seven days to pay. The clerk of the court, Mr Cecil Geeson, asked Bunton if he appreciated that the Wireless Telegraphy Act required anyone using apparatus to have a licence. Bunton replied: 'Yes but £1 goes to the Government and £3 to the BBC.' He then told the court that he watched only Independent Television programmes and never the BBC, before reading out a statement: 'Undoubtedly, free viewing will come. I just want it to come quicker. Meantime I say that the aged folk should have it right away ...' He then said, 'I have no intention of paying the fine.'[2]

Initially only available in the capital, Independent Television had been introduced to most of Britain by September 1955. The North East, however, was to be the last of the English regions to get its own television transmitter. It wasn't until 12 December 1957 that a contract was awarded to a consortium led by the film producer Sydney Box and the *News Chronicle* executives George and Alfred Black. Just over a year later, Tyne Tees Television went on air at 5 p.m. on 15 January 1959. Harold Macmillan, a local MP but also prime minister at the time, was interviewed on the first night. This was followed by a programme called *The Big Show* which was notable, despite its name, for being broadcast from an extremely small studio.

Mary Crozier of *The Manchester Guardian*, and daughter of a former editor of the same newspaper, wrote about Tyne Tees Television in 1960. After commenting about the airy canteen at the top of their building being like the south of France on a sunny June day – except for the view – she went on to describe the Tyne Tees Television programming: 'It makes no pretension whatever to meet highbrow tastes. Which must be in a great minority anyway ... In light entertainment and comedy it has certainty and speed, and it was here that I saw some programmes fresher and saltier than some I see on the main network. I left Newcastle with the loud echoes of some "live" and many Ampexed programmes ringing in my ears and a new almost alarmed respect for the toughness of Tyneside television.'[3]

Mary Crozier implied that Tyne Tees knew its audience and she was right; by 1960 that station had 150,000 more viewers than the BBC in the same region. Meanwhile Kempton Bunton continued his fight with the authorities over the non-payment of his television licence and by now the affair had caught the interest of the national newspapers. On 29 May 1960 it was reported that the magistrates gave Bunton a further seven days to pay his £2 fine, otherwise he would be imprisoned for thirteen days by default. Bunton then told the magistrates: 'Since I started this argument I have treated the BBC levy with the contempt it deserves. I say that the old folk should have free viewing right away. They are sick of empty promises given by forgetful governments. I would suggest that the red tape be cut, precedent forgotten and a quick Act passed through the House of Commons allowing old folk to take for nothing that which is already offered free.'

In September, as he had still not paid a penny in fines, Bunton gave himself up to the police to serve a fifty-six-day prison sentence. Bunton again made a statement: 'This is a matter of principle for me. I believe that the air should be free. Why should millions of people be deprived of the pleasures of TV? Four pounds for a Licence is not a lot of money, but to some people it is a huge sum. The standard of programmes on television may at times be ridiculed but I still maintain that it is a grand time-killer and of a special benefit to our old folk. Tyne-Tees offer me a free programme and I take it. I shall go on refusing to pay this ridiculous tax.'

The 'ridiculous tax' had first been introduced in November 1922 and was originally called the Broadcasting Receiving Licence. It cost 10 shillings (50 pence but about £25 in 2015) and it covered the existing BBC radio broadcasts. Later it also included the BBC's 405-line television service, introduced in November 1936 before it was suspended at the beginning of the Second World War in September 1939. The Television Licence was introduced after the war in June 1946, to coincide with the post-war resumption of the BBC TV service that same month, and it cost anyone with a television set £2. It was increased to £3 in 1954 and when Kempton Bunton refused to buy his licence in 1960, they had increased it to £4 (£86 in 2015).

It didn't take long after the theft of the Goya from the National Gallery for the press to start enjoying the confusion of the authorities. The *Daily Express* headline on 23 August 1961 was: 'No Goya – No Clue', while the *Daily Mirror* joined in with: 'Who Stole it? Crook, Crank or Joker'. Ten days after the theft a Fleet Street news agency received an anonymous letter, optimistically and succinctly addressed: 'Reuters News, London' and dated 30 August 1961. Written in capital letters on cheap notepaper the letter read:

> Query not that I have the Goya. It has a stick label on back saying F Gallais and Son. Date 22.8.58. It has six cross ribs each way (back). The act is an attempt to pick the pockets of those who love art more than charity. The picture is not damaged, apart from a couple of scratches at side. Actual portrait perfect. The picture is not, and will not be for sale – it is for ransom – £140,000 – to be given to charity. If a fund is started – it should be quickly made up, and on the promise of a free pardon for the culprits – the picture will be handed back.

Almost one year later, in July 1962, another letter arrived from the Goya thief, and this time they enclosed a label from the back of the painting to prove they had the painting:

> Goya Com: the Duke is safe. This temperature cared for – his future uncertain. The painting is neither to be cloak-roomed or kiosked as such would defeat our purpose and leave us to ever open arrest. We want pardon or the right to leave the country – banishment? We ask that some non-conformist type of person with the fearless fortitude of a Montgomery start the fund for £140,000. No law can touch him. Propriety may frown – but God must smile.

At about an hour into the first James Bond film, released in October 1962, the evil Dr Julius No shows 007 around his lair. At one point millions of people around the country laughed while, presumably, members of the Metropolitan Police involved in the investigation flinched when Bond does a double-take as he realises it's Goya's Duke of Wellington portrait perched on an easel by some stairs.

Nothing was heard from the actual thief until the end of the year in 1963, when on 30 December another letter was received by Reuters:

> Terms are same. Rag students kidnap living persons for ransom – they are not charged. An amnesty in my case would not be out of order. The Yard

are looking for a needle in a haystack, but they haven't a clue where the haystack is ... I am offering three-pennyworth of old Spanish firewood in exchange for £140,000 of human happiness. A real bargain compared to a near million for a scruffy piece of Italian cardboard.

The thief was not far wrong when he mentioned needles and haystacks and the Metropolitan Police knew it. The newspapers were still occasionally having fun with the situation and *The Times* in January 1964 suggested that the thief should act like his forerunner Raffles, when in the story 'A Jubilee Present' a gold vase that had been stolen from the British Museum was returned via Buckingham Palace. The newspaper suggested that the culprits should 'return the painting and get it into the present exhibition at Burlington House. If the world woke up one morning and found the masterpiece appropriately among its fellows, then eyes would be rubbed, and the thieves become immortal'.[4]

There had been silence from the anonymous thief until March 1965, when he sent a letter to the *Daily Mirror* suggesting that the portrait should be exhibited privately until £30,000 had been raised for charity. Then, and only then, would it be returned to the National Gallery. The *Daily Mirror* enthusiastically took up the challenge of organising such an exhibition and suggested that: 'This great national art treasure should be taken IMMEDIATELY to the shop of any newsagent in the land. The newsagent to whom the painting is delivered will then IMMEDIATELY telephone the Editor of the *Daily Mirror* in London at Fleet Street 0246.'[5]

The chairman of the trustees of the National Gallery, Lord Robbins, after already saying that if the picture was returned 'the probability of further search for whoever temporarily appropriated it would be virtually nil', also described what he thought he knew of the thief: 'I feel I know him pretty well already ... He is still probably fairly slim and physically fit, and the cunning with which he carried out the raid suggest that he was probably a commando or something like that. A man without fear.'[6]

It all went quiet again for almost a month. Then, on 21 May, the *Daily Mirror* received an envelope containing a receipt for a parcel left at New Street Station, Birmingham. The next afternoon, Detective Inspector John Morrison presented the ticket, paid the surcharge of 7 shillings and carefully opened the parcel labelled, 'Glass. Handle with Care.' It was the Goya, albeit without its frame. It had been at New Street for just over two weeks among suitcases, knapsacks, handbags and other left luggage. On the same day Michael Levey, the assistant keeper at the National Gallery, identified the Goya portrait. The portrait was displayed at a press conference on 24 May 1965, and then was quickly put back on display, almost four years after it had been reported stolen.

On Thursday 27 May one final 'com' was sent to the *Daily Mirror* and by now the letter-writer was starting to have some fun:

> Goya. Extra Com. Lost – one sporting offer. Propriety has won – charity has lost. Indeed a black day for journalism. I wonder if he is worthy of £2500 reward or should he be drummed out. We took the Goya in sporting endeavour – your Mr Editor pinched it back by a broken promise. You furthermore have the effrontery to pat yourself on the back in your triumph. Animal – vegetable – or idiot.

Just a few weeks later, on 20 July 1965, a large man, 6 feet tall, about sixteen stone and wearing a grey suit and hat, stopped a policeman in central London and asked to be directed to the West End police station on Savile Row. When he arrived he told the desk sergeant: 'My name is Kempton Bunton and I am turning myself in for the Goya.' When Bunton was asked whether he was saying that he had stolen it, he replied: 'Of course, that is why I'm here.' He handed over a written statement that he had brought with him:

> (1) My secret has leaked – I wouldn't like a certain gentleman to benefit financially by speaking to the law.
> (2) I am sick and tired of the whole affair.
> (3) By surrendering in London I avoid the stigma of being brought here in 'chains'.

The next day at Bow Street magistrates' court, Bunton was charged with the theft of the picture, demanding money from Lord Robbins with menaces, demanding money from the editor of the *Daily Mirror* with menaces, and with 'causing a nuisance to the public by the unlawful removal and wrongful detaining of a painting on display at the National Gallery'.

On 10 November 1965 Kempton Bunton pleaded 'Not Guilty' to all the charges at the Central Criminal Court. In evidence to his counsel, Mr Jeremy Hutchinson QC, Bunton said that he had never intended to deprive the National Gallery of the portrait permanently. Neither had he the intention of getting any money for himself by taking the portrait. When he was asked how he had stolen the painting Bunton told the court that it was at 5.50 a.m. and that the guards must have been playing cards. He had got in by using a ladder which had been left by builders against the outside wall. Bunton added that he had taken the painting because he had been incensed with the Government for not allowing free television licences to pensioners.

During his cross-examination of Bunton, Mr E. J. P. Cussen for the prosecution asked: 'Are you not sure your object was to steal the portrait from the National Gallery in revenge for the way you had been treated by the authorities over your television licence?' Bunton replied 'That is not correct.' Mr Cussen continued: 'When you walked out of the National Gallery carrying the portrait were you saying to yourself: I always intend to return it?' To which Bunton replied: 'It was no good to me otherwise. I would not have hung it in my kitchen!' Asked if he had ever told his wife that he had been holding the Goya for nearly four years, Bunton promptly replied: 'No, the world would have known if I had done so.' Bunton was acquitted on four of the charges but convicted of stealing the frame and sentenced to just three months' imprisonment. The judge in his summing up expressed what was generally the view of most, but especially of the National Gallery, and presumably all the museums and galleries around the country, that there couldn't be people creeping into art galleries and removing paintings only to say later they were intending to bring them back. The judge also pronounced, and again he couldn't have been alone with his opinion, that the theft was a 'remarkable feat' for the large, seventeen-stone, rather unfit Bunton who had long retired from driving because of a previous injury.

As Kempton began his jail term his wife, Dorothy Bunton, said of her husband: 'He is a clever man and a deep thinker. But he has no regard for money. He could go a whole week with a halfpenny in his pocket providing he got his meals.' Dorothy Bunton also revealed that her husband had written several plays, articles and a novel but none was ever published. 'We were struggling along on 21 shillings a week,' said Mrs Bunton. 'It used to break my heart to see my husband spending two shillings a week to buy foolscap paper to write his novel on.'[7] Kempton had been convinced that the reason the novels and plays had been rejected was because they had been written in long hand. What the publishers needed was a neatly printed manuscript. Kempton then built his own printing press of wood and bits of metal collected from local scrap heaps. It worked and he printed eight copies of a book, bound them himself and sent one off to the publishers. Unfortunately, to no avail. He had also been sending plays to the BBC, all of which had been rejected. This may have been the real reason he was so upset with the national broadcaster.

Three years later, the Kempton Bunton case led to an important clause being inserted into the Theft Act of 1968, which made it illegal to 'remove without authority any object displayed or kept for display to the public in a building to which the public have access'. Everyone involved in the Bunton affair must have thought that was absolutely that.

Less than three years later, however, on 22 June 1969, a small article appeared on the front page of the *Observer*. The journalist Barrie Stuart-Penrose reported that the police now believed it was someone else and not Kempton Bunton that had stolen the Goya portrait. The man in question had said, 'I didn't have a pre-arranged plan with Kempton Bunton to steal the picture. I did it alone. I only brought him in later. I sent a letter to Kempton Bunton in Newcastle and told him about the Goya. Bunton wrote back saying, "I'm coming to London."'[8] Rather oddly, when so many acres of newsprint were used up when covering the original heist and the subsequent arrest and imprisonment of Kempton Bunton, the story disappeared without trace. Indeed, considering he was responsible for one of the great British art heists of the twentieth century, when Kempton Bunton died in Newcastle in 1976 it went largely unreported and there were no obituaries to be found in the major newspapers.

In November 2012, a confidential Director of Public Prosecutions file was released at the National Archives. It identified the 'thief' of the Goya Duke of Wellington portrait as the twenty-year-old son of a retired Newcastle bus driver. His name was John Bunton and he was, of course, the son of Kempton. On 30 May 1969, John Bunton, aged twenty-eight, had been arrested and charged at Leeds police station for stealing a car. While at the station he made it known that he wanted to get an offence of some magnitude cleared up and off his chest, and then admitted to stealing the Goya painting. The police went to visit Kempton at 12 Yewcroft Avenue in Newcastle. He was now sixty-five and an old age pensioner and he immediately conceded that it was his son John who had stolen the painting. He also admitted that he had committed perjury at his trial at the Central Criminal Court in 1965. After reading his son's statement he agreed that it was true and described to the police officers what actually had happened.

In August 1961 John Bunton was living at the Arlington Lodging House in Camden Town, and on the 21st he stole a green Wolsley 1500 from a small lock-up in Old Street. He drove back to his lodgings, where he remained until 4.00 a.m. and then drove to St Martin's Street and parked alongside the National Gallery. He scaled the wall of the gallery in Orange Street by standing on a convenient parking meter. There had been some construction going on behind the wall and a wooden ladder about 20 feet long had been left lying around. John Bunton put the ladder up to an unlocked window, which was about fifteen feet from the ground, and without much trouble climbed through into a gent's toilet. He then made his way to the gallery, which was at the top of the main steps. The Goya painting of the Duke of Wellington was there in a roped off enclosure and standing on an easel. He just picked it up – it wasn't a particularly large painting – and briskly walked back to the gent's. He retraced his steps out of the gallery. John then gave the painting over to his father, who had travelled down from Newcastle to collect it.

Four years later in May 1965 Kempton requested that his son should come and visit him in Newcastle. He gave John the Goya and asked him to take it to Birmingham and leave it at the Left Luggage at New Street station. Following his father's instructions, it was John who actually sent the letter to the *Daily Mirror* soon after. When John was asked by the police why he hadn't come forward when his father was charged with the offence of stealing it, he said: 'He told us not to. Ordered us. It was his wish.'

Sir Norman Skelhorn, the Director of Public Prosecutions, told the police that John Bunton's admission of guilt was almost certainly not sufficient to prosecute him; and for his father, Skelhorn ruled that it would be difficult to prosecute him for perjury as they would have to rely on the evidence of the son, who was clearly an unreliable witness. No further action was ever taken. John Bunton, with the help of his father, managed to completely get away with one of the twentieth century's greatest art heists.

In 1967, the Royal Academy invited Harold Wilson, the prime minister, to their annual dinner to be held on 27 May. Wilson wrote back saying: 'I'd love to come, but with Jennie Lee.' The Royal Academy agreed with his request that he would come but only if he was accompanied by his arts minister, and thus, for the first time since 1769, a woman was present at a Royal Academy dinner. It was decided to invite some other eminent women as guests and they included, among others, Dame Barbara Hepworth and Dame Peggy Ashcroft. *The Times* Diary, describing the event, reported that Lady Gaitskell looked 'striking in a dress of wild silk in a pleasing shade of yellow, and as for Miss Gertrude Hermes, A.R.A., she was seen smoking a thoroughly masculine cigar after dinner'.[9] On the very same night as the prime minister and the other prestigious guests of both sexes were enjoying their dinner at the Royal Academy, Kempton Bunton was presumably watching Tyne Tees Television in his Newcastle council house. He probably enjoyed the 1955 Humphrey Bogart film *We're No Angels* which was broadcast early in the evening, and if he stayed up later he may have watched a precursor of *Monty Python* – the comedy series called *At Last the 1948 Show* – which featured a sketch entitled 'Thief in the Library'...

METROPOLITAN POLICE

£5,000 REWARD

STOLEN

from

THE NATIONAL GALLERY

on 21st August, 1961

Portrait of

THE DUKE OF WELLINGTON

by Francisco de GOYA

The above reward of £5,000 will be paid by the Trustees of the National Gallery to the first person giving information which will result in the apprehension and the conviction of the thief or thieves, or receiver, and the recovery of this famous picture, the property of the Nation.

Information should be given at the Metropolitan Police Office, New Scotland Yard, London, S.W.1, or at any Police Station.

Printed by the Receiver for the Metropolitan Police District, New Scotland Yard, S.W.1.   62358/8,700

QUERY NOT, THAT I HAVE THE GOYA.

IT HAS A STICK LABEL ON BACK SAYING
F Le GALLAIS & SON. DEPOSITORIES. JERSEY.
NAME DUKE OF LEEDS. DATE 23.9.58

no 2. IT HAS 6 CROSS RIBS EACHWAY (BACK)
THE ACT IS AN ATTEMPT TO PICK THE
POCKETS OF THOSE WHO LOVE ART MORE THAN
CHARITY.
THE PICTURE IS NOT DAMAGED APART
FROM A COUPLE OF SCRATCHES AT SIDE.

ACTUAL PORTRAIT PERFECT,
THE PICTURE IS NOT, AND WILL NOT BE FOR
SALE — IT IS FOR RANSOM — £140,000 — TO BE
GIVEN TO CHARITY.
IF A FUND IS STARTED — IT SHOULD BE QUICKLY
MADE UP, AND ON THE PROMISE OF A FREE
PARDON FOR THE CULPRITS — THE PICTURE WILL
BE HANDED. BACK.
NONE OF THE GROUP CONCERNED IN THIS
ESCAPADE HAVE ANY CRIMINAL CONVICTIONS.
ALL GOOD PEOPLE ARE URLED TO GIVE, AND HELP
THIS AFFAIR TO A SPEEDY CONCLUSION.

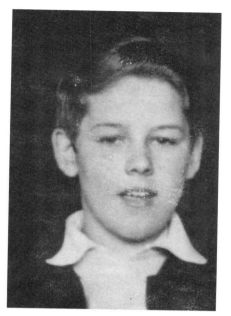
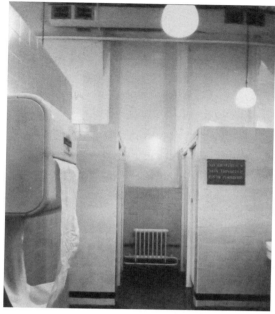

Above left: The real thief, John Bunton, in 1957. (Courtesy of Chris Bunton)

Above right: The gent's in the National Gallery, the window through which John Bunton climbed to get into the gallery.

Opposite above left: The British general Arthur Wellesley, 1st Duke of Wellington, by Francisco de Goya, 1812–14. The Duke of Wellington fought Napoleon's troops in Spain and entered Madrid in August 1812, after which Goya painted this portrait. Wellington finally defeated the French forces in 1814 and the painting was modified by Goya after Wellington received further honours.

Opposite above right: Metropolitan Police reward notice of £5,000.

Opposite below: Kempton Bunton letter to the Reuters news agency dated 30 August 1961, ten days after the disappearance of the Goya portrait.

CHAPTER 22

The Prostitutes' Padre and the Lyons' Tea-Shop Nippies

The Reverend Harold Davidson in his pulpit at Stiffkey church.

It is very hard to be good, once you have been bad.

Barbara Harris

The Reverend Harold Francis Davidson, rector of the small Norfolk coastal village of Stiffkey for twenty-five years, was utterly besotted and bewitched by pretty young girls. Of that there is no doubt. How he behaved in the company of said pretty young girls was more up for debate; and in 1932 it seemed that the whole country, including the highest echelons of the Church of England, was debating exactly that.

Every Sunday, from 1906 to 1932, with a break for the First World War when he joined the Royal Navy, the Reverend Davidson was always at his pulpit at the Stiffkey church. He then spent the rest of the week, however, in London, usually Soho, catching the first train every Monday morning and the last one back to Norfolk on Saturday night. It was said that the only time he spent the entire week in his parish was during the General Strike of 1926. The Stiffkey locals joked that it was best not to die on a Monday morning as the body, especially in the summer, would be decomposing by the time the reverend made it back for the funeral. Wedding services were either deputised or the ceremony was held on a Sunday. All the same, he was well liked by most of his parishioners.

During the week Davidson, often without his 'dog collar', would walk around the streets of the West End, essentially stalking and pursuing girls and young women wherever he went. Whether it was attractive young actresses, shop girls or waitresses, none of them was particularly safe from the glint in the reverend's eye. He always argued, until the day he died, that as he was wandering around Soho he was doing nothing but God's work. His aim in life, he claimed, was helping young women from falling into a life of prostitution, particularly shop assistants and tea shop waitresses, many of whom had left an acrimonious home for the first time and were on very low wages.

It had all started in 1894 when Davidson was working as a comic actor in London. He had come from a long line of clergymen (he would eventually be ordained in 1903 at the age of twenty-eight) but had always loved amateur dramatics at school, and subsequently toured for several months with friends, performing as travelling entertainers. One evening, walking along the Thames Embankment in a thick fog, he came across a sixteen-year-old young woman who was about to throw herself into the Thames. Davidson managed to stop her from her suicide attempt and found out that she had run away from home and had no money or anywhere to stay. He persuaded her to go back home with a letter from him to her mother: 'Her pitiful story made a tremendous impression on me ... I have ever since ... kept my eyes open for opportunities to help that kind of girl.'[1]

During the first part of the twentieth century and before the beginning of the First World War, however, most of Davidson's early work was with underprivileged boys in the East End. He helped set up the Newsboys' Club to help out young London newsboys, who were often badly treated and exploited by Fleet Street. Clubs were created where the young boys could get a meal and play games and generally be kept out of mischief. Davidson, with others, helped the boys secure better wages and improve their working conditions. His work with young women, however, became more prominent after he returned home from war service as a naval chaplain, to an adulterous and pregnant wife.

At his own estimation, Davidson had made the acquaintance, in one way or another, of 2,000–3,000 girls between 1919 and 1932: 'I was picking up in this way roughly, as my diaries show, an average of about 150 to 200 girls a year, and taking them to restaurants for a meal and a talk, of these I was definitely able to help into good jobs of work a very large number.' When the reverend talked about 'restaurants', he almost certainly was referring to cafés such as the J. Lyons tea shops, of which there were many around London in the twenties and thirties.

J. Lyons & Co. was established in 1885 by four entrepreneurs – Isidore and Montague Glickstein, Barnett Salmon and Joseph Lyons. From modest beginnings as a supplier of catering to the Newcastle Exhibition in 1887, the company went on to become, at its height, the largest food company in Europe. The first of the Lyons' teashops opened at 213 Piccadilly in 1894 (it's still a café today and you can still see the original stucco ceiling of the original Lyons café). Soon there were more than 250 white and gold fronted teashops occupying prestigious locations on many of London's high streets and also around the country. Food and drink prices were the same in each teashop, irrespective of locality, and the tea was always the best available – although the Lyons blend was never sold or made available to the public. The J. Lyons flagship shops were the London Corner Houses situated on or near the corners of Coventry Street, the Strand and Tottenham Court Road. They were started in 1909 and remained until 1977. They were gigantic places with food being served on four or five floors. In its heyday the Coventry Street Corner House served about 5,000 covers and employed about 400 staff. There were hairdressing salons, telephone booths and even at one point a food delivery service. For a time the Coventry Street Corner House was open twenty-four hours a day.

In 1924 the directors at J. Lyons & Co. had decided to update their image and specifically their waitresses. The dresses were to be modernised and they removed the ban on bobbed hair. The (mostly) young women had to wear starched caps with a big, red 'L' embroidered in the centre, a black Alpaca dress featuring a double row of pearl buttons sewn with red cotton, with white detachable cuffs and collar, finished off with a white square apron worn at dropped-waist level. There was a staff competition to choose a nickname for the newly styled Lyons' teashops' waitresses. The former name of 'Gladys' was now seen as very old fashioned. The name 'Nippy' was eventually chosen, probably for the connotation that the waitresses nipped speedily around (in an attempt to avoid the advances of middle-aged men like Harold Davidson presumably). If 'Nippy' sounds odd as a nickname for a waitress, it's worth noting that rejected suggestions included 'Sybil-at-your-service', 'Miss Nimble', Miss Natty', 'Busy Bertha', 'Speedwell' and even 'Dextrous Dora'.

The 'Nippy' made her first appearance on New Year's Day in 1925, and by 1939 there were around 7,600 of them working around the country, all selected on deportment, condition of hands, an ability to add, and the competence to handle crockery deftly. A pleasant personality was judged more important to Lyons than good looks and it seems there were a lot of men on the look-out for a 'pleasant personality'. The *Daily Mail* in September 1930 reported that during the previous six weeks, 144 girls, including eighty waitresses, employed by J. Lyons & Co. had got married: 'To find a husband in these competitive days one cannot do better than became a Lyons waitress. A pretty "Nippy" is nipped up in no time. Clerks, Stockbrokers, sailors, soldiers, shipping men, visitors from the provinces, are all temptingly arrayed, so to speak, on her matrimonial menu.'[2]

Picture Post in March 1939 reported that there were a total of between 800 and 900 Nippy marriages every year and J. Lyons & Co. claimed that the marriage rate among Nippies was higher than any other class of working girl and that the job was good training for a housewife. In the same article the magazine featured a London Nippy called Miss A., who said: 'Nippies appear to agree that men are easier to serve than women. They are less fussy. Women seem to want to report you to the manager for the least little thing. And often quite unjustifiably. There are, of course, exceptions, but men generally are seldom unreasonably annoyed, and they don't mind waiting a bit if they see we are very busy.'[3]

It was a Nippy that was once involved in an incident with Harold Davidson. A friend of the reverend, called J. Rowland Sales, remembered a time when they were having a cup of tea in the Coventry Street Corner

House between Piccadilly and Leicester Square. Davidson had become visibly upset while telling a very sad story about a homeless couple he had recently found sleeping under a hedge in Norfolk. All of a sudden his demeanour changed. It was almost like he was a completely different person, recounted Sales. A young 'nippy waitress' had just walked by and Davidson leapt to his feet and called out 'Excuse me, Miss. You must be the sister of Jessie Matthews.' He then promised the startled waitress that he would get her a part in a new play that was opening in London.

Davidson, with the Bishop of Norwich's full support, had become the chaplain to the actors' Church Union and he started using this as an excuse to appear backstage at various West End theatres. He became known as a 'voyeuristic pest' and would often open doors backstage: 'Oh, excuse me ladies, I didn't know this was your dressing room ...' Tales like these and other bizarre stories of the Reverend Davidson's behaviour around Soho eventually came to the notice of his employer – the Church of England. A complaint was made, via a handwritten letter, to the Bishop of Norwich, the Right Reverend Bertram Pollock, by a seventeen-year-old young woman called Barbara Harris. In 1931 the Bishop decided to investigate Davidson, and soon the self-styled 'Prostitutes' Padre' was charged with five offences against public morality under the 1892 Clergy Discipline Act. He was to be tried in a Consistory court, an ecclesiastical court used by the Church of England to this day for the trial of clergy (below the rank of bishop), and it opened in the Great Hall of Church House in Westminster on 29 March 1932. A Consistory court has no jury and is presided over, in place of a judge, by what is called a Chancellor of the Diocese. In Davidson's case it was before F. Keppel North, the Chancellor of the Diocese of Norfolk. It was never revealed at the time, and certainly should have been: not only had Bishop Pollock and Chancellor North been to the same university together, but Mr North was the godfather to the Bishop's daughter.

The court case was a sensation and front-page news. Davidson wasn't slow in courting the press, and on the first day of the trial arrived in flamboyant style while smoking a characteristically large cigar. He even signed autographs. Among what seemed like dozens of Nippies, theatre girls, and domestic servants brought up to give evidence, the prosecution's star witness was a young woman called Barbara Harris whom Davidson had befriended in 1930. He had first seen her at Marble Arch – a popular haunt of prostitutes at the time – and he used his old tried and tested trick of comparing Barbara to a famous actress, this time Greta Garbo. Barbara was just sixteen and already a prostitute and suffering from gonorrhoea.

She had never known her father and had been abandoned by her mother, who was suffering from mental illness. Harris initially welcomed what seemed a kind gentleman's offer of help and was soon pouring out her life-story to Davidson, no doubt in a Lyons' café in the near vicinity. Davidson helped her find lodgings and they became friends over the next eighteen months.

The rector had given Barbara money and even found her a job in domestic service at Villiers Street in Charing Cross, but she quickly tired of both the job and the reverend's repeated attentions. At one point she gave him a black eye and threw coins at him but he continually came back for more. One morning, at 9 a.m., Davidson had appeared at the room where she was sleeping. During the court case the prosecution asked Barbara about this:

> Prosecution: You say you kissed him?
> Barbara: Yes.
> Prosecution: How often was he kissing you?
> Barbara: He was always kissing me.
> Prosecution: Did he ever ask you to do things?
> Barbara: Yes, he once asked me to give myself to him body and soul …

As the trial was coming to its end it was thought that the evidence against Davidson would not be enough to find him guilty. That is until the prosecutor, Roland Oliver, brought out two small photographs. To Davidson's utter shock and horrified disbelief, one of the photographs was of the reverend standing between an aspidistra plant and a bare-bottomed teenage actress. The girl was called Estelle Douglas and was the daughter of a close friend of his – an actress called Mae Douglas, whom he had helped to get on stage some twenty years before. In turn she had asked Davidson to try and get her daughter into films. A photoshoot had been organised at the Stiffkey rectory with the idea of taking publicity shots of Estelle in her bathing suit. At one point the photographer told Estelle that the strap of the bathing suit and her chemise were both showing and, apparently out of earshot of the reverend, asked her to remove them, leaving her with a black tasselled shawl to protect her modesty. A series of photographs were then taken. According to Davidson, the photographer offered £50 to take a photograph of him and Estelle with the intention of selling it to the newspapers. Davidson was completely broke and needed the money and so he rather stupidly agreed to the request. Whether the photograph was set up or not (there is much evidence to suggest that it was), it was the end for the 'Prostitute's Padre' and Chancellor North found him guilty of five counts of immoral conduct. He was charged £8,205 costs and was left in financial and professional ruin.

Davidson's legal team were let down by the eccentric rector's antics. He performed a tap dance at one point in the witness box, and for some reason always refused to question the truthfulness or character of any of the prosecution witnesses, including Barbara Harris. The defence were also at fault for Davidson's conviction, however. Letters between Harold Davidson had been produced in court as evidence – most of the letters from Davidson were signed 'Your sincere friend and Padre', while the relatively mundane letters from Harris were either thanking Davidson for his help or confirming an appointment with him – but Harris's original letter of complaint to the Bishop of Norwich was written in a completely different handwriting style. It was almost certainly written by someone else. Crucially this wasn't noticed by the defence team. Another major mistake occurred when they failed to call Molly Davidson, the reverend's wife, as a witness. She had always been completely aware of Davidson's charity work with young girls and, generally, had always supported him. She even often hosted 'sleepovers' with the girls at the rectory in Stiffkey.

In October 1932 Davidson was summoned to appear in front of Bishop Pollock at Norwich cathedral, where he was subjected to a humiliating and demeaning public defrocking. 'Removed, Deposed and Degraded' shouted a *Daily Mirror* headline. At one point the bishop knelt in prayer and after a reference to 'Our sentence duly passed,' declared the office of Rector of Stiffkey and Morston to be vacant. 'It appears to us,' he said, 'that the Rev. Harold Francis Davidson has been found guilty in our Consistory Court of certain immoral conduct, immoral acts, and immoral habits ... we do hereby remove, depose and degrade him.'

While the bishop and his procession reformed to leave the high altar, the loud high-pitched voice of Davidson was heard again protesting his innocence. The bishop completely ignored him and Davidson was left pleading his case in an increasingly hysterical voice as the clerical procession swept past him on their way out.

Harold Davidson was not alone in criticising his prosecutors and the fairness of his trial. While most of the national press saw him as little more than a joke figure, the *Church Times*, no less, was more on the ex-rector's side. While they criticised Davidson's conduct as 'foolish and eccentric', they wrote in July 1932 that: 'There can be no doubt that he was originally moved by a high Christian impulse, and that he is still regarded by many as a champion of the outcast and the wretched. However necessary the proceedings may have been, the spirit in which they were conducted has shocked the public conscience. The secret inquiry agents, the characters of some of the unnecessary witnesses, above all, the photograph, made the trial both undignified and unChristian.' The article also mentioned that under the Clergy Discipline Act of 1892 a clergyman could be found guilty from one single immoral act and that, 'It was therefore perfectly superfluous to bring forward numerous witnesses of doubtful character and to heap up a number of charges.'[4]

The Reverend Davidson wasn't the first member of the establishment who spent much of their time helping fallen women in central London. William Ewart Gladstone was often found wandering around the darker environs of the West End. With almost reckless abandon he searched for young women to 'rescue', often asking them back to his house. A shocked private secretary once asked him, 'What would your wife say?' 'Why,' Gladstone answered, 'it is to my wife that I'm bringing her.' His wife Catherine would indeed feed the women and give them a place to sleep before finding, not always entirely gratefully, a temporary shelter to stay. Although Gladstone was completely open about the 'rescuing' of the young street women and he even wrote in his diary that he occasionally committed 'adultery of the heart' and 'delectation morosa' (enjoying thinking of evil without the intention of action). It was estimated that Gladstone spent a minimum of £2,000 a year helping prostitutes and providing shelters for them.

A fellow parliamentarian called Henry Labouchere, MP for Northampton, noted that Gladstone seemed to prefer the young and pretty prostitutes and wryly noted that he 'manages to combine his missionary meddling with a keen appreciation of a pretty face. He has never been known to rescue any of our East End whores, nor for that matter is it easy to contemplate his rescuing any ugly woman and I am quite sure his convention of the Magdalen is of incomparable example of pulchritude with a superb figure and carriage'. Similarly, Ronald Blythe in his book *The Age of Illusion*, published in 1964, wrote in one chapter of the Stiffkey clerical scandal: 'The Reverend Mr Davidson's downfall ... was girls. Not a girl, not five or six girls even, not a hundred, but the entire tremulous universe of girlhood. Shingled heads, clear cheeky eyes, nifty legs, warm, blunt-fingered workaday hands, small firm breasts and, most importantly, good strong healthy teeth, besotted him.'

After the public humiliation at Norwich cathedral, Harold Davidson picked himself up and started to use his experience on the stage as a young man. He turned himself into a travelling showman in order to attract as much publicity for his case as possible. He also desperately needed money. He wanted to appeal his court case and believed he should have been tried by a jury. One infamous stunt involved him fasting inside a barrel at Blackpool. The container was fitted with an electric light and also a small chimney from which his cigar smoke could escape. Through a grille he'd protest his innocence to anyone who would listen and even invited Gandhi to meet him there for tea. To no avail.

Despite his stunts becoming more and more outrageous – at one point he was being roasted in an oven while being prodded in the buttocks with a pitchfork by a mechanical devil – the erstwhile clergyman's fame was beginning to wane. In the summer of 1937 Davidson tried one more stunt, and at Thompson's Amusement Park in Skegness he was billed as: 'A modern Daniel in a lion's den.' Davidson stood in a cage with a lion called Freddie and a lioness called Toto. Again he shouted to any passer-by about the injustice he had been dealt. This was merged, as usual, with a torrent of loud abuse against his former church leaders.

On 28 July, Davidson accidentally stood on Toto's tail. The lioness's sudden movement made Freddie attack the former rector. The *Daily Mirror* described the attack: 'In a flash the angry beast had torn open both the ex-rector's shoulders with its claws, and though Davidson bravely tried to strike with his stick he crashed to the floor of the cage with the lion on top of him. It gripped him by the back with its jaws and began to maul him, while spectators screamed in horror.'[5] At this point it was the turn of a sixteen-year-old girl to attempt to save Davidson. A young assistant lion-tamer called Renée Somer picked up a whip and an iron cage and leapt into the cage. After raining blows on the lion with the whip, when it lurched towards her on the attack she rammed the iron bar into its jaws and then dragged Davidson across the cage out of immediate danger. Davidson was taken to Skegness Cottage Hospital, fatally injured. It is said that the ex-reverend, always hungry for publicity to help his cause and with blood pouring from his neck, still had the presence of mind to say: 'Telephone the London newspapers – we still have time to make the first editions!'

The owner of the amusement park, with rather indecent haste, put up a notice that said: 'See the lion that mauled and injured the rector.' The next day he was asked to take the notice down, and then soon after the badly injured Davidson died of his horrific wounds. A verdict of misadventure was returned at the inquest. Davidson was buried in Stiffkey churchyard and with the help of the police to control the crowds, over two thousand mourners attended the funeral. His epitaph reads: 'He was loved by the villagers, who recognised his humanity and forgave him his transgressions. May he rest in peace.'

After the Second World War there were seven Lyons teashops operating on Oxford Street alone although the idea of Nippies, especially in London, was beginning to seem old-fashioned. By now Lyons & Co. was operating large hotels, many of which they built themselves – the last of them was the 'brutalist', and much maligned, Tower Hotel next to the Tower of London. During the war they had run one of the largest bomb-making factories in Britain while producing millions of rations for troops all over the world. They also 'bequeathed' large teashops for the use of the American troops, notably 'Rainbow Corner' next to Piccadilly Circus. The company continued to grow after the war and acquired Baskin-Robbins, Dunkin Donuts and the Wimpy hamburger chain. Notably, they also built and operated the world's first business computer, which they called LEO (Lyons Electronic Office).

J. Lyons' decline came as fast as the company had initially grown, and in the early 1970s when the UK was hit by recession, inflation and the oil crisis, the company's aggressive expansion meant that they became seriously overstretched on their borrowing. In 1978 Allied Breweries Ltd made an offer for the company which was accepted and at that point Lyons lost its independence. It struggled on for a few more years, but different parts of the old company were all eventually sold off. J. Lyons & Company, which had survived for over a hundred years and always traded proudly under the same name, was no more.

The PERFECT NIPPY

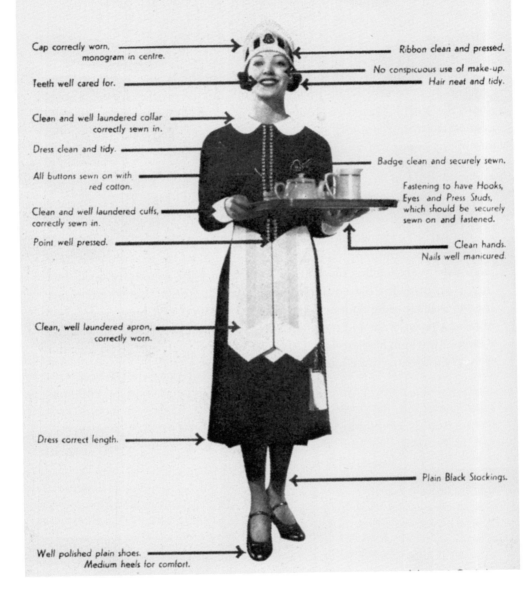

Cap correctly worn, monogram in centre.

Teeth well cared for.

Clean and well laundered collar correctly sewn in.

Dress clean and tidy.

All buttons sewn on with red cotton.

Clean and well laundered cuffs, correctly sewn in.

Point well pressed.

Clean, well laundered apron, correctly worn.

Dress correct length.

Well polished plain shoes. Medium heels for comfort.

Ribbon clean and pressed.

No conspicuous use of make-up.

Hair neat and tidy.

Badge clean and securely sewn.

Fastening to have Hooks, Eyes and Press Studs, which should be securely sewn on and fastened.

Clean hands. Nails well manicured.

Plain Black Stockings.

Right: Barbara Harris arriving at Church Hall in Westminster.

Opposite: As far as J. Lyons & Co. were concerned, this was how the perfect Nippy should look.

Left: Lyons' Teashop advert from 1932.

Below: The trial at the Great Hall of Church House in Westminster. Harold Davidson can be seen on the right, cupping his ear, and a waitress called Violet Lowe is giving evidence and sitting to Chancellor North's left.

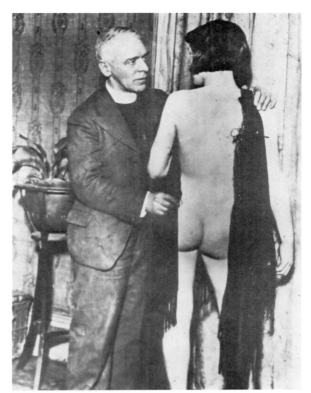

Right: The Reverend and an undraped Estelle Douglas.

Below: Davidson preaching to villagers outside the locked church, July 1932.

REV. H. DAVIDSON M A
WELL KNOWN AS THE RECTOR OF STIFFKEY.
PHOTOGRAPHED AT THE FAMOUS BARREL EXHIBITION BLACKPOOL 1933.
PHOTO BY SNOMAN. BROS. BLACKPOOL.

Left: Davidson posing in front of his Blackpool barrel, 1933.

Below: Davidson in the lions' cage in Skegness during the summer of 1937 and just before his death.

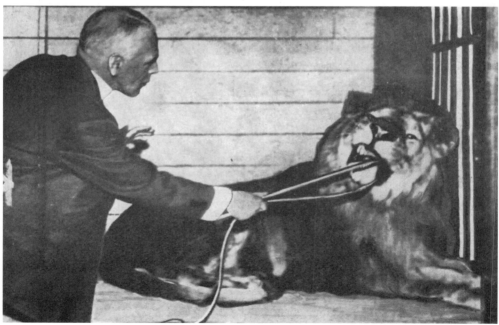

The Wonderland Theatre in Skegness shortly after Davidson had died.

CHAPTER 23

The Hippy Squat at 144 Piccadilly

144 Piccadilly on 9 September 1969. (© Keystone Pictures USA/Alamy)

On 8 July 1908, Lady Allendale, née Alexandrina Vane-Tempest, dressed in a beautiful gown of black velvet with a great cluster of Lilies of the Valley in the centre of her bodice, entertained at dinner at 144 Piccadilly. The Prince and Princess Alexander of Teck were there, as was the Russian ambassador, the Countess Benckendorff, the Duke of Marlborough and also Lord Willoughby de Eresby. *The Times* reported the next day that 'afterwards there was a dance, with the hall and reception room decorated with pink and white flowers against a background of green ferns and foliage. Herr Gottlieb's orchestra supplied the music'.[1] In July 1914, just seventeen days before the start of the First World War, Lady Allendale gave another soirée at 144 Piccadilly, this time a dance for her two daughters. The *Observer* wrote that it was the most successful dance given that week and the 'lovely rooms were gay with exquisite flowers sent up from Lord Allendale's country place ... and the garden was prettily illuminated and set out with rugs and seats'.[2]

Fifty-five years and two world wars later there was also illumination at a party, of sorts, at 144 Piccadilly. Although the 21 September 1969 edition of the *Sunday People* hardly thought it was pretty: 'In some upstairs room I found three boys and a girl sitting round a tiny little oil-light breaking up some sort of drug and mixing it with tobacco ...' Underneath the headline 'Hippie Thugs – The Sordid Truth' the reporter described the scene she found: 'Drug-taking ... couples making love while others look on, rule by a heavy mob armed with iron bars ... foul language ... filth and stench ... that is the scene inside the hippies' fortress in London's Piccadilly. These are not rumours but facts, sordid facts which will shock ordinary decent living people. Drug taking, squalor and sex.'

Lady Allendale almost certainly wouldn't have approved. It did, however, amuse her grandson, the 3rd Viscount Allendale who, when he heard the news of the hippies moving into the house where he was born in 1922, said: 'I had a good laugh. All I can say is, the best of luck to them. It must be jolly uncomfortable, especially if they put in 500 people as they were talking about yesterday. In my time we had a dozen family and staff there at most.'[3]

The five-storied Piccadilly mansion where Lady Allendale once held so many soirées, dinners and parties had always been a prestigious address; Lord Palmerston had lived at 144 the year before he became prime minister and next door, 145, had been Queen Elizabeth's childhood home. When the future queen's parents, the Duke and Duchess of York, moved into their house in October 1926, the *Daily Mirror* described the house as 'one of those fine stone mansions which stand between Hamilton place, where the traffic turns in to Park Lane, and Apsley House, the Duke of Wellington's house at the entrance to Hyde Park. No nicer situation could be imagined, for from all the front windows there is a clear view across the Green Park'.[4]

Since three o'clock on 15 September 1969, when a scarlet banner of the London Street Commune had been raised on the roof over a surprised Mayfair, 144 Piccadilly was now the home of 400 hippies. On the same day as the *Sunday People* was giving the country the 'sordid truth', two men, Claude Moore and John Howe, aged thirty and thirty-one respectively and members of the Fairoaks Flying Club, flew their small, pale grey Chipmunk through the Tower Bridge, under Albert Bridge and then 'buzzed' other central London bridges along a three-mile stretch of the Thames. After they had landed back at Blackbushe airport, John, a Kingston-on-Thames heating engineer, said: 'Call it a stand against long hair, hippies and similar horrors – a hope that we have still got a spirit of 1940 in this country.'[5]

Mr Moore and Mr Howe weren't the only people making a stand against hippies that morning. At 11.30 a.m., the slightly built Metropolitan Police Chief Inspector Michael Rowling, under the pretext that someone inside was about to have a baby, convinced the 'Hells-Angels' who were guarding 144 to lower an improvised wooden drawbridge that led into a ground floor window. As soon as it was down, a whistle blasted and Rowling, who weighed less than 11 stone, flung himself across the barricaded opening and out of nowhere 100 policemen rushed forward and stormed right across the back of the sprawled chief inspector. Missiles of all sorts were hurled down by the hippies including roofing slates and, rather oddly, hundreds of water-filled plastic boules, boxes of which had been found in a small room in the basement. It was to no avail, and only four minutes after the breach of the drawbridge, a policeman was seen at the top of the mansion raising his truncheon in triumph.

Not long after, and to cheers from what were now many hundreds of onlookers on the street below, the Hells Angels' flag was lowered from the flagpole. As he was being led outside by the police, 'Dr John', the 'so called' leader of the squatters, shouted at the press and the crowds in the street: 'They conned us! They tricked us!'

About two years before 144 Piccadilly had been squatted and subsequently raided by the police, a group of about twenty young hippies, although at the time they would have called themselves 'Freaks', had almost made Piccadilly Circus their home. Nearby Covent Garden was still a fruit and vegetable market in those days, and the hippies took advantage of the unwritten rule that once fruit was on the floor it was fair game. The bakery on Bourchier Street in Soho was still thriving and 'produced a supply of bread and cakes for the asking'.[4] The busking pitches were uncrowded and 'in those days it was easy to live on the streets'. As a last resort, if anyone ran into real difficulties, there was the Salvation Army on the Embankment or the crypt underneath St Martin's, but the 'freaks' hardly ever resorted to that. Richard Gardner, one of the group and known as Richie, remembered that time: 'We didn't live in squats in those days, we lived in "derris" – slang for a derelict house, of which there were thousands in the sixties. They had a certain short life and when the bulldozers moved in we moved on.'

At one point a man called Phil Cohen arrived on the 'Dilly'. No one seems to remember why, but he was called Dr John. He looked a bit different from the rest, and while everyone else was wearing loons, cheesecloth and beads, he wore a worn suit jacket and mismatched trousers. He was, according to Gardner, into Agitprop, Tariq Ali, Che and all that stuff, 'whereas we were more inclined to skin-up and see if we could get the Dilly record shop to play the new Jefferson Airplane on its outdoor speakers'. It was Dr John's idea to start the London Street Commune and their first squat was a corner building on Broad Court next to Bow Street Magistrates' Court. It was a warren of small rooms, and the ground floor sash windows 'yielded instantly to Coventry Johnny's thin blade'. The next squat under the LSC banner was a rambling old church school at Endell Street, right opposite the Oasis public baths. It was completely enclosed, with a narrow side entrance that was easy to defend. A small advance party secured the squat and printed up the relevant legal documents that explained to the police that squatting was not a criminal offence. The police had no power to evict them, and a Civil Court application for eviction had to be left with the owners of the property.

At the same time as the Endell Street property was secured, another advance party of hippies managed to get inside the old disused mansion at 144 Piccadilly. The main doors of the building facing Hyde Park Corner were quickly nailed shut and completely barricaded. The entire property was surrounded by a deep dry moat with sheer sides, so a reception room was established with a plywood drawbridge to the right of the main doors. Gloria Lovatt, one of the early squatters and eighteen at the time, remembered the first day at 144: 'We ran through the whole building, yelling with delight like kids at what we found. Not only did it have running water but also all the main electricity switches were connected. There were even elevators that worked. In the back garden there was a gold fish pond and from the top-floor windows you could look right over Hyde Park. In the morning we were able to do the laundry and hang our clothes over the balcony rail to dry.'[7]

The fact that dozens of hippies had moved into a large house in 'aristocratic Mayfair' quickly became news. Just two days after they had arrived, a crowd of photographers and reporters were outside, all desperate for stories from inside the squat. Lovatt later wrote that she made £300 in five days giving 'exclusive' interviews to almost every newspaper she could find. Although most of it was just made up: 'Everyday life in the commune was about as exciting as watching paint dry. People came in, slept and went out again. The reporters didn't want to hear that, so I gave them what they did want to know – stories of drugs and drinking and orgies – and they lapped it up.'[8] After a few days, the squat at 144 Piccadilly became news around the world. Even *Life* magazine had a story: 'A London hippie commune went house-hunting and found a splendid crash pad.' *Life* also commented on the increasing crowd outside 144: 'Soon mobs of middle-class squares gathered outside to shout insults ("Dirty layabouts, take a bath!").'

Richard Gardner, one of the original Piccadilly hippies, would later write: 'Some people choose to remember the London Street Commune as a motivated alternative group committed to the cause of freedom but honestly folks, we were a bunch of "Dilly dossers" who were having a whole load of fun. For us the revolution had landed right on our doorsteps and we were loving every minute of it. Phil [Dr John] was certainly the politico of us but he was as much of a space cadet as anyone else. He had a great way with words about him though ...'[9]

'We believe in people,' said Dr John while he was stirring baked beans on a camp stove in an improvised kitchen behind the barred front door. The *Daily Mirror* reporter Stanley Bonnett had managed to get an interview with the hippy leader from inside 144: 'These people. Not those out there who are still hoodwinked with all the trappings of a society which is dead but will not lie down. We are socialists in the real sense; in the old sense. Not in the Wilson way. He's not a socialist at all. Put this down: "We are prepared to pay for the gas and the electricity we use here and the water. You can say we are determined to keep the lavatories clean and flushed. After all, it is Piccadilly."'[10]

The name 'Piccadilly' came from the word 'Picadils' or 'Pickadils', which were stiff collars with scalloped edges and a broad lace or perforated border. At the beginning of the seventeenth century they were particularly fashionable. A man called Robert Baker made a lot of them and made his fortune. He bought land around the area we now know as Piccadilly and his house became known as Pikadilly Hall. He bought more land with the help of money from a second marriage and a map published in 1658 by Faithorne, the engraver, described the street as 'the way from Knightsbridge to Piccadilly Hall'. Which is what Piccadilly, essentially, is today.

Two centuries later, several members of the Rothschild family had mansions on the Knightsbridge end of the street. Nathan Mayer Rothschild moved his banking premises to No. 107 in 1825, but also built other large buildings, complete with ballrooms and marble staircases. This led to the street becoming known as Rothschild Row. The houses at 144 and 145 Piccadilly were built at the end of the 1790s by Sir Drummond Smith. They were erected, *The Times* wrote of the properties, 'without regard for expense. Great solidity is visible in its construction and the interior is arranged to unite every possible luxury and comfort'.[11] Lord Palmerston lived at 144 between 1855 and 1856, and was living there when he became prime minister. After that, Lady Margaret Beaumont and Wentworth Blackett Beaumont moved in not long after they were married in 1856. Beaumont became Lord Allendale in 1906.

Lady Allendale, the daughter-in-law of the first Lord Allendale, died just a few weeks after VE Day, and the Allendale family sold 144 Piccadilly not long after. Next door had been badly bombed and subsequently demolished during the Blitz. Alexander Korda's film company occupied 144 and what was left of 145, but *The Guardian* reported in 1961 that: 'The London branch of the Arts Educational School is settling down with happy adaptability in its new home at 144 Piccadilly.'[12] This was where Liza Goddard, Jane Seymour and Nigel Havers learnt their trade. The school moved out a few years later, and 144 Piccadilly remained empty for several years until September 1969, when members of the London Street Commune decided to make it their home.

On 20 September (the day before the police raid on the squat) there had been a free festival at Hyde Park. It was the third of the free festivals in the park that summer and the one that has been mostly forgotten (the first featured the super group Blind Faith and the second was the famous Stones performance two days after the death of Brian Jones). The third festival featured Soft Machine, the Deviants, Quintessence, Al Stewart and the Edgar Broughton Band who, as usual, finished with their fans' favourite, 'Out Demons Out'. Many of the visitors to the Hyde Park concert that day would have come from out of town, and many of them went to visit 144 Piccadilly, which had been extensively in the news for the last three weeks. Some stayed the night at the run-down mansion, not having anywhere else to go, and must have unfortunately been caught up in the raid the next day. Nineteen-year-old Chris Hedley had come for the Hyde Park concert from Sydenham and, with a friend, decided to stay at 144: 'When we got into the house we were amazed by the amount of people in there. Most were very friendly and welcoming even though it must have been obvious we were not homeless. We took part in throwing the boules that were in boxes in the basement. As the evening went on we noticed things getting a bit aggressive, in particular two or three Hells Angels walking around with a pair of very scary Alsatians just pushing people around and telling people they were 'taking over'. We eventually got some sleep, but woke up early and saw two or three people next to us injecting into their feet and one of the Hells Angels kicking one of them. We decided there and then to get out and we were greeted by two police, but they let us go telling us if they see us in the area again we would be nicked.'[13]

Paul Chambers, who was nicknamed 'The Colonel' by the press, essentially because he wouldn't tell them his name and because he wore an old First World War army jacket, wrote that the police 'destroyed everything with great gusto. I watched my mate's guitar (his livelihood) being pounded into matchsticks, sleeping bags, clothes ripped up terrible'. Richie, one of the original 'Dilly Dossers', had a similar experience: 'Everyone was thrown onto the streets as they were. Property that survived the trashing was collected and taken to West End Central police station where we glumly queued and gave our names until we were reunited with, in my case, the razor slashed remains of my doss bag and a caved in guitar that would never play again.'[14]

The nice round number of 100 people were taken into custody, with twenty-seven adults and three juveniles arrested for offences ranging from assault to drug possession. There were no bad casualties, although many of the occupants complained of being beaten by the police. The occupation of 'Hippydilly' was over, just three weeks after it had begun.

The police raid so impressed the property developer Ronnie Lyon ('Business is just like driving a car – of which I have four, by the way,' he once observed. 'I moved up in stages, like changing gears.') that he walked into the West End Central police station and wrote a cheque for £1,000 for the Police Benevolent Fund. Lyon said: 'I feel that these hippies had no legal or moral right to be in that building. One is very ready to criticise the police when parking and speeding, but when there is a real problem you run to the British bobby and he is pretty good at his job.'[15]

In August 1970, not quite a year after the end of the 'Hippydilly' squat, the architect Sir Frederick Gibberd spoke at a public enquiry about a proposal to demolish number 144, to be replaced by a luxury hotel. Gibberd had designed Liverpool's Catholic cathedral, the first three Heathrow terminals, the mosque in Regent's Park, and was the master planner for Harlow new town (which was where, to his credit, he lived all his life). He was asked his opinion of the empty mansion at 144 Piccadilly and replied: 'The desecration and squalor were indescribable, and rain was pouring through the roof.' The architect then told the enquiry (from the totally unbiased perspective that he was the designated designer of the proposed hotel to be built on the same location) that he thought: 'It would be totally unreasonable to leave this site underdeveloped. That there is pressing demand for luxury hotels is incontrovertible.'[16]

Westminster Council agreed, as did the Royal Fine Art Commission, and plans were made for the mansion at number 144 to be knocked down. If it seems surprising today that historical Georgian houses at the western end of Piccadilly were demolished for the sake of a relatively nondescript hotel, unsuited, especially in size, to its surroundings, it is worth being reminded that at that time large amounts of Piccadilly were due to be razed to the ground, including most of the area around Piccadilly Circus.

Sir Alfred Gilbert, who sculpted the Shaftesbury Memorial Fountain, commonly known as Eros, and less commonly known to be made out of aluminium, ironically had no liking for Piccadilly Circus at all. In 1893 he described the Circus as 'a distorted isochronal triangle, square to nothing of its surroundings – an impossible site, in short, upon which to place any outcome of the human brain, except possibly an underground lavatory!'[17] Plans had been made after the death of King Edward VII in 1910 to clear the area and create a rectangular open space with an adjacent Shakespeare Memorial Theatre and a National Opera House. The First World War came along, as did the Second, and the asymmetrical chaos that made up Piccadilly Circus remained … until 1954 that is.

That year Coca-Cola starting advertising at the famous London landmark and has done so ever since; but, more importantly, the property developer Jack Cotton bought the Monico site (named after the Café Monico that had been there since 1877) on the north side of Piccadilly Circus. His plans for a huge office block at Piccadilly Circus passed almost unhindered and unnoticed through the various planning stages – many newspapers reported on it at the time as if the redevelopment was a *fait accompli*. As soon as the plans were released, however, there was a public outcry with most Londoners wanting Piccadilly to remain exactly how it was. The Conservative government, however, asked for proposals for a grand integrated rebuilding plan that covered not only Piccadilly Circus but also much of the surrounding area. They were particularly worried about the expected future growth of traffic.

Lord Holford, acting for the Greater London Council and Westminster Council, proposed a 'double-decker' scheme that segregated pedestrians on elevated concrete concourses sixty feet above the ground while several lanes of traffic roared past below. There was also to be a ring of office towers which would be overshadowed by a 132-metre tower block on the Criterion Theatre site to the south of the Circus. This plan, with minor changes here and there, was kept alive throughout the rest of the sixties. It is mentioned in the short documentary film *Goodbye, Piccadilly*, produced by the Rank Organisation in 1967 as part of their *Look at Life* series, when it was seriously expected that Holford's recommendations would still be acted upon.

There was yet another scheme, put forward in 1972, that consisted of three octagonal towers, the highest of which was to be 73 metres tall, to replace the Trocadero, the Criterion and the 'Monico' buildings. That year, with the wholesale destruction of Piccadilly Circus more than still on the cards, Hugh Cubitt, Westminster Council's planning chairman, let it be known that he hoped the scheme could be started as soon as possible, so as to combat the decay of what he called 'little more than a down-at-heel, neon-lit slum'.[18]

Most Londoners thought, 'Yes but it's our down-at-heel, neon-lit slum and we'd like to keep it that way, thank you!' A year later the *Observer* wrote: 'Piccadilly Circus, more than anywhere else in the country, is a place for the people. It is not, first of all, a traffic junction nor an office centre. It is somewhere people go to wander about, gawp and gossip, and generally amuse themselves. Those who have drawn up successive plans for its redevelopment have failed to understand its real nature, and, one after the other their efforts have been laughed to scorn.'[19] The so-called 'Dilly Dossers' that hung about Piccadilly Circus at the end of the sixties were only doing what people, many of whom felt outside mainstream society for many reasons, had been doing around that part of the West-End for decades.

After the hippies had been thrown out of 144 Piccadilly, the building remained empty for three more years, and was then demolished. Sir Frederick Gibberd got his wish, and his large, unimaginative Hotel Intercontinental was built on Hyde Park Corner. It's slightly more expensive to stay there than at 144 back in 1969, although there is now, apparently, hot water. The prices range, for one room, as of the summer of 2015, from £450 – £900 per night.

In May 1979, after almost eighty years of different redevelopment plans of Piccadilly Circus, the latest plans were unveiled. At last, all the grand projects featuring massive office blocks and 'pedestrian walkways in the sky' were rejected in favour of what Mr 'Sandy' Sandford, chairman of GLC's central area planning committee, begrudgingly called the 'least change' plan. Essentially, except for some pedestrianisation on the south side, it meant that it was to remain roughly how it had always looked, and what we see at Piccadilly Circus today.

Coventry Street looking towards Piccadilly Circus, 2 April 1956. (Allan Hailstone)

Piccadilly Circus in 1908.

657.K.   **PICCADILLY CIRCUS & SHAFTESBURY AVENUE, LONDON.**   BEAGLES' POSTCARDS.
THIS FAMOUS CIRCUS WITH ITS FOUNTAIN MEMORIAL TO THE EARL OF SHAFTESBURY
IS ONE OF LONDON'S BRIGHTEST AND BUSIEST SPOTS, BEING IN THE MIDST OF THE GREAT WEST-END STORES
AND ADJACENT TO MANY NOTED THEATRES AND PLACES OF AMUSEMENT.

Postcard of Piccadilly Circus in 1911.

'Dr John' or Phil Cohen, 9 September 1969. (© Keystone Pictures USA/Alamy)

Piccadilly Circus tower block proposed for the Monico site in 1959.

Piccadilly Circus in 1959 by Graham Knott.

'Freaks' hanging out at Piccadilly
Circus in 1969. (Dezo Hoffman,
REX Shutterstock)

Piccadilly looking towards
Piccadilly Circus in 1969. (Bernd
Loos)

The Intercontinental Hotel, designed by Sir Frederick Gibberd, on Hyde Park Corner where 144 Piccadilly once stood, seen in 2015. (Rob Baker)

CHAPTER 24

The Men's Dress Reform Party, 'Bare-Leg Tennis' and Little Miss Poker Face

Helen Wills ('Little Miss Poker Face') at Wimbledon in 1929.

Charlie Chaplin once wrote that the most beautiful sight he had ever seen, and presumably he had seen a few, was 'the movement of Helen Wills playing tennis'. Wills, a pretty twenty-three-year-old American, played the game with an unhurried and what seemed an effortless style. She was in her heyday when *Vogue* magazine in their June 1929 issue wrote: 'One very noticeable thing about our girl champions at Wimbledon is their grace, distinctly the reverse of what some people have prophesied – that hard exercise and strain would thicken the ankles, coarsen the complexion, and lead to general ungainliness.'

Helen Wills was never accused of ungainliness but her composed and rather dispassionate on-court behaviour meant that she was often called 'Little Miss Poker Face'. The designer and tennis player Teddy Tinling described her as the Garbo of tennis, not only because of her undoubted beauty, but because she 'always wanted to be alone and away from her fellow competitors ...'

In 1929 Helen Wills, at the age of just twenty-three, was appearing at the famous south London tennis tournament for the sixth time, and was already five times Wimbledon singles champion. That year she wore a white sailor suit with a pleated knee-length skirt, white shoes and the white visor for which she was famous and made popular. The Wimbledon crowd were more than used to seeing her on the centre court but that year they took a particular interest in her. Especially her legs.

Earlier that summer there had been an enthusiastic debate in much of the press about the wearing, or more specifically the non-wearing, of stockings by female tennis players. The Lawn Tennis Association along with the All-England Club were considering prohibiting at Wimbledon what was known at the time as 'bare-leg tennis'. Anna Mallory, the former Ladies Wimbledon champion, had never heard anything so ridiculous: 'Bare legs are a great advantage to a woman, and I do not agree that they look ugly. If a woman has nice legs they look very pretty without stockings.' The British tennis player and Wimbledon Doubles champion Mrs Shepherd-Barron had a different point of view: 'I think that the bare-leg fashion is hateful. I am sure that most of the married women will not adopt the fashion as their husbands would object violently. Women's legs do not look handsome when they are bruised and scarred.'[1] Incidentally, her son John was far more forward thinking than his rather conservative mother, and in 2005 won an OBE for services to banking as 'inventor of the automatic cash dispenser'. He was, apparently, inspired by the chocolate vending machine and had the idea in the bath after he had been locked out of his bank.

The *Daily Mail* reported that some players were 'indignant' with the possible ban and that even the women players who thought that bare legs were ugly resented the idea that men officials of Wimbledon should dictate what clothes they wear. Mrs Lambert Chambers, who had won the Wimbledon title seven times, thought that what 'a woman wears is her own business and not that of the Lawn Tennis Association'.[2] The two leading American tennis stars of the time – Helen Wills and Helen Jacobs – were reported as surprised with the proposed veto as 'bare-leg tennis' was already popular in America and in France.

The committee of the All-England Club finally decided against a formal ban but they firmly let it be known that they would rely on the good taste and good sense of the players involved. Indeed, Miss Wills stated in London's *Evening News*: 'I definitely have decided to wear stockings in the Wimbledon tournament. As soon as I heard that the Wimbledon authorities might object to bare legs I reached a definite decision and I shall not alter it.' Wills went on to easily beat Helen Jacobs 6-1, 6-2. The only singles match Helen Wills ever lost at Wimbledon was her first final when, at the age of eighteen, she lost against the British player Kitty Godfree in 1924.

The stockings (or lack thereof) controversy was brought about by changes in the manufacturing of stockings during the previous thirty years or so. At the turn of the century, nineteen out of twenty pairs of stockings were black, and of course very rarely on show, but with the relatively short skirts of the 1920s, more and more stockings were made with finer knits and in a range of paler colours. The stockings were held in place with a combination of suspenders and garters, although the French tennis player Suzanne Lenglen, the first proper international female tennis celebrity, wore white silk stockings with the tops rolled over her garters in what was called the 'American' style. She was also the first major tennis player, early in her career, to play without a corset, for which she was often known by many Wimbledon tennis fans as 'the French Hussy'.

Lord Aberdare in his definitive *Willis Faber Book of Tennis* described when Lenglen first appeared at Wimbledon in 1919: 'Suzanne acquired strength and pace of shot by playing with men, and for playing a man's type of game she needed freedom of movement. Off came the suspender belt, and she supported her stockings by means of garters above the knee; off came the petticoat and she wore only a short pleated skirt; off came the long sleeves and she wore a neat short sleeved vest.'

Lenglen's look, her coloured bandeau (known to some as a 'headache band'), rolled stockings, knee-length pleated skirts, became the symbol of the flapper in the 1920s. It may have been the first time a sports figure influenced general fashion around the world. Helen Wills and Suzanne Lenglen only played one match together, at a small tournament in Cannes in 1926. It was billed as Match of the Century because the two players, up to then, had studiously avoided playing each other. It was estimated that 7,000 spectators crammed into the stands at the Carlton Club. Lenglen won in straight sets 6-3 8-6 but it seemed that she realised her reign was close to coming to an end and she turned professional soon after. They were never to play together again.

It was a more polite and deferential time and, without exception, the women players at the 1929 Wimbledon championships all wore stockings. As far as tennis-playing women were concerned, however, it was now the beginning of the end for the restrictive garments. Later that summer the *Daily Mail*'s prurient eyes were turned away from the legs of female tennis players, and the newspaper started studying what men were wearing instead. After reporting that men were 'shy creatures' and would 'rather die than wear anything unconventional in public', on 31 August 1929 the *Daily Mail* wrote: 'It seems to be universally agreed that male dress at the present time is the most unhygienic, inartistic, sombre, and depressing form of costume that the mind could well imagine. But the difficulty is to get the idea of a brighter, more hygienic, and more picturesque attire into the mind of the mere male.'

Recently the press had featured a photograph of the renowned radiologist Dr Alfred Charles Jordan cycling to his office in Bloomsbury. What fascinated and slightly horrified the readers was that the picture showed him wearing shorts with his jacket. This was utterly unknown at the time for anybody working in a city – shorts were for Scouts, sport, and maybe a hiking holiday. They weren't even worn by men playing tennis at the time. Jordan was the honorary secretary of the Men's Dress Reform Party, which had announced its existence on 12 June 1929, just twelve days before the be-stockinged Helen Wills had walked out for her first round match on the Centre Court at Wimbledon. The organisation's first aim was to improve men's health by changing what they wore and early MDRP literature complained that:

> Men's dress has sunk into a rut of ugliness and unhealthiness from which – by common consent – it should be rescued … Men's dress is ugly, uncomfortable, dirty (because un-washable), unhealthy (because heavy, tight and unventilated) … it is desirable to guard against the danger of mere change for change's sake, such as has often occurred in women's fashion.

All change should aim at improvement in appearance, hygiene, comfort and convenience.[3]

While most men at the time would have taken some convincing to wear this new style of clothing, an article in the tailoring magazine *Tailor and Cutter* thought it was almost the end of civilisation: 'If laces are unfastened, ties loosened and buttons banished, the whole structure of modern dress will come undone; it is not so wild as it sounds to say that society will also fall to pieces ... Such restraints were not noxious: they were the foundation upon which civilisation rested and protected men from savagery and decadence.'[4] A man called D. Anthony Bradley agreed and spoke at a debate in 1932 entitled 'Shall Man be Redressed?'. Mr Bradley patently thought not and argued: 'The man who, alone in the jungle, changes into his dinner jacket does so to convince himself that he is not a savage – soft sloppy clothes are symbolic of a soft and sloppy race ... It did not matter very much what health cranks, exhibitionists or men of misplaced sex wore,' but, he continued, 'man – sturdy and virile man, capable of withstanding the rigours of a stiff shirt, must maintain conservative standards of dress.'[5]

The MDRP was an off-shoot of, and shared premises with, the New Health Society formed in 1925 and situated at 39 Bedford Square in Bloomsbury. Dr Jordan was a founding member of the Party but the chairman of the organisation was another doctor, Caleb William Saleeby, who had originally chaired the clothing sub-committee of the New Health Society but had also founded the Sunlight League in 1924.

The Sunlight League had been formed in London to educate the public about 'Nature's universal disinfectant, stimulant and tonic' and advocated heliotherapy – direct exposure to the sun. The league campaigned for a variety of causes including mixed sunbathing and the relaxation of the rules for what was considered appropriate attire when in the sun. Towards the end of the 1920s, new-fangled sunbathing clubs were opening around London, including Finchley and Sidcup, while the Yew Tree Club, devoted to physical culture and nudity, opened in Croydon. Compared with on the continent, especially in Germany, nudism remained a minority activity in England and it rarely strayed from its suburban, Home Counties roots. The clubs had strict conventions, and rules of etiquette were designed to convince a doubting public that sex was the last thing on the nudists' minds. And maybe it was.

Dr Saleeby, as chairman of the MDRP, wrote a letter to the Lawn Tennis Association in 1929 encouraging it to 'persuade men to give up the handicap of heavy trousers and play in shorts'. The first man to have famously worn shorts at Wimbledon was Henry 'Bunny' Austin (his nickname comes from a character in the comic strip 'Pip, Squeak and Wilfred') in 1932. Except he wasn't. In reality the first man to experience fresh air against his legs while playing tennis at Wimbledon was actually the relatively unknown English player Brame Hillyard. A year after Saleeby's letter, the fifty-six-year-old Hillyard wore them on Court 10. Despite the freedom his shorts must have given him while playing, he promptly lost, and he was hardly ever heard of again.

Two years later, in 1932, the twenty-four-year-old Henry Wilfred 'Bunny' Austin, born in South Norwood, 8 miles or so away from Wimbledon, but educated at Repton and Cambridge, became the first person to wear shorts on Centre Court, and thus the first in front of the world's press. A man wearing shorts to play tennis looks utterly normal these days, but in the early 1930s it attracted much derision. John Kieran wrote about Austin in the *New York Times* that year: 'With his white linen hat and his flannel shorts, the little English player looked like an AA Milne production.'[6] Austin had to overcome considerable embarrassment when he decided to wear them for the first time:

> I myself took over two years to summon up enough courage to wear shorts, although for years I had known how much more healthy, comfortable and reasonable they were for tennis. I hovered in my bedroom … putting them on, taking them off, putting them on again, wrestling with the problem of Hamlet – 'to be or not to be'. At last I summoned up all my courage, put and kept them on, and wearing an overcoat to conceal them as much as possible, went out of the hotel to play. My bare legs protruded beneath the coat and I slunk through the lounge self-consciously. As I passed through the door an agitated porter followed me. 'Excuse me, Mr Austin', he whispered diffidently, 'but I think you've forgotten your trousers.[7]

Bunny Austin lost in the final to the American Don Budge, who was happy to be weighed down by long flannel trousers. The Englishman's reward as runner-up was a £10 gift voucher redeemable at a high-street jeweller's. Austin was the last English man to appear in a Wimbledon Singles Final, when he was runner-up in 1938. During the war he became active in the Christian pacifist movement and lived in the US. He was criticised in the press as a conscientious objector. It wasn't until 1984 that Austin was again allowed to be a member of the All-England Club.

The MDRP, almost forgotten these days, had some success in getting its message across during the first years of its existence. It held annual parties, in order to 'give every man a chance to show how he can look and feel his best by the costume he will evolve for this unique occasion', and it was possible to find MDRP approved clothing in some shops in London, including the famous Austin Reed on Regent Street. It also had an official shop and a relatively successful mail-order service. In 1937, the Men's Dress Reform Party lost the support of the New Health Society because of financial trouble and eventual bankruptcy. Then, in 1940 the Sunlight League was wound up. A bomb destroyed their offices and then the founder, Dr Saleeby, died that year too. There is no evidence of the Men's Dress Reform Party continuing to exist after this date.

The MDRP, realistically, did little to turn general male fashion around except maybe in holiday and athletic wear. A major shift in men's clothing didn't happen until after the war, when new fabrics and the rise of American style, with its preoccupation with leisure-wear, radically changed men's appearances in the 1960s.

In 1931, two women players flouted the unofficial clothing rules at Wimbledon. Joan Lycett, who was actually born Joan Austin and was the sister of Bunny, played without stockings, but by now the newspapers and the watching crowds, used to seeing stockingless players away from Wimbledon, seemed to hardly notice. Lycett's opponent, however, did cause a sensation. Lili de Alvarez, 'the gay señorita' from Spain, played at Wimbledon wearing a 'white trousered frock'. *The Times* on 24 June 1931 wondered, 'which were the more wonderful things – divided skirts or bare legs?' On the same day the *Daily Sketch* saw de Alvarez's 'trousered tennis frock' as yet more evidence that women had a 'masculine fixation':

> The claim of women to equality with men is understandable, but that so many of them should wish to imitate the appearance of the less beauteous sex is not so easy to understand. It began with bobbing, and reached its logical hirsute conclusion in the Eton crop. And, having lost her hair, many a girl is now making strenuous attempts to lose her curves. And concurrently with these changes the conquest of trousers had been steadily proceeding ... although mere man may regret the lose of feminine furbelows more than he resents the theft of his trousers, he realises that it is useless to rail against the spirit of the age. Whether we like it or not, girls will be boys.[8]

Helen Wills, who became known as Helen Wills-Moody after marrying the business man Frederick Moody in December 1929 (she met him at the match with Suzanne Lenglen), went on to win thirty-one Grand Slam tournament titles during her career, including eight singles titles at

Wimbledon. Incredibly, she reached the final of every single Grand Slam singles event she entered but, as was common in those days, she never played at the Australian championships.

The rivalry between the two Californian Helens reached a head when they played against each other in the final of the 1933 US championship at Forest Hills. Wills had always beaten Jacobs and had won seven US championships out of seven, but after being broken on serve twice and falling behind 3-0 in the final set, she suddenly advised the umpire that she could not continue, citing a bad back. A reporter for the Associated Press called Will Grimsley wrote: 'The spectators were stunned. The newsmen were outraged. They called her a quitter and a poor sport. They accused her of depriving Miss Jacobs of her moment of glory.'

That wasn't the only reason why their rivalry had turned so bitter; Helen Jacobs had controversially worn shorts that year at Forest Hills, and Wills reputedly said that there was nothing more unflattering to the female form than shorts and that it was hard to distinguish whether the wearer was a man or a woman. It wasn't a pleasant thing to say but it was also a very pointed comment, as Wills would have known, unlike the great majority of the public, that Jacobs was gay.

The final time the two Helens met was in the 1938 Wimbledon final. During the first set at 4-4 Jacobs strained her right Achilles tendon straining to meet a passing shot from Wills-Moody. Jacobs didn't win another game but bravely continued to the end of the match graciously, but maybe pointedly, allowing her opponent the full taste of victory in a championship final which she herself hadn't been given five years previously. After she had won the final point Wills ran up to the net and without exchanging a smile said, 'Too bad, Helen,' after beating her for the eleventh time out of twelve matches.

Helen Jacobs became a writer while still playing tennis and wrote two tennis books, but also fictional works such as the novel *Storm against the Wind* in 1944. She served as a commander in the US Navy Intelligence during the Second World War, one of only five women to reach this rank. She had a life-long companion called Virginia Gurnee, and she died of heart-failure in East Hampton in 1997.

Helen Wills, if not always the audience's favourite, was undoubtedly one of the greatest ever tennis players. She also was a writer and wrote first-hand reports of her tennis matches for the British and American press. She died aged ninety-two on New Year's Day 1998, and left her $10 million fortune to the University of California, where she is now remembered by the Helen Wills Neuroscience Institute.

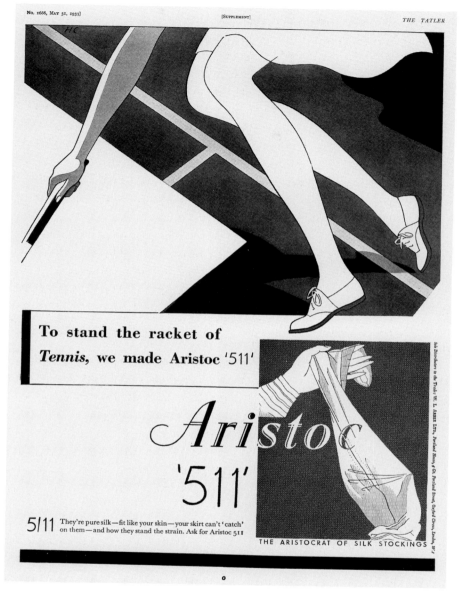

An advert for Aristoc tennis stockings from 1933. (Courtesy of Mary Evans Picture Library)

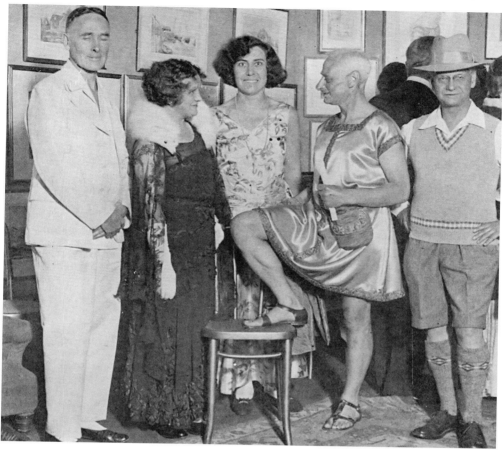

'The Countess of Mayo chatting with Dr A. C. Jordan, whose motto is apparently, "In London do as Rome did." If his notion of dress-reform is generally adopted, our scientists will have a greater incentive than ever to find a means permanently to exterminate mosquitoes.' (Courtesy of the Mary Evans Picture Library)

Opposite above: Bunny Austin and his wife in 1936. (Willem van de Poll, courtesy of the National Archives of the Netherlands and under a Creative Commons Licence)

Opposite below: 'Members of the Men's Dress Reform Party airing their sartorial notions and their limbs at a "Revel" at the Suffolk Galleries.' (Courtesy of the Mary Evans Picture Library)

Notes

1. The Empire Theatre on Leicester Square and the Arrest of Bobby Britt

1 *Manchester Guardian*, 15 April 1926
2 *Life* magazine, 25 August 1941, p. 79
3 *Daily Mail*, Thursday, April 15 1926, p. 10
4 Grant Richards, *Memories of a Misspent Youth*, 1932
5 Joseph Donohue, *Fantasies of Empire: The Empire Theatre of Varieties and the Licensing Controversy of 1894*, p. 35
6 Judith R. Walkowitz, *Nights Out: Life in Cosmopolitan London*, p. 58
7 David F. Cheshire, *Music Hall in Britain*, p. 41
8 Ronald I. Cohan, *Prudes on the Prowl: A Rant Against Mrs. Ormiston Chant*, p. 44
9 Donohue, p. 41

2. The Pop-Artist Pauline Boty and the Anti-Uglies

1 William J. Dowlding, *Beatlesongs*, 1989, p. 225
2 *The Caterer and Hotel-Keeper's Gazette*, 16 September 1907, p. 388
3 James Bone, *London Echoing*, 1948, p. 102
4 *Daily Express*, 16 March 1959, p. 3
5 Adam Smith, 'Now You See Her: Pauline Boty' (unpublished ms), p. 40
6 Nell Dunn, *Talking to Women*, 1965
7 Ian Nairn, *Modern Architecture in London*, 1964, p. 46

3. The Day the Traitors Burgess and Maclean Left Town

1 Matt Wells, 'BBC drama high on sex and espionage', *The Guardian*, Tuesday, 8 April 2003
2 Marc E. Vargo, *Scandal: Infamous Gay Controversies of the Twentieth Century*, p. 84
3 Torin Douglas, 'Spy Burgess's spell at the BBC', news.bbc.co.uk, 18 August 2009

4 Ibid
5 *The Age*, 'Guy Burgess: the Spy who went to Eton', 4 November 4 1967 p. 12
6 Donald Seaman, *The Great Spy Scandal*, 1955
7 Phillip Knightley, *The Second Oldest Profession: Spies and Spying in the Twentieth Century*, 1980
8 Bruce Page, David Leitch & Phillip Knightley, *The Philby Conspiracy*, 1968, p. 231
9 *The Great Spy Scandal*, Donald Seaman, 1955
10 Jenny Rees, *Looking for Mr. Nobody: The Secret Life of Goronwy Rees*, 1994, p. 168
11 Elizabeth Jane Howard, *Slipstream: A Memoir*, 2002, p. 218
12 *Daily Mail*, Frederic William Wile, 6 December 1916, p. 3
13 A. S. Byatt, *Still Life*, 1985, p. 273
14 *Daily Mail*, Saturday, 9 June 1951
15 Jenny Rees, *Looking for Mr. Nobody: The Secret Life of Goronwy Rees*, p. 170
16 *The Age*, 4 November 1967, p. 12

4. Warren Street, Spivs, and the Gruesome Murder of Stanley Setty

1 Tattersalls horse auctioneers was founded in 1766, and is the oldest bloodstock auctioneers in the world. It was still based at Hyde Park Corner at the beginning of the twentieth century and still exists, albeit at Newmarket and Fairyhouse outside Dublin
2 *Daily Telegraph*, 22 September 2010
3 *Daily Mail*, Tuesday, 31 May 31 1904, p. 3
4 David Kynaston, *Austerity Britain, 1945–1951*, p. 104
5 *Daily Express*, Wednesday, 6 November 1946, p. 4
6 *Time* magazine, Monday, 16 June 1958
7 Double jeopardy has been permitted in England and Wales in certain

(exceptional) circumstances since the Criminal Justice Act, 2003
[8] *Time*

5. The Protests at the 1970 Miss World Competition and its Motley Crew of Judges

[1] Nicholas de Jongh, 'Beauty overshadowed by the women's Lib', *The Guardian*, 21 November 1970, p. 1
[2] Chrissie Russell, 'The Great Miss World Cover-up', *Irish Independent*, 7 July 2013
[3] Alan Parker, 'Our Cissy and Footsteps', alanparker.com
[4] 'Courtesy prince who carried a democratic bat', *The Guardian*, 5 September 1988, p. 39
[5] 'Glen Campbell Tells it like it is', *Daily Telegraph*, 9 October 2008
[6] *Miami News*, 20 November 1970, p. 2

6. The Café de Paris and the Trial of Elvira Barney

[1] Barry Paris, *Louise Brooks: A Biography*, p. 78 and referring to a letter Brooks sent to the film historian William K. Everson
[2] *Manchester Guardian*, 25 April 1931, p. 12
[3] Judith R. Walkowitz, *Nights Out: Life in Cosmopolitan London*, 2012 p. 22
[4] Sir Patrick Hastings, *Cases in Court*, 1956, p. 202
[5] Macdonald Hastings, *The Other Mr Churchill: A Lifetime of Shooting and Murder*, 1963
[6] Peter Cotes, *Trial of Elvira Barney*, 1976, p. 15
[7] Hastings, p. 202
[8] *Daily Mirror*, July 7 1932, page 3
[9] William Hickey column, *Daily Express*, 28 December 1936
[10] *Manchester Guardian*, 19 March 1941, p. 5
[11] Ibid

7. The Deaths of Cass Elliot and Keith Moon in Harry Nilsson's Bed

[1] *Daily Express*, Wednesday, 17 July 1974, p. 7
[2] *Daily Express*, Friday, 19 July 1974, p. 10
[3] *Daily Express*, May 3 1974 page 12
[4] Alyn Shipton, *Nilsson: The Life of a Singer-Songwriter*, 2013
[5] Ibid
[6] *Daily Mirror*, Saturday, 9 September 1978, p. 2
[7] Jerry Hopkins interview, *Rolling Stone*, 21 December 1972

8. Mary Richardson – Suffragette, Iconoclast and Fascist

[1] *Daily Express*, 8 June 1934, p. 1
[2] Jennifer Birkett, *Margaret Storm Jameson: A Life*, p. 132
[3] *Daily Mail*, 8 January 1934
[4] *Daily Mirror*, 19 November 1910, p. 1
[5] *Daily Mirror*, 23 November 1910, p. 7
[6] Kenneth Clark, *The Nude: A Study in Ideal Form*, 1956
[7] Anthony Bailey, *Velázquez and the Surrender of Breda: The Making of a Masterpiece*, p. 222
[8] *The Times*, 25 January 1906, p. 9
[9] Mary Richardson interview with Sorrel Bentinck, BBC Home Service, 23 April 1961
[10] Ibid
[11] Rachel Williams, *The Guardian*, 25 June 2012
[12] *Daily Express*, 9 March 1914
[13] *Woman's Dreadnought*, 21 March 1914
[14] *Daily Mail*, Friday, 10 October 1913, p. 7
[15] Annabel Venning, *Daily Mail*, 27 April 2012
[16] *Morning Post*, 11 March 1914
[17] *Fascist Week*, 22–28 December 1933
[18] Ed Glinert, *London Compendium*,
[19] Julie V. Gottlieb, *Feminine Fascism: Women in Britain's Fascist Movement, 1923–45*, p. 162
[20] *Daily Mail*, Wednesday, 8 November 1961
[21] *The Suffragette*, 20 March 1914

9. How the GLC Almost Destroyed Covent Garden

[1] *The Observer*, 18 April 1971, p. 6
[2] *The Changing Life of London*, George Gardiner, 1973
[3] Ibid

4 'Romance in Five Acts', *Daily Telegraph*, 13 April 1914

5 'Mr Bernard Shaw on First Nighters', *Daily Telegraph*, 8 April 1914

6 G. R. Strauss, M.P. for Vauxhall House of Commons debate, 26 June 1972

7 Anthony Crosland, M.P. for Grimsby House of Commons debate, 26 June 1972

8 *The Guardian*, 29 July 1972, p. 11

9 George Gardiner, *The Changing Life of London*, 1973

10 *The Observer*, 18 January 1914, p. 9

11 *The Guardian*, 5 November 1977, p. 15

10. When Lord Haw-Haw Met Mr Albert Pierrepoint, Albeit Briefly

1 Michael Kronenwetter, *Capital Punishment: A Reference Handbook*, 2001 p. 27

2 *The Independent*, Friday 7 April 2006 *Capital Punishment in Britain: The Hangman's Story*

3 Jonah Barrington, *Daily Express*, 14 September 1939

4 Jonah Barrington, *Daily Express*, 18 September 1939

5 *Daily Mirror*, Wednesday, 10 January 1940, p. 10

6 *Daily Express*, 18 January 1940, p. 6

7 Andrew Gimson, *The Spectator*, 22 November 2003

8 William L. Shirer, *Berlin Diary: The Journal of a Foreign Correspondent, 1934–1941*

9 Mary Kenny, *Germany Calling: A Personal Biography of William Joyce, 'Lord Haw-Haw'*

10 John Alfred Cole, *Lord Haw-Haw and William Joyce: The Full Story*, p. 302

11. Christine Keeler and the Fight at the Flamingo All-Nighter

1 *Daily Express*, Friday, 13 March 1959

2 Ibid

3 Interview with author

4 Barbara Windsor, *All of Me: My Extraordinary Life*

5 Simon Napier Bell, *Black Vinyl, White Powder*, p. 50

6 Part of an interview from Julian Temple's film *London: The Modern Babylon*

7 Anthony Summers & Stephen Dorril, *Honey Trap*, p. 187

8 Paolo Hewitt, *The Soul Stylists: Six Decades of Modernism: From Mods to Casuals*

9 Ibid

10 *Melody Maker*, 16 November 1961

11 James Maycock, *The Independent*, Friday, 16 January 1998

12 Judith R. Walkowitz, *Nights Out: Life in Cosmopolitan London*, p. 235

13 *Melody Maker*, 7 March 1936

14 Walkowitz, p. 240

15 Maycock

16 Ibid

17 Christine Keeler & Douglas Thompson, *Christine Keeler: The Truth at Last*, p. 143

18 Johnny Edgecombe, *Black Scandal*,

19 *Daily Mail*, 15 February 2014

20 *The Observer*, 4 August 1963, p. 1

12. The Blind Beggar and the Death of George Cornell by Ronnie Kray

1 Christopher Berry-Dee, *Gangland UK: The Inside Story of Britain's Most Evil Gangsters*,

2 Reginald & Ronald Kray, *Our Story*

3 Dan Farson, *Never a Normal Man*, 1997

13. When James Earl Ray Came to Earl's Court

1 *Daily Express*, Wednesday, 3 July 1968

2 *Montreal Gazette*, 14 June 1968, p. 4

3 Hampton Sides, *Hellhound on his Trail: The Stalking of Martin Luther King, Jr.*,

14. The Death of Benny Hill and the Windmill Theatre in Soho

1 Robert Ross, *Benny Hill – Merry Master of Mirth: The Complete Companion*

2 Max Decharné, *King's Road*, p. 32

3 Frank Muir, *A Kentish Lad*, p. 127

4 David Kynaston, *Austerity Britain 1945–51*, p. 261

5 *Daily Mirror*, Saturday, 30 April 1955.
6 John Howard Davies, Gavin Gaughan obituary, *The Independent*, 25 August 2011
7 Leon Hunt, *British Low Culture: From Safari Suits to Sexploitation*, p. 46

15. When Fifty Hoxton Schoolchildren Met Charlie Chaplin at the Ritz

1 Kenneth Schuyler Lynn, *Charlie Chaplin and His Times*, p. 175
2 David Robinson, *Chaplin: His Life and Art*, p. 157
3 Robinson, p. 185
4 Charlie Chaplin, *My Wonderful Visit* (Hurst & Blackett, 1922)
5 Ibid
6 *Manchester Guardian*, 12 September 1921, p. 7
7 Ibid
8 Charlie Chaplin, *My Autobiography*, 1966
9 The Queen's Head is still there although the road has been called Black Prince Road since 1939
10 *The Times*, 12 September 1921
11 Robinson, p. 282
12 *Manchester Guardian*, 12 September 1921, p. 7
13 *The Times*, 12 September 1921
14 *Brisbane Courier*, Saturday, 17 August 1929, p. 25
15 Charlie Chaplin, *My Wonderful Visit* (Hurst & Blackett, 1922)
16 Ibid
17 Ibid
18 Eric James, *Making Music with Charlie Chaplin: An Autobiography*
19 *My Trip Abroad*, Charlie Chaplin. Reprint. London: Forgotten Books, 2013. pages 68-9
20 Noel 'Boy' McCormick fought Joseph 'Joe' Beckett, with the latter winning by a 12th-round TKO in a fight at the Royal Opera House, Covent Garden.
21 *Maoriland Worker*, 6 September 1922, p. 12
22 Robinson, p. 272
23 Ibid. Wheeler's grandson, Charlie's nephew, was called Spencer Dryden and became the drummer for the rock band Jefferson Airplane.

16. The Rise and Fall of Colin Wilson and how he Met Marilyn Monroe

1 Terry Eagleton, *The Guardian*, 4 August 2013
2 Colin Wilson, *Dreaming to Some Purpose*, p. 119
3 Wilson, p. 22
4 Interview Lynn Barber 'Now they will realise I am a genius', *The* Observer, 30 May 2004
5 Wilson, p. 117
6 Introduction entitled 'The Outsider' Twenty Years on', *The Outsider* (Diversion Books, 1976)
7 Colin Wilson, *The Angry Years: The Rise and Fall of the Angry Young Men*, p. 16
8 Interview Jasper Gerard 'Still an angry man, always an Outsider', *Sunday Times*, 20 June 2004
9 *The Observer*, 14 October 1956, p. 3
10 Ibid
11 *Daily Express*, 12 October 1956, p. 17
12 *Time* magazine, 4 March 1957
13 *The Guardian*, 12 August 2006
14 *Daily Express*, 14 September 1956

17. David Hemmings, Blow-up and the Red Buildings on Stockwell Road

1 *The Independent*, Monday, 5 June 2006
2 Ibid
3 Mark Bostridge & Nicholas Kenyon, *Britten's Century: Celebrating 100 Years of Benjamin Britten*, p. 49
4 Antonioni interview with Roger Ebert in 1969
5 *Daily Mail*, Saturday 9 September 1967
6 The average weekly wage was £23 for men and £12 for women. A pint of beer cost less that 10p (2 shillings)
7 Paul McCartney & Barry Miles, *Many Years From Now*
8 *Daily Express*, Friday, 20 January 1967
9 *Hansard* vol 285, House of Lords debate, 21 July 1967, cc 522–6

18. Two 'Perfect' Women – Prunella

Stack and Gertrud Scholtz-Klink

1 *Daily Mail*, 8 March 1939, p. 11
2 *Daily Mail*, Wednesday, 15 July 1936, p. 9
3 *Daily Mirror*, Wednesday, 27 November 1935
4 Michael Bloc, *Ribbentrop*, p. 127
5 *The Times*, Friday, 11 1938, p. 15
6 *Daily Mirror*, Thursday, 15 June 1939
7 Prunella Stack, *Movement is Life: An Autobiography*
8 *Daily Express*, 15 September 1939
9 *Daily Express*, Thursday, 4 March 1948

19. Mary Quant, the Mini-Skirt and the Chelsea Palace on the King's Road

1 Brenda Polan & Roger Tredre, *The Great Fashion Designers*, pp. 103–4
2 'Coffeeless Coffee and Milkless Milk', *The Guardian*, Monday, 17 April 2000
3 H. G. Wells, *Christine Alberta's Father*, 1925, p. 51
4 Shawn Levy, *Ready Steady Go*, p. 54
5 *Daily Mail*, Saturday, 11 June 1966, p. 4
6 Kieran Curran, *Cynicism in British Post-War Culture: Ignorance, Dust and Disease*, p. 52
7 John Osborne, *Looking Back*
8 *The Stage*, 27 December 27 1956
9 Max Décharmé, *King's Road: The Rise and Fall of the Hippest Street in the World*, p. 79
10 Décharmé, p. 114
11 *Life* magazine, 26 May 1967, p. 24

20. Winifred Atwell – The Honky Tonk Woman

1 *Daily Express*, 14 July 1953 p. 1
2 Peter Ackroyd, *London: The Biography*, p. 753
3 Stephen Bourne, *Black in the British Frame: The Black Experience in British Film and Television*, p. 93
4 Keith Kyle, *Suez: Britain's End of Empire in the Middle East*, p. 441
5 Bernard Delfont, *East End, West End: an Autobiography*, p. 161
6 Sharon Osbourne, *Extreme: My Autobiography*

7 Ibid
8 Bourne, p. 96
9 *Daily Express*, Wednesday, 12 April 1961
10 *The Guardian*, 8 November 1971
11 'Winnie makes a big entry', *Sunday Mirror*, 4 February 1971

21. Kempton Bunton and Britain's Greatest Art Heist

1 *Daily Express*, Thursday, 5 December 1963, p. 5
2 *Daily Mirror*, Friday, 20 May 1960, p. 20
3 *Manchester Guardian*, 8 June 1960, p. 7
4 *The Times*, Monday, 6 January 1964, p. 11
5 *Daily Mirror* Thursday, 18 March 1965, p. 1
6 Ibid
7 *Daily Mail*, 17 November 1965, p. 11
8 *The Observer*, 22 June 1969 p. 1
9 *The Times*, Thursday 27 April 1967 p. 10

22. The Prostitutes' Padre and the Lyon's Tea-Shop Nippies

1 Jonathan Tucker, *The Troublesome Priest*, 2007
2 *Daily Mail*, 11 September 1930, p. 8
3 *Picture Post*, 4 March 1939, pp. 29–32
4 *Church Times*, 15 July 1932, p. 68
5 *Daily Mirror*, Thursday, 29 July 1937

23. The Hippy Squat at 144 Piccadilly

1 *The Times*, Thursday, 9 July 1908, p. 13
2 *The Observer*, 19 July 1914, p. 8
3 *Daily Mail*, Wednesday, 17 September 1969, p. 4
4 *Daily Mirror*, 5 October 1926
5 *Daily Express*, 22 September 1969 p. 1
6 Richard Gardner interview with author
7 Gloria Lovatt, *A Nice Girl Like Me*, p. 126
8 Lovatt, p. 128
9 Richard Gardner interview with author
10 *Daily Mirror*, Wednesday, 17 September 1969, p. 15
11 *The Times*, Tuesday, 28 July 1835
12 *The Guardian*, 10 February 1961 p. 10
13 Interview with author

[14] Article about the London Street Commune on wassu.com by Richard Gardner (Supercrew)
[15] *The Guardian*, February 10 1961, p. 10
[16] *The Times* Thursday, 6 August 1970 p. 3
[17] *Easter Art Annual*, 1903, pp. 13–17
[18] *Toledo Blade*, 3 May 1972, p. 39
[19] *The Observer*, 28 October 1973, p. 12

24. The Men's Dress Reform Party, 'Bare-Leg Tennis' and Little Miss Poker Face

[1] *Daily Mail*, 28 Tuesday 1929, p. 11

[2] Ibid
[3] Robert Ross, *Clothing: A Global History*, p. 145
[4] *Tailor and Cutter*, 205 December 1931
[5] Joanna Bourke, 'The Great Male Renunciation: Men's Dress Reform in Inter-War Britain', *Journal of Design History*, vol. 9, no. 1, 1996, pp. 23–33
[6] Frank Litsky, *New York Times*, 28 August 2000
[7] Jennifer Craik, *The Face of Fashion: Cultural Studies in Fashion*, p. 153
[8] Rob Steen, *Floodlights and Touchlines: A History of Spectator Sport*, p. 479

Selected Bibliography

Archer, Fred, *Killers in the Clear* (London: W.H. Allen & Co. Ltd, 1971)

Berkeley, Roy, *A Spy's London* (Great Britain: Leo Cooper, 1994)

Bourne, Stephen, *Black in the British Frame: The Black Experience in British Film and Television* (London: Continuum 3PL, 2005)

Cotes, Peter, *Trial of Elvira Barney* (London: David & Charles, 1976)

Davenport-Hines, Richard, *An English Affair: Sex, Class and Power in the Age of Profumo* (London: HarperPress, 2013)

Décharné, Max, *King's Road: The Rise and Fall of the Hippest Street in the World* (London: Weidenfield & Nicolson, 2005)

Donahue, Joseph, *Fantasies of Empire: The Empire Theatre of Varieties and the Licensing Controversy of 1894* (US: University of Iowa Press, 2005)

Gardiner, George, *The Changing Life of London* (Great Britain: T. Stacey, 1973)

Glinert, Ed, *London Compendium* (expanded edition) (Great Britain: Penguin, 2013)

Gottlieb, Julie V., *Feminine Fascism: Women in Britain's Fascist Movement, 1923–45* (Great Britain: I.B. Tauris, 2000)

Green, Jonathan, *Days in the Life: Voices from the English Underground 1961–1971* (Great Britain: William Heinemann Ltd, 1988)

Hastings, Sir Patrick, *Cases in Court* (London: Wm. Heinemann Ltd, 1949)

Hewitt, Paolo, *The Soul Stylists: Six Decades of Modernism – From Mods to Casuals* (Great Britain: Mainstream Publishing, 2003)

Houlbrook, Matt, *Queer London* (Chicago and London: The University of Chicago Press, 2005)

Keeler, Christine & Thompson, Douglas, *The Truth At Last: My Story* (London: Sidgwick & Jackson, 2001)

Kenny, Mary, *Germany Calling* (London: Max Press, 2008)

Klein, Leonora, *A Very English Hangman: The Life and Times of Albert Pierrepoint* (London: Corvo Books, 2006)

Kynaston, David, *Austerity Britain 1945–51* (London: Bloomsbury Publishing, 2007)

Levy, Shawn, *Ready, Steady, Go! Swinging London and the Invention of Cool* (Great

Britain: Fourth Estate, 2002)

Linnane, Fergus, *London's Underworld, Three Centuries of Vice and Crime* (London: Robson Books, 2004)

Mort, Frank, *Capital Affairs, London and the Making of the Permissive Society* (New Haven and London: Yale University Press, 2010)

Napier-Bell, Simon, *Black Vinyl, White Powder* (Great Britain: Ebury Press, 2007)

Pugh, Martin, *Hurrah For The Blackshirts!: Fascists and Fascism in Britain Between the Wars* (Great Britain: Pimlico, 2006)

Quant, Mary, *Quant by Quant* (Great Britain: Cassell & Co. Ltd, 1966)

Rees, Jenny, *Looking for Mr Nobody: The Secret Life of Goronwy Rees* (Great Britain: Orion, 2007)

Robinson, David, *Chaplin: His Life and Art* (New York: McGraw-Hill, 1987)

Ross, Robert, *Benny Hill, Merry Master of Mirth* (London: Batsford Ltd, 1999)

Shapiro, Jill Millard, *Remembering Revudeville 1932–1964* (United Kingdom: Obscuriosity Press, 2014)

Shipton, Alyn, *Nilsson: The Life of a Singer-Songwriter* (USA: OUP, 2013)

Smith, Adam, 'Now You See Her: Pauline Boty' (unpublished ms)

Stack, Prunella, *Movement Is Life: An Autobiography* (London: Collins and Harvill Press, 1973)

Stack, Prunella, *Zest for Life: Mary Bagot Stack and the League of Health and Beauty* (London: Peter Owen Publishers, 1988)

Summers, Judith, *Soho: A History of London's Most Colourful Neighbourhood* (London: Bloomsbury, 1989)

Tate, Sue, *Pauline Boty, Pop Artist and Woman* (Wolverhampton: Wolverhampton Art Gallery, 2013)

Thomas, Donald, *An Underworld at War* (UK: John Murray, 2003)

Thomas, Donald, *Villain's Paradise, Britain's Underworld from the Spivs to the Krays* (Great Britain: John Murray, 2005)

Tucker, Jonathan, *The Troublesome Priest: Harold Davidson, Rector of Stiffkey* (Norwich: Michael Russell Publishing Ltd, 2007)

Walkowitz, Judith R., *Nights Out: Life in Cosmopolitan London* (New Haven and London: Yale University Press, 2012)

White, Jerry, *London in the 20th Century* (London: Viking, 2001)

Wilkes, Roger, *Scandal: A Scurrilous History of Gossip* (London: Atlantic Books, 2002)

Wilson, Colin, *Dreaming to Some Purpose, an Autobiography* (London: Century, 2004)

Wilson, Colin, *The Angry Years: The Rise and Fall of the Angry Young Men* (London: Robson Books, 2007)

Index